ADMINISTRATIVE ASSISTANT'S & SECRETARY'S

HANDBOOK

ADMINISTRATIVE ASSISTANT'S & SECRETARY'S

HANDBOOK

J. STROMAN & K. WILSON
Edited by
SUSAN HEYBOER O'KEEFE

amacom
American Management Association
New York · Atlanta · Boston · Chicago · Kansas City · San Francisco · Washington, D.C.
Brussels · Mexico City · Tokyo · Toronto

This publication is designed to provide accurate and authoritative information in regard to the subject matter covered. It is sold with the understanding that the publisher is not engaged in rendering legal, accounting, or other professional service. If legal advice or other expert assistance is required, the services of a competent professional person should be sought.

Library of Congress Cataloging-in-Publication Data

Administrative assistant's & secretary's handbook / J.
  Stroman & K. Wilson ; edited by Susan Heyboer O'Keefe.
     p. cm.
  Includes bibliographical references and index.
  ISBN 0-8144-0273-9
  1. Secretaries—Handbooks, manuals, etc.   2. Office prac-
tice—Handbooks, manuals, etc.   I. Stroman, James.
II. Wilson, K. (Kevin). 1958– .   III. O'Keefe, Susan
Heyboer.
HF5547.5.A247   1995
851.3—dc20   95-8662
                                   CIP

Printing number

10 9 8 7 6

Special thanks to
**Jennifer Wauson, Kathy Stose,
Judy Courtney,** and **Susan Heyboer O'Keefe**
for their help on this project

Contents

Preface   xi

Section One: General Procedures   1

1 Overview for the New Secretary   3
   *Why are you needed? * What do employers want? * Interview tips * Your*
   apprenticeship
2 Daily Routine   7
   *Your office * Your workstation * Office supplies * Reference works * Work*
   *planning * Dictation * Transcription * Dictating machines * Your*
   *employer's office * The intangibles*
3 Telephone Usage   15
   *Telephone manners * Taking and transferring calls * Taking messages **
   *Screening calls * Often-used numbers * Long-distance calls * Conference*
   *calls * Ship-to-shore calls * Air-to-ground and ground-to-air calls * Calls*
   *to trains * Telegram airport delivery * New telephone equipment*
4 Mail Services and Shipping   23
   *Beyond a letter and a stamp * Addressing for success * Postal automation:*
   *Encoding for business mailers * Metering * Packaging * Important U.S.*
   *Postal Service mail services * Other classes of mail * Electronic mail*
   *services * Other special mail services * International mail * Alternatives*
   to the USPS
5 Travel Arrangements   77
   *Today's business traveler * Getting the trip underway * Doing it yourself*
   *ic Using a travel agency * The itinerary * Foreign travel*
6 Keeping Accurate Records   88
   *A critical duty * Getting ready * Basic filing systems * File*
   cabinets

Section Two: Office Equipment and Computers   95

7 Office Machines   97
   *Typewriters * Copy machines * Calculators*
8 Telecommunications Equipment   104
   *Telephones * Voice mail and answering machines * Special telephone*
   *services * Long-distance services * Cellular telephones * Pagers **
   Facsimile machines

9 Computer Systems 113
*Office computers * Hardware * Memory * Input devices * Output devices
* Storage devices * Software*

10 Database Management Systems 132
*Creating and using a database * Fields, records, and files * Sorting and
searching * Types of databases * Applications*

11 Computer Communications 139
*Connecting with other computers * Modems * Communications software
* Online databases * Bulletin boards * Networking * Electronic mail*

12 Computerized Spreadsheet Software 146
*What is a spreadsheet? * Navigating around a spreadsheet * Spreadsheet
data * Functions * Editing spreadsheets * Other spreadsheet functions *
Spreadsheet software*

13 Data Security 153
*Information = profit * Computer crime * Protecting your company's data
* Coping with disaster*

14 Keyboarding skills 158
*Keyboards * Function keys * Macros * The mouse * Using typewriters*

15 Word Processing 163
*A boon for secretaries * Creating documents * Editing documents *
Formatting documents * Printing documents * Saving and loading
documents * Advanced word processing features * Popular word
processing software*

16 Glossary of Computer Terms 172

Section Three: Business Documents **183**

17 The Business Letter 185
*Appearance * Paragraphing * Beginning the letter * Contents * Closing
the letter * A last look*

18 Other Written Communications 194
*Letters written by the secretary * For the employer's signature * Routine
letters * Sample model letters * Interoffice memorandums * Postcards *
Mailing lists * Meetings*

19 Forms of Address 210

20 Legal Documents and Terms 225
*Grammalogues * Document formats * Case titles * Notary public forms *
Codicils to a will * Agreements and contracts * Proxy * Legal glossary,
including real estate terms*

Section Four: Language Usage **239**

21 Correct English Usage 241
*Language: Key to your success * Correct usage * Additional
examples*

22 Spelling   253
*Dictionary uses * Plurals * The suffix * Irregular spelling * Capitalization*

23 Pronunciation   261
Perfecting your speech

24 Punctuation   265
*Purpose of punctuation * The period * The comma * The question mark *
The exclamation point * The semicolon * The colon * Quotation marks *
The apostrophe * The dash * Ellipses * Parentheses * Italics*

25 Numerals   279
*Words or figures? * Printed text * Large numbers * Separating digits *
Dollars and cents * Decimal points * Time * Dates * The hyphen * Age *
Dimensions * Weights and measures * Percentages * Page numbering *
The abbreviation for* number *Plurals of numbers * Roman numerals*

Section Five: Financial Activities   **289**

26 Bookkeeping and Accounting   291
*Financial record keeping * Property rights * Accounting statements * The
account * Payroll * Travel-and-entertainment and auto-expense records *
Cash budgets * Records for lenders*

27 Business and Personal Taxes   308
*The secretary's role * Business taxes * Employee or independent
contractor? * Property and net worth taxes * Business licenses * Tax
assistance*

28 Banking   312
*The company's bank * Checking accounts * Petty cash * Savings accounts
* Investment accounts * Trust services * Other services * Checks *
Deposits * Withdrawals * Special situations * Credit cards * Reconciling
bank statements*

29 Special Business and Financial Information for the Small
    Business Secretary   326
*Frequently asked questions * Trading with other countries * Sources of
financing * Small Business Administration * Selling to the federal
government*

Section Six: Career Advancement   **335**

30 Your Future   337
*Growing as the company grows * Recognizing a time for change * Finding
a job * Presenting your credentials * The plus element*

Index   345

Preface

One of the most important positions in any company is that of secretary, also referred to as executive secretary, private secretary, personal secretary, or administrative assistant. The job requires versatility, skill, precision, efficiency, and a constant willingness to increase one's knowledge.

Being a top-notch secretary in the business or the professional world is a satisfying and rewarding career in itself. It also provides, for those who want it, an excellent opportunity for advancement.

This manual covers the many aspects of a secretary's job—from opening the mail to handling bookkeeping, from making travel arrangements to operating computers. It's both an ideal how-to book for newcomers and a handy reminder for veterans: a compact, yet comprehensive, all-purpose business reference that provides the information you need quickly and concisely.

We hope that the *Administrative Assistant's and Secretary's Handbook* will sharpen your interpretation of this exciting vocation and provide you with everything you need to become a valued, competent, indispensable secretary on your way up the wonderful ladder of success.

Section One
General Procedures

A good secretary can be an indispensable part of any business team.

Photo by Jennifer Wauson.

Chapter 1

Overview for the New Secretary

Why Are You Needed?

A secretary is hired to relieve the busy employer of a great deal of work, especially the details of office procedure and other matters that do not require the employer's personal involvement. You'll act as a liaison between your boss and the rest of the company; sometimes you'll act as a buffer. Depending on the size of the company, you may also be called on to perform tasks normally outside the secretarial role, in sales, banking, billing, payroll, accounting, advertising, public relations, purchasing, and more. Everything you do for your employer must duplicate as closely as possible what he or she would do if not absorbed in work that couldn't be delegated.

Every businessperson dreams of having the perfect secretary, and every secretary dreams of having the perfect boss. Hopefully you and your boss will become so well adjusted to each other that you'll work as a team, each trusting the other to carry part of the load in harmony.

What Do Employers Want?

It's helpful to know what an employer expects of a "perfect secretary" so that you can present yourself at your best during both the job interview and those critical first weeks on the job. Here are a few of the most important qualities:

- *Punctuality.* An employer wants a secretary who is consistently punctual and always on hand during office hours. A secretary who continually arrives even a few minutes late or who is ill frequently can cause havoc in a busy office. The employer knows from experience that such a secretary isn't truly interested in the work. This person will be passed over or terminated in favor of someone with greater respect for the job and for the employer—a secretary who is always punctual and always there when needed.

During an interview, the employer may try to see where your attention is focused, asking such questions as how many sick days you used on your previous jobs, how many outside activities you engage in , and so on. Previous sick days can and will be checked, so don't lie. If you have many outside interests, mention only those that in some way contribute to your job, such as night courses or professional associations. You don't want to give the impression that you're "too busy" to work.

▪ *Dependability.* An employer considers the applicant's disposition and personality, trying to judge whether he or she is dependable. Would the candidate rush home at precisely five o'clock despite an office crisis, for example, or take enough responsibility to volunteer to remain after hours if an emergency arises?

▪ *Ability to learn.* An employer wants to know the extent of the applicant's education—not only formal programs and degrees but self-instruction and single courses. This information indicates the applicant's willingness and capacity for learning. For example, an employer may hope that you know the specific computer software the company already uses but not be too concerned if you aren't familiar with it if you show the potential to learn quickly.

▪ *Willingness to follow instructions.* An employer wants a candidate who follows instructions carefully and willingly. Of course, a good secretary will soon take initiative and perform certain tasks differently to save time or improve results. But the secretary who always demands complete control may ultimately become unwilling to follow instructions, debating or questioning every one of the boss's directives. Though intelligent input from a secretary is prized, an employer usually prefers not to argue points that he or she has already decided. There are more important matters than explaining all the reasons for pursuing a particular policy. Therefore, the employer looks for a secretary who will execute a decision no matter how many alternatives may seem obvious or no matter what a former boss did in the same situation. In other words, the employer wants an efficient tool whose personality will be an asset rather than a handicap.

▪ *Loyalty and confidentiality.* Although these qualities are impossible to discover during an interview alone, every boss wants his or her secretary to possess them. In an office there is nothing more unwelcome than the "human sieve" who constantly chatters about every conversation heard, spreads idle rumors like wildfire, and must constantly be screened from confidential projects and information. No matter how efficient, how educated, how experienced that secretary is, his or her employment will be short-lived.

And something else: A keen employer wants more in a prospective secretary than these general qualifications. During an extended interview, the employer will be looking for quick-wittedness, flexibility, commitment to work, a certain quality and level of conversation, and a sense of courtesy. This last attribute is essential in establishing cordial relations with clients and fellow employees.

Interview Tips

During your interview, it's wise to be as relaxed as possible, despite a natural tendency to be nervous. Appear on time, of course, and be well groomed and neatly dressed. Otherwise the appointment may be cancelled at the reception-ist's desk.

You'll make a poor impression if you try too hard to sell yourself. Allow the employer to form his or her own first impression. After all, he or she knows what kind of secretary is needed and, in addition, may prefer to work with a certain type of person. If you're not what the employer wants, it's wiser for both of you that another applicant be chosen.

If you receive a job offer, the salary may be less than what you think you're worth. There's often a discrepancy between what we'd like to make and what we can make. Job applicants fresh from school in particular may feel this until they become more familiar with what the market is actually paying. Before refusing a position on the basis of salary alone, first be sure you know what the salaries are for comparable secretarial positions in your area and for someone with your education and experience. Then find out whether you'll be eligible for a raise after a short period of probation. And finally, consider whether the position has opportunities for increased responsibility and advancement. While it may not seem true to you right now as a job applicant, a big salary is rarely more im-portant than professional satisfaction.

A secretary prepares to send a fax.

Your Apprenticeship

Even if you are already well experienced, once you have a new position, you must be prepared to serve an apprenticeship with your new employer. Your past experience may be useful only in that it has taught you to learn quickly and to evaluate new situations. At your new office, there may be a different method for almost every daily procedure, even for distributing and opening the mail. No doubt there will be a filing system you haven't used elsewhere. You may be asked to use letter formats, paragraphing, punctuation, and abbreviations that were vetoed by a previous employer.

You may also discover that your new boss has an extensive vocabulary with many words you'll need to learn, or just the reverse—a poor vocabulary that needs your assistance. Will your new boss wish you to type a letter exactly as dictated, or do you have permission to "add to and take from"? Or will the boss furnish only the essentials of what he or she wishes to convey and request that you put the letter together in proper form?

Your need to be flexible extends to the computer system in the new office. You may find many differences between the hardware and software you used in school or a past job and what you must use now. Even an updated version of the same software package may have a different user interface and functions. You need to familiarize yourself with the new computer and software even if it means staying after work to read the manual and to experiment.

Stimulated by your brand-new environment and your past experience, you may find yourself coming up with dozens of ideas and suggestions your first few weeks on the job. Remember that when you do have a suggestion to offer, it may very well have been made before and rejected for excellent reasons. When one of your ideas is refused, don't take it personally. After you're more familiar with the company and its operations, you'll soon be able to make a better suggestion. At the same time, don't be reluctant to give input freely when the boss asks for it.

A new employee's overeagerness to offer advice, recommend changes, and carry over methods from old jobs may just disguise a need to be recognized for one's capability. In this situation, the best way to prove yourself is to do your best, learn quickly, follow instructions accurately and intelligently, and cooperate with fellow employees. Show consideration for others beyond the call of duty. A little extra giving will cost you absolutely nothing and will bring huge dividends in trust and friendship among your coworkers and your employer.

Chapter 2
Daily Routine

Your Office

Office conditions for secretaries vary. Your employer may be an entrepreneur working from a small office or even from home. You may find yourself in a law firm, a doctor's office, a sales office, a warehouse front office, a retail business, or a service business. Your company may have branches in several states or even several countries. The general activity of the business—selling, servicing, or perhaps manufacturing—may be located in the same area where you're expected to perform your job, or it may be far removed from where you work. And all these conditions may change over time as the company does.

Your Workstation

The location and conditions of where you do your day-to-day work can be critical to how effectively you perform. Look first at how your workstation is placed physically within the entire office setup. Is there a reason that your desk is where it is? Analyze the traffic patterns around and through your workspace. Do co-workers have to pass through it to get from one operation to another? Study your own work patterns. How often do you go back and forth to the filing cabinets each day? How far away from your desk are they? Do other workers share these files? Is there a more efficient way to organize the office?

You may find it helpful to draw a sketch of your office and try out alternative arrangements on paper before you make suggestions to your employer. Each proposed change must consider two questions: Will you work more effectively in a different office layout? Will your proposed changes affect another worker's effectiveness?

Whether or not you have input on the physical placement of your workstation, your desk and immediate workspace are yours to organize in a way that makes you comfortable and allows you to be as productive as possible. Your immediate workspace may include a desk, chairs, files, bookshelves, credenza, and portable tables. As you arrange these items, plan a layout that considers your work habits as well as the travel patterns for yourself, other employees, and clients.

Here are just a few factors to consider:

☐ *Desk chair.* Your chair should help promote good posture and back support, and it should be adjustable so you will not tire quickly. If possible, try to obtain an ergonomically designed chair.

☐ *Lighting.* Proper lighting is highly important in any office. Your work area should have sufficient lighting to avoid causing you eyestrain and headaches yet be positioned to minimize glare on your computer monitor.

☐ *Desk.* Your desk should be large enough to hold the office supplies and equipment you work with most often and to provide a clear area on which to work. Keep your most often-used supplies and equipment, such as telephone, memo pad, in and out box, and stapler, within easy reach when you are seated at your desk. Any reference books that you use frequently should also be easy to reach from your desk. A desk organizer should also be easy to reach from your desk. A desk organizer with slots is useful to store various work-in-progress folders so they can be quickly found when needed.

☐ *Supplies.* In your own desk, keep enough frequently used supplies to last for a week. At the beginning of each week, restock your supply. Neatly arrange these materials in drawer organizers, can tops, small boxes, or other containers. Store ink pads upside down.

☐ *Computer or typewriter.* Your computer or typewriter should be on a surface apart from your desk, preferably its own desk or table. In any case, you should be able to fit your legs under this surface comfortably as you work. Power cords should be kept out of the way so you will not inadvertently disconnect them with your feet. Multiple power cables can be connected together with twist-ties.

Besides a computer, keyboard, monitor, and printer, your computer workstation will most likely also be equipped with a mouse, a good-quality mouse pad for extra traction, a modem for telephone communications using the computer, a hard disk drive, an external storage drive, diskette files, a diskette storage system, and software reference manuals. Other useful accessories to help organize and protect this equipment include plastic dust covers for both computer and keyboard when not in use, a computer fan to prevent overheating, an antiglare monitor cover to reduce eyestrain, and acoustical hoods for printers. All expensive office equipment such as memory typewriters and computers should be equipped with a surge protector.

If you work for a small company, you may have to arrange all these elements so they can also be used by fellow employees without interfering with your other secretarial work.

Office Supplies

Depending on the size of the company and your own responsibilities, you may have to order office supplies for yourself, your department, or the entire business. You can purchase supplies at an office supply store, either in person or by telephone, or order them by telephone or by mail from an office supply catalog.

When determining an order, do not overestimate your need. A multiple-item discount is not always useful because certain items, such as printer ribbons, cannot be stored too long. Keep an inventory of your supplies and when you use them. A log book is a useful way to keep a record of supply consumption.

In addition to everyday supplies like pens, pencils, staples, paper clips, and file folders, some items may need special consideration. For example, replacement typewriter ribbons, fax paper, computer printer ribbons or ink cartridges, copier and laser printer replacement cartridges, toner, computer diskettes, and copier paper must each be ordered with your exact office equipment in mind.

Office supplies should be kept in a supply cabinet, shelf, or file cabinet. If coworkers have access to these supplies, consider labeling the shelves to help stay organized. Keep the supply storage orderly and clean. Items that you use most often should be stored at eye level, where they will be easy to see and reach. Those that might spill should be kept on the bottom shelf. Ink pads work best when stored upside down. Try to keep the label from the original packaging attached to the supplies; the information will be helpful when reordering the item. For the same reason, keep opened reams of copier and office paper inside the wrapper, leaving the label on one end. There are many different types and weights of office paper, and some are better suited for certain applications than others. For example, most copiers work best with 20-pound uncoated paper stock. Saving the label will help ensure you have the right product for the right job.

Reference Works

Every office should have a minimum number of reference works and other sources of information. These are invaluable in writing, taking dictation, and transcribing and will help you improve your work by enlarging your knowledge of the subject covered in correspondence or in reports. By telephoning a specific question to the reference department of the local public library, you can often obtain the information you need or else advice on how it may be found. But try to anticipate problems by having good reference books in the office.

The book you will consult most often will be an abridged dictionary; it should be on your desk. There are a number of good dictionaries; the one recommended here is *Webster's New Collegiate Dictionary* because it contains most of the information a secretary requires for daily work: spelling, syllabication, pronunciation, meaning, usage, derivation, and even synonyms in many cases. Also of value are *Dictionary of American Synonyms* and *Roget's Thesaurus,* though in a busy office there is seldom time to consult these works.

If your employer has a literary bent and inserts quotations in dictation now and then, a copy of *Bartlett's Familiar Quotations* will help prevent misquotations.

You should have a world atlas. Also try to have *World Almanac* and *Book of Facts* and a good single-volume encyclopedia. A copy of *Who's Who* will simplify your search for the addresses of people with whom your employer might correspond (or, again, you could call the reference librarian). A *Directory of Directors,* a *Director of Merchants and Manufacturers,* and similar books appear annually. Ask the reference librarian at your local public library to advise you which are best for your purpose.

Moody's *Investment Service* can provide information your employer may need if he or she invests in stocks and bonds. Your work will soon reveal whether you have use for a *List of Chambers of Commerce in the United States, Aver's Directory of Newspapers and Periodicals,* or other specialized business compilations. *The Martindale-Hubbell Law Dictionary* is used in law firms, along with other specific references.

Planning the day's activities.

Photo by Jennifer Wauson.

Work Planning

The first thing to do when you arrive at the office every day should be to air the rooms and regulate the heat or air conditioning (unless it's set on a permanent basis by building maintenance). Then arrange your desk for maximum efficiency and replenish your supplies. Prepare your notebook and pencils for taking phone messages or in case your employer gives you a task that requires taking notes.

Consult your desk calendar or your computer's calendar to be sure you're aware of all you must do during the day. Check your list of recurring matters: appointments, meetings, payroll dates, bill payments, and tax or insurance deadlines. Give your employer a reminder list of appointments and other activities, and prepare any material from the files he or she will need.

As part of your normal daily routine, try to order your activities in the most productive way. When you have to leave your desk to run an errand, for example, do other errands at the same time. Whenever possible, use the telephone instead of delivering a message in person (unless, of course, your employer asks you to do so). If you have tasks that involve mailing or shipping, plan them with pickup and delivery times in mind. Maintain a daily "to-do" list on paper or in your computer, and check off each item as it is accomplished. When new projects come in, try to complete them as quickly as possible. Prioritize your work. If you have several ongoing projects and a new one comes in, ask your employer which one has the highest priority.

Each evening before you leave the office, make a list of what you need to do the following workday. Then put away all of your work and work-in-progress files, either in your desk drawers or in a filing cabinet. Work that is especially sensitive, such as client lists or accounting records, perhaps should be put away in a locked file cabinet.

Your regular routine includes keeping your work area clean. Clean out your desk drawers periodically. Your computer, typewriter, and other office equipment should be cleaned using a slightly damp towel. Compressed air in a can is useful for blowing dust off your computer keyboard and monitor screen. Disk-drive cleaning kits use a special diskette to clean the internal working parts.

In addition to maintaining your immediate area, schedule regular servicing for all office equipment as part of a preventive maintenance program. Do not wait for equipment to break down in the middle of a big project with a firm deadline. Here the old adage is so important: An ounce of prevention is worth a pound of cure.

Finally, always be thinking of ways you can improve your own performance and the efficiency of the office. Look for problems, and try to find ways to solve them. An orderly, smoothly running business has a greater chance for success— and your company's success will help ensure your own.

Dictation

Besides storing notebook and pens in your own desk, keep a notebook, pencil, and pen in an inconspicuous place in your boss's office so you'll always be ready to take dictation, even if you've just looked in to announce a caller or deliver a message. You will save your boss valuable time since you won't have to retreat to your own desk for supplies.

Each day when you begin dictation, first write the date at the top of the notebook page. When the dictation ends, write the date once more and draw a line across the page. Though there may be several dictation periods each day, you will find this notation very helpful, if only in times of emergency, for you will be able to refer to your notes rapidly should questions arise.

When you take dictation from more than one person, keep separate notebooks with the name of each person on the outside in a prominent place. If you are asked a question about one of the letters, you will be able to reply without hesitation, especially if you've remembered to write the date before and after each session of dictation.

During regular dictation, your employer will often include faxes, telegrams, or other communications that should be sent out promptly, though he or she may continue dictating for an hour or more before you can take care of them. In such an event, immediately after taking the dictation of the fax, telegram, or urgent letter, turn down the page in your notebook so that you can find the material as soon as you reach your desk.

Occasionally when your employer is dictating, he or she may make a remark that you cannot hear distinctly. It's imperative that you ask the boss to repeat the statement before continuing. Accuracy is more important than an unwillingness to interrupt, and your employer will respect you the more.

When the dictation contains names of correspondents, companies, and products that are unfamiliar to you, ask the boss if these names are in the files or whether there are explanatory papers you should have. Ask before you close that bit of dictation, and plan to refer to those papers before beginning your notes.

Transcription

Ideally your shorthand is so reliable you can count on reading it even after the lapse of years; just the same, sometimes it is not. When the material you've taken in shorthand is an unfamiliar subject and you have to wait until the next workday before transcribing, take the time before leaving the office to scan your notes and check that they will be comprehensible later. A few minutes now may save an hour of puzzling later.

While transcribing your notes, always allow yourself to doubt a spelling now and then rather than hastily type what may be incorrect. When you have the slightest doubt, refer to the dictionary. If the word is one of those demons that you seemingly first have to know how to spell before you can even look it up, ask for help. Usually at least one person in the office will welcome your inquiry. Computers, of course, have dictionaries built into them to check for spelling or typographical errors, but not every word is in every spell-check program.

An employer who is intelligent, well read, and well traveled will have an extensive vocabulary that he or she will naturally use in dictation. Take every opportunity to improve your own vocabulary, day by day adding to your knowledge of language. When dictation contains a word unfamiliar to you, place a large question mark on the page, and when the particular fax or letter is finished, ask your boss—without embarrassment—to spell the word for you. This shows that you want to learn and make your employer's vocabulary your vocabulary.

Be careful when you are correcting what you think is an error on your employer's part. Check a dictionary or a book on language usage as it may be you who's mistaken.

After transcription of your notes, be sure to read over what you've typed. If there is even one error, it's better for you to find it rather than another person.

With computers and word processors, correction can be made in a second, and you can produce a perfect, well-spaced, and balanced page.

Dictating Machines

If you have taken dictation using shorthand in a previous job and enter an office where a dictating machine is used, you may not always welcome this new complication. Don't let such prejudice prevent you from adapting. These machines save you the double job of taking dictation before transcribing the letter. While the employer is dictating into the machine, you can finish other tasks that once otherwise had to be neglected. In addition, some employees have difficulty dictating to another person but can speak into a machine with ease; therefore, their dictation is actually easier to comprehend this way.

Portable dictating machines fit into an attaché case, purse, or even a pocket, enabling the boss to get dictation done at home or while traveling. The tape, wire, or disk is delivered or dropped off with you, to transcribe when convenient.

If your boss has noted that there are several corrections to make, take the time to listen before you type. You may save yourself a second typing this way, especially if your employer failed to mark the end of the letter or if you want to estimate its length before you begin. In such a situation, perhaps you'll prefer to do a rough draft instead of merely listening. Using a rough draft is also a good idea when you begin to transcribe for a new dictator because your ear may have to accustom itself to the voice. A rough draft using a computer or word processor is simple to do, with corrections made quickly and effortlessly.

Your Employer's Office

Some employers consider their offices sacred ground that is not to be touched; others appreciate having their secretaries dust and straighten up. You'll soon learn your own boss's preferences. If he or she doesn't mind, start by stacking the files being consulted and replacing in the cabinet those already consulted. But ask before removing papers or documents from your boss's desk, especially those you have noticed there for quite some time. Discretion is always necessary; you must not overstep your role by touching or mentioning papers that your employer considers personal or private. In addition, many employers maintain their own unique filing system atop their desks and will advise the secretary not to touch those stacks unless absolutely necessary.

One such necessity might be if the boss telephones from out of the office and asks you to retrieve a letter or document from atop the desk. If this happens, turn the stack to the side at the point you found the letter so that you can later replace it exactly where it was.

When you make appointments for your employer, record them on both the boss's calendar and your own. Be sure to remind the employer of these appointments—even though they're clearly on the calendar—so that he or she won't schedule too much work, for example, on the morning of a conference.

The Intangibles

Besides performing the usual office duties, all secretaries encounter many situations that are a test of character, judgment, and memory. The secretary must know exactly what the employer wants kept confidential. In some instances, your employer may frankly explain when something is not for public consumption, but do not assume otherwise if he or she says nothing. When someone asks you about a confidential matter, it should never be necessary to lie. A graceful "I couldn't say" is sufficient, especially in response to those who understand and respect your position.

A secretary must exercise self-control every moment, even when courtesy is strained. While on the job, you are not living your personal life but rather representing your employer. Because of this you cannot succumb to mood swings or to criticism of those around you. You must always think before speaking and keep yourself open like an impersonal channel for the fulfillment of your role as secretary. Think of how a diplomat must act while representing his or her country in a foreign land.

A great many little matters between a secretary and his or her boss will be left unmentioned between them. In a good working relationship, a type of telepathy develops between employer and secretary; their understanding of each other contributes to their mutual success.

Chapter 3

Telephone Usage

Telephone Manners

Secretaries must have a pleasing telephone personality and a well-modulated voice that conveys dignity and courtesy. Because you are not seen by the person at the other end of the line, you are judged, and more important your employer is judged, by your telephone manners. Show interest in what is being said. Reply in clear tones, never raising your voice. Be a good listener, and know what the other person at the other end of the line is saying to you.

When the telephone rings, answer it as quickly as possible. If you must leave your desk, ask someone else to answer your telephone during your absence and explain where you can be located. At all times, have a memo pad and pen near the telephone. If it's necessary to delay for some reason, make a polite request such as, "Please wait a moment while I check the record for you." If you must spend some time finding the desired information, offer to call back. If the caller prefers to hold the line, put down the receiver gently to avoid unpleasant noises in the caller's ear.

For the sake of out-of-town visitors who may call you to ask directions, keep a map of the area on a nearby wall or in a desk drawer. You can provide extra courtesy by plotting their trip from the airport or freeway.

Taking and Transferring Calls

If there is no switchboard, state the name of your company and your own name when answering an incoming call: "The Brown Company, Ms. Robertson speaking." If the business is large enough to have several departments and the operator has already answered the call before ringing your extension, state your department and your name: "Accounting Department, Ms. Robertson speaking." If there is no department and a call is referred to you, give only your name: "Ms. Robertson speaking."

Answering a Colleague's Telephone

When answering a colleague's extension, state the colleague's name and your own: "Ms. Scott's office, Ms. Robertson speaking." If the person called is unavailable, ask if the caller wishes to hold the line, leave a message, or call back. If the preference is to hold, go back on the line at short intervals to explain the delay, asking if the caller wishes to leave a message. (See the next section, on taking messages.) Be sure that the person called receives the message as soon as he or she returns.

Transferring a Call

If you can take care of the matter yourself, do not transfer the call. If you must, first tell the caller: "Mr. Jack Phillips is in charge of insurance, and I am sure he will advise you promptly. I'll transfer you." If the transfer must be made through the switchboard operator, always provide full information so that the caller doesn't need to be questioned again: "I have Mr. Black on the line. Please connect him with Mr. Phillips in the insurance department." Or, if the caller has not identified himself: "Please transfer this call to Mr. Phillips in the insurance department."

If you do not know to whom the call should be directed, advise the caller: "I'll have the proper person call you back in just a few minutes."

Handling Your Boss's Calls

When answering your employer's telephone, you may sometimes discover that the caller's secretary has placed the call. In that case, say: "Thank you. Just a moment, please." Then announce the call. Your boss will pick up the telephone (if he or she is courteous) and wait until the person calling is connected. Never ask the calling secretary to put his or her employer on the line first, unless your employer is a high-ranking personage requiring special consideration. When one businessperson calls another, both should be treated equally.

When you place a call for your boss, you naturally expect the secretary of the person called to put his or her employer on the line before you connect your own. If you are calling Mr. Fisk and the secretary answers, say: "Is Mr. Fisk there, please, for Ms. Barrett of the Barrett Company?" If Mr. Fisk's secretary knows the proper response, he or she will put Mr. Fisk on the line. Then you say to your employer: "Mr. Fisk is on the line, Ms. Barrett." If Mr. Fisk's secretary is not cooperative, continue to speak courteously. Return to your boss and explain that the other secretary insists that Ms. Barrett go on the line before Mr. Fisk will be connected.

Taking Messages

Many companies have neither a central switchboard with an operator nor a computerized voice mail system. In this case, the secretary will be asked to answer incoming calls and place outgoing calls. It's useful for the secretary to keep an accurate written record of both, particularly incoming calls when the employer is not in the office. You should record the caller's name, telephone number, purpose of call, and any message.

When a caller has a message to leave for your employer or another employee, take the message verbatim. Write it exactly as stated, taking time and being patient with the caller. If you don't understand what the caller is saying, ask to have it repeated. The message may be very important to your employer, and a single word omitted or out of place could make a significant difference in the meaning. If you are unfamiliar with the caller's name, ask for its spelling. Also, make sure you note whom the message is for.

All office supply stores have telephone message slips to make this record keeping easy. (Figure 3-1 shows a typical message slip.) Some message slips come in booklets with carbon copies. The original can be placed on the employer's desk,

Figure 3-1. A telephone message slip.

To _____ ☐ URGENT
                                       A.M.
Date _____ Time _____ P.M.

WHILE YOU WERE OUT

From _____

Of _____

Phone _____
        Area Code   Number   Ext

Telephoned		Please call	
Came to see you		Wants to see you	
Returned your call		Will call again	

Message _____
_____
_____
_____
_____
_____

_____ Signed _____

Notes _____
_____
_____
_____

while a copy is maintained in the booklet, perhaps for later use or reference when the original might have been destroyed.

A major advantage of using printed telephone message slips rather than blank scraps of paper is that you are more likely to take a complete message by filling in the printed form. A telephone message slip has lines for the name of the person being called, the date and time of the incoming call, the name of the person calling, the name of that person's company or organization if given, the caller's telephone number, and the message, if any. The last line of the slip is for your initials as the taker of the message. By placing your initials at the end, you will be advising yourself as well as your employer that the information is complete and accurate.

Screening Calls

Although many employees answer their own telephone, you'll be expected at one time or another to screen the boss's incoming calls. In this case you become the judge as to whether your boss should be disturbed.

When screening calls, be extremely tactful so the caller will not be affronted. You want to be able to meet the caller face to face the next day without feeling embarrassed about the way you treated him or her over the telephone. A simple question—"May I tell Mr. Jones who's calling?"—should encourage the caller to give a name without hesitation. If the caller refuses, explain that your employer is unable to accept a call without knowing whom it's from and suggest that a letter be written.

Many callers will ask for your employer by name and will tell you the question they need answered. You then need to confer with your boss to know if screening should be done or the call put through immediately.

Protecting Your Employer

Don't be overly zealous in trying to "protect" your employer by screening calls when not asked to do so. When a business is just getting underway, for example, many executives welcome all calls and don't want the secretary to screen any potential clients. If that is the case, then simply say to the caller: "Thank you. I will connect you with Mr. Jones." Then, on your intercom telephone, tell Mr. Jones the name of the person calling.

If you answer the telephone for all of the employees in the company and a caller does not request a specific person, inquire as to the nature of the call so you can transfer it to the proper department or employee. When you realize what the caller's needs are, you could say: "Ms. Johnson in our accounting department should be able to assist you with this. I will transfer your call to her."

Courtesy

All callers should be treated with great respect and a patient tone of voice. If another call comes in while you're speaking, ask the first caller to hold the line,

A secretary takes a message from a caller.

answer the second call, ask if the second caller can hold for a moment, saying you are on another line, and then return to the first. Never keep a caller waiting or on hold for any length of time. When you return to the line, thank the caller for holding. Keep in mind that his or her time is valuable.

Never put one line on hold without informing the caller, not even when two or more incoming calls arrive simultaneously and two or more lines are ringing. Many callers will hang up when this happens, and your employer could very well miss a much-needed business call. You've no doubt experienced this yourself as a caller and will always retain negative thoughts concerning that company. Always have the courtesy to say: "Hello. Can you hold a moment, please?" And wait until the caller answers yes or no. It is frustrating for a caller to be asked, "Can you hold a moment, please?" and then be cut off before the caller has had a chance to say no.

Often-Used Numbers

Your employer no doubt will use certain personal telephone numbers regularly. You will soon memorize many of them without effort, but it's useful to keep a short alphabetical list of these numbers close to the telephone for quick consultation. The list might include numbers for the boss's spouse's workplace, schools his or her children attend, stores the boss and family frequent, as well as their country or health clubs, plus the boss's physician, dentist, mechanic, accountant, and personal friends. Modern telephone equipment can be programmed to dial frequently called numbers automatically, saving you time and effort. Some computers also have this function and can dial frequently used numbers quickly and efficiently.

On any directory that you make up, the telephone numbers opposite each name should contain the area codes if not in your immediate area. For long-distance areas, also note the time differentials between other cities and your own to avoid disturbing people at awkward times. Some secretaries leave their directory fitted beneath the desk blotter or taped to a pull-out shelf of the desk. Others like to keep their desk uncluttered; still others prefer to keep the boss's personal numbers confidential.

Long-Distance Calls

Secretaries often place long-distance calls.

Station-to-Station Calls

When you are willing to speak with anyone who may answer, dial the number yourself. Charges for the call begin as soon as an answer is heard, including an answering machine. A station-to-station call is considerably less expensive than a person-to-person call but should be used only when you are relatively sure that anyone who answers can be of service to you.

Person-to-Person Calls

A person-to-person call—when you want to speak only to a specific individual— is made through the operator. Charges for a person-to-person call do not begin to accrue until the person called answers. This service is more expensive than a station-to-station call but may prove to be more economical if you are not sure the person you're calling will be available to come to the telephone. To make this call, say to the operator: "I wish to make a person-to-person call to Mr. Sullivan at (212) 555–7900."

Collect Calls

In any long-distance call made through the operator, if you expect the person on the other end to pay for the call, say: "This is a collect call. My name is Miss Scott for the Brown Company." If you are willing to speak to a second person when the first person is unavailable, give this information to the operator before he or she places the call. If you have reason to believe that the person called may be at another telephone number or in another city, explain that as well: "If Mr. Greene is not at 555–1860, please try 555–8430."

Conference Calls

A conference call allows as many people as desired to speak with each other. To place such a call, ask for the conference operator, and give the operator the names and telephone numbers of all of the persons to be convened. When all of them are on the line, the operator will connect you, and the charge will begin at that time. Modern telephones allow you to make these conference calls yourself, but the equipment installed must allow for this specific service. Your telephone company representative can explain the many services available.

Ship-to-Shore Calls

You may call a ship at sea (if the ship has facilities for receiving the call; most ships do) by asking for the ship-to-shore operator.

Air-to-Ground and Ground-to-Air Calls

Many airlines now provide air-to-ground and ground-to-air calls while a plane is in flight. Many planes are equipped with telephones that require the use of credit cards when placing a call from air to ground. When placing a call from ground to air, tell the long-distance operator the person's name being called, the airline (e.g., American or Delta), the flight number, the destination of the flight, and the passenger's seat number if known.

Calls to Trains

On a message to be delivered to someone on a train, give the person's name, train number or name of train, direction the train is traveling, car and reservation number if known, station, city and state, and arrival date and time. Also say that the message is to be delivered in care of the conductor of the train—for example:

Mr. Philip W. Wade
Care of the Conductor
AMTRAK, Westbound
Car 9, Bedroom 22
Due at LaSalle Station
Chicago, Illinois
December 1, 5:30 P.M.

Telegram Airport Delivery

When calling in a telegram to be sent to an airport for delivery to a plane passenger, provide the person's name, airline, flight number, direction of travel, airport destination, city and state, and arrival date and time—for example:

Ms. Janet Harrold
A Passenger
American Airlines, Flight 88, Northbound
Due at Chicago (Illinois) O'Hare Airport
May 5, 1:20 P.M.

New Telephone Equipment

The telephone company will advise you how to increase the efficiency of the telephone service in your company. Because new technology is constantly coming on the market, many of its devices and services may not be familiar to you, and an inquiry can be worthwhile. Ask about switching, hold buttons, exclusion buttons, cut off, pickup audible signal, visual signal, speaker telephones, automatic dialing, automatic answering and recording equipment, and intercommunicating features. Keep in mind that the more efficient your office equipment is, the more efficient you will be.

Many of these services, as well as facsimile or fax machines, are described in Chapter 8, Telecommunications Equipment.

Chapter 4

Mail Services and Shipping

Beyond a Letter and a Stamp

Mail is an important method of communication between a company and the outside business world. The daily processing of mail is usually handled by the secretary. This may include sorting the mail and distributing it to the proper departments or individuals. It may also include opening the employer's mail, prioritizing it, and gathering the necessary preliminary information needed to answer specific requests or problems.

Sending out business mail involves much more than a letter and a stamp, even when those letters are sent by the hundreds of thousands. There are larger documents and packages to be mailed, varying timetables to be met, and destinations ranging from next door to around the world. Dozens of work-saving, time-saving, money-saving strategies can help move the mail more efficiently.

A competent secretary should become acquainted with these profit-boosting moves, from the best physical ways to prepare the mail to the advantages of one mail service over another. He or she should also keep abreast of U.S. Postal Service (USPS) rules and regulations and methods of moving the mail. Neither you nor the company may need all this information at the present, but companies constantly change and grow. The secretary who can fulfill a company's new mailing needs—or who knows where to get the information quickly—is invaluable.

Addressing for Success

A company is judged by the way its letters are composed and spaced on the pages, and even by the manner in which its envelopes are addressed. All of this does more than simply create a good impression; it affects whether the mail is even delivered in a timely fashion.

The USPS relies on computerized mail processing machines—optical character readers (OCRs) and bar-code sorters (BCSs)—designed to increase the speed, efficiency, and accuracy of processing mail while keeping postal operating costs down. Consistently accurate delivery, faster mail turnaround, and greater profits are just some of the ways your company can benefit from this state-of-the-art system.

This high-speed equipment is programmed to "read" and sort up to 36,000 pieces of mail per hour. That's 10 pieces every second. But if your company's mail is not technically compatible, these sophisticated machines will not be able to sort it. Your mail will have to be sorted by hand, and the company will miss the related benefits of the equipment.

Two factors determine whether mail is considered technically compatible: (1) mail that is "machinable" or, in other words, the right size and shape to speed with ease through the equipment, and (2) mail that is electronically "readable" or capable of being read, coded, and sorted by the equipment.

How Your Company Can Receive the Benefits

Size

Begin by making sure that your letter mail is the proper size. Envelopes and cards with dimensions that fall between the minimums and maximums listed below will speed through the machines without a hitch.

Dimensions	Minimum (inches)	Maximum (inches)
Height	3 1/2	6 1/8
Length	5	11 1/2
Thickness	0.007	3/16 (card stock not to exceed .0095)

Envelopes or cards smaller than the minimums will not be delivered. Letter mail larger than the maximums may be mailed, but it must bypass the OCR and be processed through slower and less efficient manual or mechanized methods. It may also be subject to a surcharge even though the postage is correct for the weight.

Address Location

The OCR looks for the address within an imaginary rectangle on each mail-piece called the **OCR read area** (Figure 4-1). Make some quick measurements of your company's envelope stationery. The OCR will not have trouble finding the delivery address if it's located within the following boundaries:

SIDES OF THE RECTANGLE:	1/2 inch in from the right and left edges
BOTTOM OF THE RECTANGLE:	5/8 inch up from the bottom edge
TOP OF THE RECTANGLE:	2 3/4 inches up from the bottom edge

Figure 4-1. The OCR read area on an envelope.

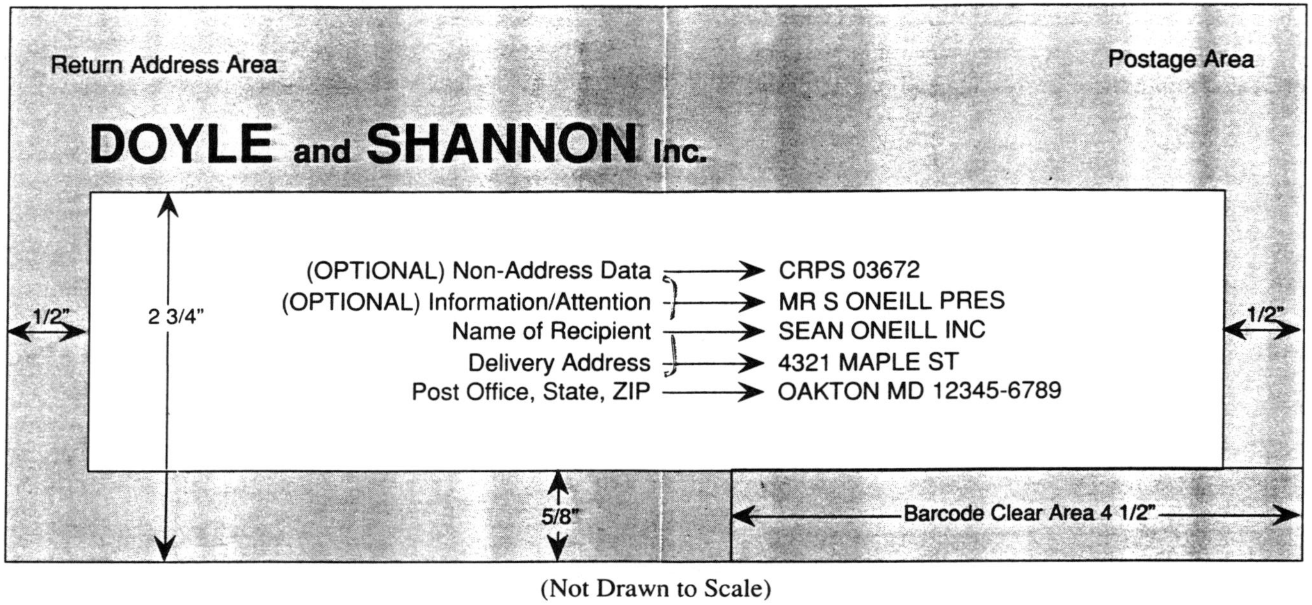

Return Address Area

Postage Area

DOYLE and SHANNON Inc.

1/2"

2 3/4"

1/2"

(OPTIONAL) Non-Address Data → CRPS 03672
(OPTIONAL) Information/Attention → MR S ONEILL PRES
Name of Recipient → SEAN ONEILL INC
Delivery Address → 4321 MAPLE ST
Post Office, State, ZIP → OAKTON MD 12345-6789

5/8"

Barcode Clear Area 4 1/2"

(Not Drawn to Scale)

Courtesy of the United States Post Office.

To provide the OCR with the information needed for the finest sort, put all the lines of the address within the above area. If that is not possible, it will still help to place as many address lines in the OCR read areas as you can.

A WORD OF CAUTION. Make sure no portion of the return address appears in the read area.

Lines of the Address

The OCR cannot rearrange address information that is out of proper sequence, so keep your address lines in the order shown in Figure 4-1. Make sure addresses are complete, including apartment or suite numbers and proper delivery designations (e.g., street, road, avenue). Often there will be in a single city streets with the same name—for example, a Hanford Street, Hanford Court, Hanford Lane, and Hanford Avenue—so always use the proper designation. Two-letter state abbreviations (listed in Figure 4-2) should always be used because the OCR recognizes them at a glance. Do not place a period after each initial of the abbreviation—that is, use AR instead of A.R.

Foreign Addresses

Foreign mailings should have the country name printed in capital letters as the only information on the bottom line. The postal delivery zone, if any, should be included with the city, not after the country. For example:

Mr. Thomas Clark
117 Russell Drive
London W1P6HQ
ENGLAND

Nonaddress Information

Extraneous (nonaddress) printing that appears in or near the OCR read area can cause the piece of mail to be rejected. To ensure that the equipment locates and reads only the delivery address, nonaddress information (advertising copy, company logos, etc.) that must appear in the read area should be positioned above the delivery address line. In other words, the space below and on either side of the delivery address line within the read area should be clear of all printing and other markings not actually part of the address. Positioning such information as far away from the address as possible also helps.

Bar-code Area

After reading an address, the OCR will print the appropriate bar bode on the bottom of the piece of mail. Then, by reading the code, BCSs quickly route each envelope and card to its destination. But BCSs recognize only bar codes and will reject mail that has some other type of printing where the bar code goes. Make sure the bar code area (see Figure 4-1) remains free of all markings.

Figure 4-2. Two-letter postal abbreviations for states, territories, and the District of Columbia.

Here is a list of the 2-letter abbreviations for states, territories, and the District of Columbia:

Alabama	AL	Nebraska	NE
Alaska	AK	Nevada	NV
Arizona	AZ	New Hampshire	NH
Arkansas	AR	New Jersey	NJ
American Samoa	AS	New Mexico	NM
California	CA	New York	NY
Colorado	CO	North Carolina	NC
Connecticut	CT	North Dakota	ND
Delaware	DE	No. Mariana Islands	CM
Dist. of Columbia	DC	Ohio	OH
Florida	FL	Oklahoma	OK
Georgia	GA	Oregon	OR
Guam	GU	Pennsylvania	PA
Hawaii	HI	Puerto Rico	PR
Idaho	ID	Rhode Island	RI
Illinois	IL	South Carolina	SC
Indiana	IN	South Dakota	SD
Iowa	IA	Tennessee	TN
Kansas	KS	Trust Territory	TT
Kentucky	KY	Texas	TX
Louisiana	LA	Utah	UT
Maine	ME	Vermont	VT
Maryland	MD	Virginia	VA
Massachusetts	MA	Virgin Islands	VI
Michigan	MI	Washington	WA
Minnesota	MN	West Virginia	WV
Mississippi	MS	Wisconsin	WI
Missouri	MO	Wyoming	WY
Montana	MT		

Window Envelopes

If your company uses window envelopes, be certain that the entire address is always visible, even during full movement of the insert. If part of the address is hidden, the OCR will reject the envelope and send it off for manual or mechanized processing.

Address Characters

The OCR will read most typewritten and other machine-printed addresses. It cannot read type styles such as script, italic, and highly stylized characters. It also has trouble deciphering dot-matrix print if the dots that form each character are not touching each other. Among the best typeface designs to choose from are those known as sans serif. (See the examples in Figure 4-3.)

Print Quality and Color

Print quality is of great importance to the OCR. It quickly reads clear, sharp print but may not be able to distinguish characters that are faded, broken, or smudged. Black ink on a white background is best. Although certain color combinations are acceptable, the OCR cannot read the address if there is not enough contrast between the ink and paper. Keep the ink as dark as possible and the background as light as possible. (See the examples in Figure 4-3.)

Spacing

Spacing between characters, words, and address lines is equally important. The OCR must see a clear vertical space between each character and each word, or it will not know where one ends and the next one begins. For similar reasons, it needs a clear horizontal space between each line of the address.

Postal Automation: Encoding for Business Mailers

Even if an address is sharply imprinted and speeds through the OCR, the letter itself won't be deliverable if the information in the address is incorrect. If your company maintains its address list on computer, the postal service can help you here too. Suppose your company has an in-house list of its best customers. The Postal Business Center for your area may be able to clean up your list and add valuable ZIP+4 (5-digit zip code plus 4-digit addendum) and carrier route information at no charge.

The postal service provides this service for your company because the benefits are mutual: for your company, more accurate and readable addresses, which provides faster sorting of mail and fewer undeliverable pieces (undeliverable third-class mail is money thrown away), and for the USPS, more efficient moving of the mail, saving it money, which can then be passed onto customers by holding the line on rates.

When the USPS cleans up your list, here is what it specifically does:

1. Standardizes your address list, making sure cities match the zip codes on the list.

Figure 4-3. Common address problems.

Common Problems

Not Enough Contrast

> MR JAMES JONES
> 4417 BROOK ST NE
> WASHINGTON DC 20019-4649

Characters Touch

> MR JAMES JONES
> 4417 BROOK ST NE
> WASHINGTON DC 20019-4649

Script Type Font Used

> *Mr. James Jones*
> *4417 Brook St NE*
> *Washington DC 20019-4649*

Logo Below Delivery Address Line

> MR JAMES JONES
> 4417 BROOK ST NE
> GHI WASHINGTON DC 20019-4649

Address Not Visible Through Window

> JAMES JONES & COMF
> 4417 BROOK ST NE
> WASHINGTON DC 200⁻

Non-Address Information Below Delivery Address Line

> MR JAMES JONES
> 4417 BROOK ST NE
> WASHINGTON DC 20019-4649
> Attn: R. Jones

Address Slanted

> MR JAMES JONES
> 4417 BROOK ST NE
> WASHINGTON DC 20019-4649

THE RIGHT WAY

> MR JAMES JONES
> 4417 BROOK ST NE
> WASHINGTON DC 20019-4649

2. Changes all characters to uppercase for increased readability by automation equipment.
3. Corrects minor misspellings and adds missing directions and suffixes.
4. Validates or corrects each five-digit zip code.
5. Adds the extra digits of ZIP+4 codes.
6. Gives you a report on any address that cannot be coded. For example, you'll discover which address needs an apartment or suite number to be complete or which address does not exist as given.

Important: This clean-up service does not eliminate duplicate addresses.

It's not a complicated procedure to benefit from this service. All you must provide is a copy of your address list on a diskette in a fixed ASCII format (plain text with no formatting) with fixed field and fixed record lengths. Many database management and spreadsheet programs and some word processing programs already operate in this format. To see about arranging encoding for your company's list or to ask questions, contact your account representative or the Postal Business Center in your area.

Metering

What's the next step after addressing your company's mail with the most accurate address information? Putting on postage, of course, so you can get the mail out on its way. Many small companies stamp their short letters and save longer correspondence and packages for a trip to the post office. Your company can save both time and money by investing in its own postage meter instead.

A postage meter offers savings for every office, not just larger ones with a heavy flow of outgoing mail. A postage meter ensures that your office does not overpay postage or underestimate it, which results in the embarrassing situation of mail arriving at clients' offices marked "postage due." It takes much less time to put metered postage on mail than it does to apply stamps, helping make more efficient use of staff time. In addition, your business correspondence moves more quickly once it leaves your office since the post office does not have to spend time cancelling and postmarking the mail.

Fee

There is no license fee for using a meter.

Postal Authorization

To obtain a postage meter license, submit a completed Form 3601-A, Application for a Postage Meter License, to the post office where your company will deposit its metered mail. To obtain the meter itself, you may lease one from an authorized manufacturer, which will install it. The post office will then, on request, set it for the amount of postage you wish to purchase. You may purchase postage for the meter at the same post office where the company has its meter license. If you'll be using the meter for bulk rate postage, you also need to order a "Bulk Rate" or "Nonprofit Organization" slug that is inserted into the meter.

Guidelines for Using a Postage Meter

A postage meter can make any business more cost efficient, though using it properly is vital. Here are a few simple guidelines for you to follow:

☐ *Change the meter date daily.* In a small business or in a department with its own postage meter, it will probably be up to you as secretary to change the date on the meter. Be sure to set up a reminder system for yourself to change the date daily; postal regulations demand the correct current date must be shown on first-class mail or the mail has to be remetered.

No date is required for metered bulk mailings if the meter impression is placed directly on the mailing piece (Figure 4-4, examples A and B). If a date is shown, it must be the actual date of the mailing. Meter tape must show the month and year but not the day of the mailing (Figure 4-4, examples C and D).

Once you've updated the meter and have the correct impression on your mail piece, don't lose momentum by missing a scheduled mail pickup. Contact your local post office about its operating hours and pickup times so you can deposit the mail in time for that day's processing and dispatch schedule.

☐ *Apply correct postage.* A mailroom is a good place to be cost-efficient; metering only the exact amount of postage is a good place to start. Overpaying "just to be sure" can be expensive over the long run. And do not underpay when the weight is "just a hair over." It makes a bad impression on the addressee and can even delay the mail's being sent. Test your scales for accuracy every day. Then get a copy of postal rate charts at your local post office.

☐ *Check for clear, readable imprints.* A clearly defined, readable meter impression is one more calling card to your customers. When those dates are readable, your customers know when you mailed—especially important for time-sensitive material.

☐ *Use special postage meter fluorescent ink.* Properly prepared metered mail should bypass the post office's facer/canceler machine. If metered mail inadvertently passes through the machine, fluorescent ink (known as "hot" ink in the trade) will speed the process. Use the ink provided by the meter manufacturer.

Figure 4-4. Examples of metered mail.

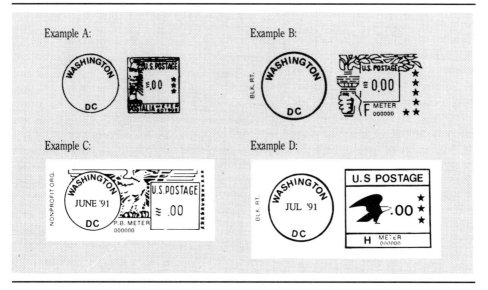

☐ *Face the mail.* As small a thing as facing all metered envelopes up and in the same direction speeds your company's mail on its way. If the post office does not have to turn pieces over to read the address before distributing each to the proper sorting area, a costly step has been saved.

☐ *Package securely.* Package five or more pieces of metered mail securely with rubber bands, and it will be handled more efficiently. Your post office will provide you with rubber bands for this purpose at no charge.

☐ *Use trays.* When preparing large volumes of letter metered mail, place it in trays secured from the post office. This method creates a cleaner environment for your employees and your mail, and it helps to direct the mail to the appropriate sorting equipment to speed up the process.

☐ *Protect the company's investment.* If your meter's printing or recording mechanism is faulty, contact your local post office and meter manufacturer for instructions.

The Secretary's Metering Checklist

Consider placing these reminders near or on your meter:

☐ Correct postage?

☐ Today's date?

☐ Scales balanced?

☐ Fluorescent (hot) ink?

☐ Clear impression?

☐ Mail faced in one direction?

☐ Rubber bands around five or more pieces?

☐ Tray large volumes of mail?

☐ Mail early?

Packaging

Much of the mail you'll be asked to send out as secretary will consist of letters and documents. But even with a mailroom on the premises, you may have to prepare and send out the occasional package yourself. For a package to arrive in good condition at its destination, it's important to observe four basic principles in packaging your shipments:

1. *Use a corrugated container.* These "cardboard boxes" come in a variety of strengths and weights. Primarily there are three basic types: single-wall, double-wall, and triple-wall containers. You can tell the difference by examining the sides of the box and noticing the number of layers. Single wall has two outside liners and a wavy corrugated medium in the middle. Double wall has two wavy corru-

gated mediums in the middle separated by a third liner. Triple wall has three corrugated mediums and a total of four liners.

Select a box that is large enough to allow some room around the contents in every direction. This will allow the contents to be safe from punctures, tears, or rips on the corners or side of the box when turning in transit.

Boxes are available from many shipping supply companies, as well as mailing and packaging chain stores. Make sure that the box will support the weight of your shipment. Every box has a stamp printed on it specifying the maximum weight it will support. Double-wall and triple-wall containers are stronger than most single-wall boxes. It is not a good idea to reuse shipping containers unless they are in good shape and will not be supporting much weight. Moisture and other shipping conditions tend to lessen the strength of corrugated containers.

2. *Protect the contents.* Use wadded-up newsprint, crumpled brown grocery bags, air bubble pack, foam peanuts, or shredded paper. Depending on the contents of the package, it may be a good idea to wrap them in plastic as well to keep the packing material from sticking to them or getting inside. The packing material should be placed on the bottom, all four sides, and the top to provide several inches of protection between the contents and the sides of the box.

3. *Close the box securely.* Most shipping companies, including the USPS, will not accept boxes tied with string. Nor should you use masking tape or regular cellophane tape; neither has enough strength to keep the box closed. Instead use carton sealing tape, pressure-sensitive place tape, water-activated paper tape, or water-activated reinforced tape. Generally apply three strips of tape to the top and the bottom. One strip should seal the box, and the other two strips should seal the sides.

4. *Use the proper labeling.* Make sure you include a zip code; as an added precaution you may want to include the addressee's telephone number. Your company's return address is also important. You never know if the recipient has moved or is out of town and cannot receive your shipment. In some cases, your shipment can be held at the destination, but there are time limits on this. It's also a good idea to pack a copy of the label with all of the identifying information inside the box so if the outside label is damaged or removed, the shipper can determine the destination by opening the box.

When applying your labels to the package, always place them on the top of the package, away from seams or box edges. Then apply several strips of clear carton sealing tape over the label to prevent it from falling off.

For odd-shaped or extremely fragile objects, it's best to check with the shipping services for advice on how to package the item and the best way to send it.

Important U.S. Postal Service Mail Services

Most of your company's mail probably goes out and comes in via the U.S. Post Office. The information following only touches the high points of the many services it offers so you'll know they are there when needed. A complete and separate brochure is available on each subject mentioned. USPS services change from time to time so it's useful to call or visit a local post office occasionally. In addition, the USPS maintains a Marketing and Communications Office in large metropolitan areas to advise the public of such services and answer questions by telephone or in person.

Should you experience a problem with any mail service, complete a Consumer Service Card, Form 4314 (Figure 4-5), available from letter carriers and at all post offices. Detailing your problem will help your postmaster respond. You may also advise the postmaster of a problem by calling your local post office.

The Consumer Advocate represents consumers at the top-management level in the postal service. If your problem cannot be solved by your local post office, write to the Consumer Advocate at:

Consumer Advocate
U.S. Postal Service, Room 5821
475 L'Enfant Plaza West SW
Washington, DC 20260-2200

Following is a brief description of the major mail services provided by the USPS.

Express Mail

Express Mail is the fastest service. It offers guaranteed delivery, or your money will be returned upon filing a refund application at your local post office. Express Mail provides several options for private and business customers who require fast (usually overnight but sometimes two days) delivery of letters and packages.

How to Use Express Mail

It's very convenient to use Express Mail. There are a variety of ways to drop off your letters or packages or have them picked up for you:

- Take your shipment to any of the over 26,000 designated Express Mail post offices, generally by 5:00 P.M. Monday through Friday and typically up to noon on Saturday.
- Deposit the shipment in one of the 20,000 Express Mail collection boxes conveniently located on streets, in shopping malls, high-rise office buildings, and post office lobbies. Pickup times are posted on the boxes.
- Hand your prepaid Express Mail shipment to your letter or rural-route carrier at the time your mail is delivered.
- Use any of the additional convenient ways to send Express Mail that are provided in many cities, including mini–Express Mail offices in storefront locations, traveling "mobile acceptance vans" that sell stamps and process Express Mail letters and packages, and a pickup service that will come to

Figure 4-5. USPS Consumer Service Card, Form 4314 and 4314-C (computerized).

1 PRINT FIRMLY   2 REMOVE TOP COPY FOR CUSTOMER RECORD (do not separate remaining copies)   3 FILL IN ADDRESS BLANK ON BACK OF LAST CARD   4 MAIL (postage free)

U.S. POSTAL SERVICE CONSUMER SERVICE CARD

No. **M** 6 477 925

Name

| Date (Mo., Day, Yr.) | | Customer Phone (8 a.m.-5 p.m.) |

Address (Apt./Suite No., No. and Street, City)

| State | ZIP Code | |

Is This

☐ Information Request   ☐ Suggestion   ☐ Problem   ☐ Compliment

Did It Involve			**This Section Is For USPS Use Only**
Delay	If This Is A Problem With A Specific Mailing, Please Complete The Following:		Recording Employee Name
Nonreceipt			
Damage	Was It	Was Mailing	Date Customer Contacted / Customer Contacted By
Misdelivery	Letter	First-Class	
Improperly Returned	Package	Special Delivery	USPS Action
Change of Address	Newspaper/ Magazine	Certified	
Vending Equipment		Registered	
Window Services	Advertisement	Insured	
Personnel	Electronic Transmission	Express Mail	
Other		Other	

Please Give Essential Facts (If this involves a change of address problem, please include previous address.)

PS Form 4314-C, July 1991   THANK YOU. You will be contacted soon by your Post Office.   CUSTOMER COPY - 1

your door and pick up an unlimited number of Express Mail pieces for $4.50 per trip. Call your Express Mail post office for the 800 pickup number for your area. If there is recurring need, pickup service can even be pre-scheduled on a regular basis.

- Take letters or packages to an airport mail facility. You will find the latest acceptance of your important Express Mail shipments at any one of 66 airport mail facilities (AMFs) nationwide.

If your shipment has been dropped off by the acceptance time, generally it will be delivered to the addressee by noon the next day if you are mailing between major markets; otherwise, it will arrive by 3:00 P.M. the next day, weekends and holidays included. The addressee can also pick up Express Mail at the destination post office as early as 10:00 A.M. the next day.

Payment

The overnight letter rate for Express Mail is $9.95 for letters weighing up to 8 ounces. A small package flat rate is $13.95. Using the special flat-rate envelope, you can send as many documents as the package will hold. There's no need to weight it: just affix $13.95 postage, and send to any destination in the United states or its protectorates. The envelope fits into any Express Mail collection box.

Pay for Express Mail with stamps, postage meter strips, or through a corporate Express Mail account. In some cities, credit cards can be used as well. The postal service will supply you with mailing containers—envelopes, boxes, tubes—plus the necessary mailing labels at no additional charge. A 2-pound flat rate envelope is also available.

To open a corporate account for your company, apply at any Express Mail post office by filling out a brief application and depositing an amount equal to your company's estimated two weeks' Express Mail postage charges or $100, whichever is higher.

Express Mail service comes with a postage money–back guarantee. Merchandise is automatically insured up to $500 against loss or damage. Compensation for loss of negotiable items such as currency or bullion is limited to $15. However, document reconstruction insurance is available up to $50,000 for nonnegotiable documents.

Service Options

Express Mail offers a variety of service options to meet all mailing needs:

Post Office to Addressee Service

This service delivers letters and packages directly to the addressee, guaranteeing delivery by noon the next day between all major business markets and by 3:00 P.M. the next day in other markets (with a few exceptions). Among all overnight mail delivery services, it is the only one that can deliver to an addressee's post office box. Check the Express Mail directory at your local Express Mail post office for all overnight destinations. The standard acceptance time is 5:00 P.M., although many Express Mail post offices and Express Mail boxes have scheduled later acceptance.

Post Office to Post Office Service

When delivery by noon is not early enough, this is the service to use. Post office to post office service delivers to the Express Mail post office nearest your addressee by 10:00 A.M. the next day, provided the letter or package was mailed by the acceptance time of your Express Mail post office. Check with your local post office to be sure the destination post office is one of the USPS's 6,400 shipment claims locations. Also, you will need to notify the addressee where and when the shipment can be picked up.

Express Mail Same Day Airport Service

This is the fastest and most economical of all Express Mail options, as low as $8.35 between any two airport mail facilities. The mailer brings a letter or package to one of the sixty-six airport mail facilities, to be placed on the next available flight to an airport mail facility in the destination city, reaching its final destination within a matter of hours.

Express Mail Military Service

This is the fastest service to and from over 290 APO/FPO addresses around the world—reliable two- to three-day delivery for the same rates as domestic Express Mail service, no matter where in the world the shipment goes.

Special Business Needs

The Post Office will personalize their services to meet the special needs of a particular business shipper. Some of these services are described here.

Custom Designed Service

Express Mail Custom Designed Service provides fast, reliable delivery to any location in the United States—24 hours a day, 365 days a year—or around the world to cities included in the Express Mail International Service Network. The service is specifically designed to fit a regularly scheduled mailing that must be delivered quickly, but at off hours. Here's how it works:

Your company selects the time and place for both acceptance and needed delivery of the shipment. If 3:00 A.M. is the best time to have urgent letters and packages picked up, the USPS will be there. Your company can have shipments picked up and delivered directly to the addressee, to any post office or airport mail facility offering Express Mail service, or to any combination. Once your company decides upon its needs, it receives from the post office a written proposal containing service details such as acceptance and delivery locations, pickup and delivery requirements, total costs, and methods of payment. Rates for Express Mail Custom Designed Service are determined by the weight of the package and the Express Mail service options used.

Express Mail Drop Shipment Service

Get extra speed by bundling individual mailings and sending them via Express Mail overnight service to key cities around the country. The next morning, Express Mail pouches are opened, and individual pieces are sent along to their ultimate destinations as normal mail.

Express Mail Re-Ship Service

Many businesses such as direct-sales organizations, film processors, stock brokerage firms, and fund-raising organizations receive payments via mail for the products or services they've sold to customers all over America. Most of these companies have their customers send payments to the home office or the site of their accounting operation. Express Mail Re-Ship Service accelerates the delivery of this incoming mail significantly by having customers send payments or orders to the business, but in care of a local post office box in a key city within a given region. Each day, for a fee of $4.50, the post office box is cleared out and the contents are packaged and sent to the company via Express Mail service. The speed of delivery can lead to better cash flow and improved order processing for the company and greater satisfaction for customers.

Express Mail COD Service

This option lets your company rush merchandise to collect-on-delivery (COD) customers who order via mail or phone and request rapid service. Upon delivery, the postal service employee collects—in cash or a check payable to sender—the total amount specified on the COD label. If the recipient pays in cash, the local post office will send the business owner a postal money order for the amount collected. Checks will be sent directly to the business owner. COD service fees are determined by the amount of money to be collected.

Express Mail International Service

This service provides speed, economy, and reliability, delivering to most foreign cities in one to three days and with surprisingly fast deliveries to remote areas too.

Express Mail Packaging

The USPS has special shipping containers for the most common types of Express Mail service shipments: the Express Mail Envelope, EP-13A, for urgent letters and documents weighing up to 8 ounces; the Express Mail Envelope, EP-13, for letters and documents and small packages; the Express Mail Box for heavier items; and the Express Mail Tube for drawings, maps, blueprints, and similar items. The Flat Rate Envelope, EP-13F, will be provided to customers who wish to take advantage of the 2-pound flat rate.

Mailers can use their own packaging as long as each package does not exceed 70 pounds in weight and 108 inches in combined length and girth. The mailer must also have the appropriate label for the type of service used. Figures 4-6 through 4-10 show various types of labels, plus a chart for Express Mail rates.

Extra Conveniences

Besides the many types of services listed above, Express Mail Service provides these extra conveniences:

Waiver of Signature

You can have overnight shipments delivered even if the recipient is not available by signing the waiver-of-signature line on the Post Office to Addressee B-Label. A postal employee will then deliver your shipment even if the addressee/agent is not available to sign for it, provided the package can be placed in a secure location. Waiver of signature is not available for Express Military Service to an FPO or APO address.

Return Receipt

If you wish to get a signed receipt from the person accepting your Express Mail shipment, fill out Form 3811, Return Receipt, and attach it to your shipment. An additional fee of $1.00 will be charged for this option. Form 3811 is available at any Express Mail post office.

Return to Sender

Express Mail service items that are not delivered or claimed after five days will be returned to the sender via Express Mail service.

Free Forwarding

If the addressee has moved, your shipment will be automatically forwarded to the new address via Express Mail service, if the addressee has provided proper notification of address change with the postal service.

Postage Refund Guarantee

The USPS is so confident in the reliability of Express Mail that it offers to refund the postage if an item was mailed by the local acceptance time but not

(text continues on p. 45)

Figure 4-6. Express Mail label 11-A.

POST OFFICE TO POST OFFICE

EXPRESS MAIL
NEXT DAY SERVICE®

Y A0316067L2

FROM:

Corporate Account Number:
Federal Agency Account No:

HOLD FOR:
Name & Firm   Telephone Number:

AT:
Branch/Station

City   State   Zip

Sender must notify addressee of claim location—See Publication 272

Press Hard. You Are Making 4 Copies
Remove The Backing Sheet To Expose Adhesive Before Applying The Label To Your Package

ORIGIN:
Initials of
Receiving
Clerk

P.O. ZIP Code

Date in   Time in

Return Receipt Service
(Additional fee required)
☐ To Whom & Date Del.

Weight
_____ lbs. _____ oz.

Postage & Fees:
$

DESTINATION:
at P.O. Window
Date Received: Time Received:

Initials of
Window Clerk:

RECEIVED:
Signature of Addressee or Agent:

Initials of
Window Clerk:

EXPRESS MAIL SERVICE
Mailing Label
Service Analysis & Proof of Delivery
Label 11-A (July 1988)

Courtesy of the United States Postal Service.

Figure 4-7. Express Mail label 11-B.

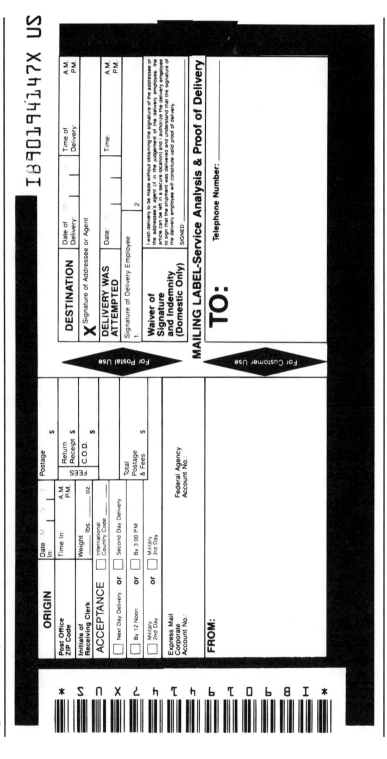

Courtesy of the United States Postal Service.

Figure 4-8. Postal Service Form 5625 and 5625-C (computerized), Express Mail, Custom Designed Service.

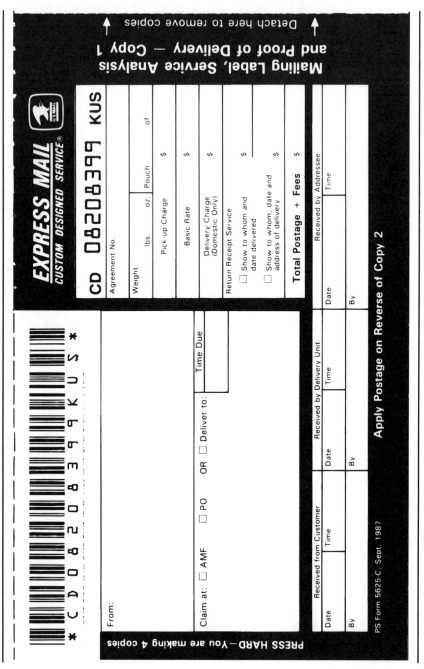

Courtesy of the United States Postal Service.

Figure 4-11.   Presort identification.

PRESORT IDENTIFICATION

All the envelopes or cards in a Presort mailing must be endorsed
"Presorted First-Class." This includes both the mail which qualifies
for the lower rate and the residual mail.

PERMIT IMPRINT MAILINGS

On mail paid by permit imprint the "Presorted First-Class"
marking must either be printed within the permit imprint, or be
printed or stamped above the address and just below or to the
left of the permit imprint.

POSTAGE METER STAMP MAILINGS

On metered mail the marking must be printed or stamped above
the address and just below or to the left of the meter stamp. It
may be printed by a postage meter special slug or by an ad plate.
If the customer has a "Drop Shipment" authorization, and uses it
with Presort First-Class Mail, the "PRESORTED FIRST-CLASS"
endorsement may be included with the "Drop Shipment"
endorsement. See example below.

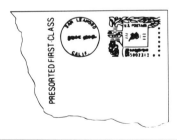
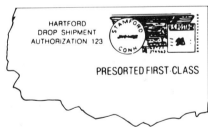

Figure 4-12. Precanceled stamp mailings.

PRECANCELED STAMP MAILINGS

On mail affixed with precanceled stamps, the marking must be printed or stamped above the address and just below or to the left of the precanceled stamp. The only exception is when the mailer uses stamps that are precanceled by the Postal Service and include the "PRESORTED FIRST-CLASS" endorsement as part of the precancelation.

Precanceled by the mailer:

May be used by all customers with local postmaster approval.	May be used only by mailers who have this die. New dies with this format will not be made.

Precanceled by the Postal Service
(Endorsement included in the precancelation):

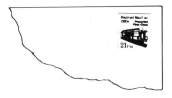 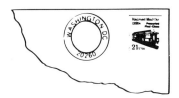

Used when the mailer's return address (city, state, ZIP Code) is shown on the mailing piece and the city and state are the same as the post office of mailing.	To be used if the mailer's return address (city, state, ZIP Code) is NOT the same as the post office of mailing.

Figure 4-13. How to prepare presorted first-class mail (500-piece minimum).

Pieces qualifying for the Presort Rate MUST be prepared in the following sequence:

DIRECT	CITY	SCF	AREA DISTRIBUTION CENTER (ADC)	MIXED ADCs
10 or more to the same 5-digit ZIP Code.	50 or more to the same first 3-digit ZIP code uniquely* assigned to a city. *Applies ONLY to those cities listed in upper case letters in the ZIP Code Prefixes Section of the National Five-Digit ZIP Code and Post Office Directory or in Exhibit 122.63b of the DMM.	50 or more to a first 3-digit ZIP Code assigned to a Sectional Center Facility.*(Each first 3-digit ZIP Code assigned to a SCF MUST be packaged separately.) *See National ZIP Code and Post Office Directory for SCF list or Exhibits 122.63c and 122.63d, DMM.	Recommended but not mandatory that remaining qualifying packages be sorted to Area Distribution Centers (ADCs) and placed in ADC TRAYS. Postmasters will provide mailers with listings of ADCs and the areas they serve from Exhibit 122.63e, DMM.	

Qualifying Direct pieces that do not fill a DIRECT TRAY must be packaged and trayed in the following priority order:

CITY TRAY – When the first three digits of the Direct packages are the same as the first three digits uniquely assigned to a city.

SCF TRAY – When the first three digits of the Direct packages are the same as any of the first three digits assigned to the SCF.

ADC TRAY (Recommended but not mandatory) – When the first three digits of the Direct packages are the same as any of the first three digits assigned to the ADC.

MIXED ADCs TRAY – When the Direct packages are not presortable in full trays to the required or recommended categories.

Qualifying City pieces that do not fill a CITY TRAY must be packaged and trayed in the following priority order:

SCF TRAY – When the first three digits of the City packages are the same as any of the first three digits assigned to the SCF.

ADC TRAY (Recommended but not mandatory) – When the first three digits of the City packages are the same as any of the first three digits assigned to the ADC.

MIXED ADCs TRAY – When the City packages are not presortable in full trays to the required or recommended categories.

Qualifying SCF pieces that do not fill an SCF TRAY must be packaged and trayed in the following priority order:

ADC TRAY (Recommended but not mandatory) – When the first three digits of the SCF packages are the same as any of the first three digits assigned to the ADC.

MIXED ADCs TRAY – When the SCF packages are not presorted in full trays to the recommended category.

Remaining (Residual) Mail
Any remaining mail not presorted into DIRECT, CITY, or SCF categories is INELIGIBLE for the lower rate. If it is included as part of the Presort mailing it must be completely segregated from the qualifying pieces, placed in separate trays and sorted by one of the following schemes:

- Sequenced by 5-digit ZIP Codes
- Sequenced by 3-digit ZIP Code
- Separated by ADCs
- Separated by in-state and out-of-state

☐ Ten or more pieces to the same first five digits of the zip code—for example, 75214—must be grouped together and banded with rubber bands.

☐ Fifty or more pieces to the same first three digits of the zip code—for example, 752—must be grouped together and banded with rubber bands.

☐ Mail that cannot be separated as above is referred to as residual mail. It can be counted toward the 500-piece minimum volume requirement but does not qualify for the lower presort postage rate.

☐ Accurately label each tray or sack of presorted mail for proper postal handling.

☐ Accompany each mailing with a properly completed Form 3602-R, Statement of Mailing with Permit Imprints (for a permit imprint mailing), or a Form 3602-PC, Statement of Mailing Bulk Rates (for a metered or precanceled stamps mailing). These forms are available at all post offices.

☐ Deliver the mail to a bulk mail acceptance unit during normal operating hours.

In certain circumstances, the postal service will provide customer mail collection. The collection must be part of an existing collection service for another class of mail. Call your post office for details.

Priority Mail

Priority mail is first-class mail weighing 11 ounces or more, with a maximum weight of 70 pounds and a maximum combined girth of 108 inches. When the speed of Express Mail is not needed but preferential handling is desired, use priority mail. It offers expedited delivery at the least expensive rate in the industry.

Priority mail should be well identified. All post offices supply priority mail stickers, labels, envelopes, and boxes at no extra charge. A presort discount is available for large mailings. A flat-rate 2-pound envelope is available, suitable for sending contracts, documents, forms, or any other important items that require prompt but not overnight delivery. The postal service also offers flat rates for shipments of 3, 4, and 5 pounds. The costs for priority mail packages weighing up to the maximum weight of 70 pounds are listed on the priority mail rate card.

Priority mail can be insured, registered, certified, or sent COD for an additional charge.

Pickup Service

As with Express Mail, the postal service will pick up prepaid priority mail packages for $4.50 per pickup, no matter how many pieces. If you prefer to mail them yourself, you can take priority mail packages to your nearest post office. You can also drop prepaid unzoned packages (weighing up to 5 pounds) in one of the many collection boxes or hand them to your letter carrier.

Priority Mail Drop-Shipment Service for Larger Mailings

When sending a large number of first-, second-, third-, or fourth-class mail pieces out of town yet to the same area, consider Priority Mail Drop-Shipment Service. Your different classes of mail are bundled up and travel via priority mail to a destination post office, where the pouch is opened and the mail is unbundled and put into the local mainstream for delivery.

Priority mail handling reduces the total delivery time. It is almost like having another office in the destination city.

Forwarding First-Class and Other Mail

First-class mail is forwarded at no charge for one year. Second-class mail, including magazines and newspapers, is forwarded at no charge for 60 days from the effective date of a change-of-address order. All post offices have information about holding mail, temporary changes of address, and forwarding and return of other classes of mail.

Other Classes of Mail

Second-Class Mail

Magazines and newspapers may be sent at second-class mail rates, which are less expensive than first class. However, only publishers and registered news agents that have been approved for second-class mailing privileges may mail at these rates; magazines and newspapers mailed by the general public must be paid for at the applicable single-piece third- or fourth-class rate. All post offices can provide additional information on second-class mail.

Third-Class Mail (Bulk Business Mail or Advertising Mail)

Third-class mail, also referred to as bulk business mail or advertising mail, may be sent by anyone but is used most often by large mailers. This class covers printed material and merchandise weighing less than 16 ounces.

There are two rate structures for this class: single piece and bulk rate. Many businesses and community organizations find the economics of bulk rate more attractive than the speed of first class. Individuals may also use third-class mail for lightweight parcels. Insurance can be purchased at the option of the mailer to cover loss or damage of articles mailed at the single-piece third-class rate. (See the following section on Insurance.)

Your post office has information on what category of third-class mail is best suited to your company's needs. If the company is planning to mail at the attractive third-class bulk rates, stop by the local post office or Postal Service Business Center in large metropolitan areas and secure a copy of USPS Publication 49, *Third-Class Mail Preparation.* (See Figures 4-14 and 4-15 for labeling, packaging, and sacking instructions.)

Figure 4-14. Packaging instructions.

PACKAGING

NOTE; SUPPLIES, INCLUDING PRESSURE SENSITIVE LABELS ("D", "3", AND "MS"), RUBBER BANDS, SACKS, AND SACK LABELS, INCLUDING PREPRINTED BARCODED SACK LABELS ARE AVAILABLE FROM THE POST OFFICE. CONTACT YOUR LOCAL MAILING REQUIRE-MENTS OFFICE OR POSTMASTER FOR DETAILS

A Package is a group of mailpieces secured together as a single unit.

The packaging instructions below were designed for you to obtain the lowest allowable rate by providing the Postal Service with mail that is easily and quickly sorted, dispatched, and delivered.

Please follow the step-by-step instructions below when packaging your mail.

GENERAL INSTRUCTIONS:

■ Face all addresses in the same direction.
■ Secure packages with rubber bands. Rubber bands are preferrable using the following recommended methods:

• One rubber band around the girth for packages up to one inch in thickness.
• Two rubber bands (one around the length and one around the girth) for packages between one and four inches (always band length-wise first, then around the girth).
■ Four-inch thick packages are preferred and *no* package may be more than six inches thick.

PREFERRED BANDING METHODS:
ALWAYS BAND LENGTHWISE FIRST
WHEN USING TWO RUBBER BANDS

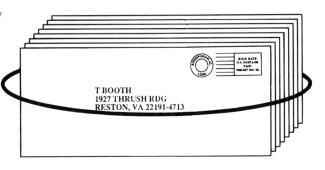

BAND WIDTH NEXT

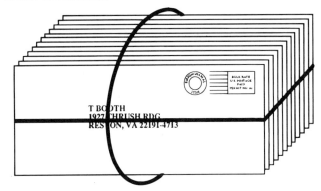

Fourth-Class Mail (Parcel Post)

Use this service for packages weighing 1 pound or more. If first-class mail is enclosed or attached, first-class postage must usually be paid for the enclosure or attachment. Ask your post office about incidental first-class attachments or enclosures that do not require separate payment of first-class postage. You can purchase insurance to cover the value of articles mailed at the fourth-class rate. (See the following section on Insurance.)

Packages mailed within the continental United States can weigh up to 70

Figure 4-15. Sacking/labeling instructions.

SACKING/LABELING

GENERAL REQUIREMENTS

Sacking is a means of combining mail for the same area of distribution. Except as noted under carrier route presort rate and basic presort rate sacking requirements, a sack of bulk third-class mail must contain at least 125 pieces or 15 pounds of mail. Although 70 pounds is the maximum allowable limit per sack, 40 pounds is preferred.

The contents and destination of each sack are described by means of a sack label. The sack label must be clearly printed as three distinct and separate lines, as shown in the illustration below.

The following abbreviations may be used:

3C	Third Class
MXD	Mixed
DG	Digit
LTRS	Letters
FLTS	Flats

Additional abbreviations that may be used for carrier route presort sack preparation may be found in Chapter 4.

EXAMPLE: This is for a 5-digit sack in which all the mail is going to the 5-Digit ZIP Code 33624. Labels for other types of sacks appear in other illustrations throughout this booklet.

Destination   TAMPA FL 33624
Contents   3C LTRS
Office of Mailing   TAMPA FL

LINE 1—Indicates the mail in this sack is for delivery to Tampa, FL 33624 only.

LINE 2—Indicates the contents of the sack are third-class letters.

LINE 3—Indicates this sack was part of a mailing from Tampa, FL.

Note: Care must be taken to prepare labels so that the top line will not be covered by the edge of the label holder.

pounds and measure up to 108 inches in length and girth combined. All post offices have information about lower local mailing rates and special mailing rates for books, catalogs, and international mailings.

The postal service sets a delivery goal for parcel post of seven days or less to most areas, depending on distance. For faster delivery of parcels, use priority mail or Express Mail service.

Electronic Mail Services

Two types of electronic mail services may also prove useful for your company: Mailgrams and INTELPOST.

Mailgram

A Mailgram (a registered trademark of Western Union Corporation) is an electronic message service offered by Western Union that provides next-day postal service delivery for messages sent to any address in the United States or Canada. The messages are transmitted for delivery with the next business day's mail.

Mailgrams are often used for short messages when you need to get someone's attention. For instance, if a company or individual is extremely late in paying a bill and is ignoring your other written correspondence, a Mailgram might help get their attention. Mailgrams are also useful as a way to get the attention of a potential client. While they are delivered with the regular mail, the Mailgram stands out and looks important.

Mailgram messages may be sent by calling Western Union and dictating your message to the operator, or you can use your office telex or TWX. For more information, call Western Union Telegraph Company. In Hawaii, call your local post office for information on how to send a message. In Alaska, call Alascom, Inc., for Mailgram service.

INTELPOST

International Electronic Postal Service (INTELPOST) is the fastest international mail service in the world. In minutes, it transmits sharp black-and-white facsimile copies of your urgent message to post offices overseas in most countries. Use it to deliver graphs, charts, contracts, invoices, retail orders, bids, price lists, sketches, itineraries—anything that can be photocopied. The service offers excellent message quality, a wide choice of delivery options, surprising economy, a free transmission test, all the security of postal correspondence, and walk-in service available in selected cities.

With 24-hour dial-in service, you don't even have to leave the office: you send facsimile messages directly from your company's fax machine to INTELPOST's fax machine at any hour of the day or night, 365 days a year. These messages are relayed electronically to post offices in participating countries.

Since the facsimile goes to a post office, not an individual, your company can deliver its message fast even if the recipient doesn't have a facsimile or you don't know its number. Depending on your choice of delivery options, your fax message will be available at the receiving post office 1 hour after transmission during business hours, delivered the same day in most major metropolitan areas, or delivered the next day in all other areas.

To find out more about INTELPOST Dial-in Service, call the nearest U.S. Postal Service Office of Marketing and Communications or your account representative. INTELPOST Service Center Dial-in Locations are in such major cities as Atlanta, Boston, Chicago, Denver, Honolulu, Houston, Long Beach (CA), Los Angeles, Miami, New York, San Francisco, Santa Ana (CA), Seattle, and Washington, D.C. Call your post office for frequent additions to this list of cities. Call the U.S. Postal Service for a list of countries served by INTELPOST. These include most countries of the world.

Other Special Mail Services

In addition to the services already outlined, the USPS offers a wide variety of other options to provide customers maximum convenience and to give individual pieces of mail special handling or protection.

Any piece traveling by one of these special services must be so labeled. The appropriate marking (registered, insured, certified, etc.) should be placed above the delivery address and to the right of the return address.

Post Office Box and Caller Services

Post office box and caller services are available at many post offices for an annual fee. Post office box delivery is a secure and private means of getting your mail any time the post office lobby is open. With post offices conveniently located near most businesses, you can get a jump on your day by picking up your company's mail at a post office box in the morning.

Caller (pickup) service, available when post office retail windows are open, is for customers who receive a large volume of mail or those who need a box number address when no boxes are available. Call your post office for more information.

Passport Applications

You can apply for a passport at more than 1,200 postal facilities nationwide. State Department regulations require that each applicant present two recent photographs, 2 inches by 2 inches, valid identification, and a certified copy of his or her birth certificate, along with the appropriate fee when applying for a new passport. The passport fee may be paid in cash, by check, or by money order. For additional information, call the Department of State information line nearest you or your local post office.

Money Orders

Because you should *never send cash through the mail*, money orders are a safe way to send money when checks cannot be used. The special color-blend, Benjamin Franklin watermark, metal security thread, and twice imprinting of the dollar amount are incorporated security features. You can buy domestic and international money orders at all post offices in amounts up to $700. Military money orders can be purchased on U.S. military ships and foreign bases.

If your money order is lost or stolen, present your customer receipt, and the money order can be replaced. For a small fee, you can obtain a copy of a money order for up to two years after the date it is paid.

Change of Address Forms

Before moving from one location to another, each company or individual should obtain from the local post office an official U.S. Postal Service Change of Address

Form 3575 (Figure 4-16). Change of address cards (Figure 4-17) are available to send to all correspondents and publishers of periodicals regularly received.

It's best to notify the post office several weeks in advance of the move to keep the mail coming without interruption. Be sure the effective date of the change is on the notification form. Your complete new address on the notification form should include directionals (North, East, South, West), the correct suffix (Street, Avenue, Road, Circle), suite number, rural route number, box number, and correct zip code or ZIP+4 code if known—all essential to proper addressing and fast delivery of your mail.

Collect-on-Delivery (COD) Service

Use COD service when your company wants to collect for merchandise and postage when the merchandise is delivered. COD service may be used for merchandise sent by first-class mail, Express Mail, priority mail, third- or fourth-class mail, or registered mail. The merchandise must have been ordered by the addressee. The fee charged for this service includes insurance protection against loss or damage, although the service is limited to items valued at a maximum of

Figure 4-16. Change of address form.

U.S. Postal Service
CHANGE OF ADDRESS ORDER

Customer Instructions: Complete Items 1 thru 9. Except Item 8, please PRINT all information including address on face of card.

OFFICIAL USE ONLY
Zone/Route ID No.
Date Entered on Form 3982 M M D D Y Y
Expiration Date M M D D Y Y
Clerk/Carrier Endorsement

1. Change of Address for *(Check one)* ☐ Individual ☐ Entire Family ☐ Business

2. Start Date — Month Day Year

3. If TEMPORARY address, print date to discontinue forwarding — Month Day Year

4. Print Last Name or Name of Business *(If more than one, use separate Change of Address Order Form for each)*

5. Print First Name of Head of Household *(include Jr., Sr., etc.)*. Leave blank if the Change of Address Order is for a business.

6. Print **OLD** mailing address, number and street *(if Puerto Rico, include urbanization zone)*

Apt./Suite No. P.O. Box No. R.R/HCR No. Rural Box/HCR Box No.

City State ZIP Code

7. Print **NEW** mailing address, number and street *(if Puerto Rico, include urbanization zone)*

Apt./Suite No. P.O. Box No. R.R/HCR No. Rural Box/HCR Box No.

City State ZIP Code

8. Signature *(See conditions on reverse)*

OFFICIAL USE ONLY

9. Date Signed — Month Day Year

OFFICIAL USE ONLY
Verification Endorsement

PS Form 3575, June 1991 ☆ U.S.G.P.O. 1992-309-315

Courtesy of the United States Postal Service.

Figure 4-17. Change of address forms for correspondents, publishers, and businesses.

As soon as you know your new address, mail this card to all of the people, businesses, and publications who send you mail.

For publications, tape an old address label over name and old address sections and complete new address.

Your Name (Print or type. Last name, first name, middle initial.)					

Old Address	No. & Street	Apt./Suite No.	PO Box	RR No.	Rural Box No.
	City	State	ZIP + 4		

New Address	No. & Street	Apt./Suite No.	PO Box	RR No.	Rural Box No.
	City	State	ZIP + 4		

Sign Here	Date new address in effect	Keyline No. (If any)

PS Form **3576**, August 1989   RECEIVER: Be sure to record the above new address.

Change of Address Request for:

Correspondents
Publishers and
Businesses

Please Type or Print

Affix
Postcard
Postage
Here

Name or Name of Publication

Address (Include Apt., Suite No.)

City, State, ZIP + 4

Courtesy of the United States Postal Service.

$600. (For further details, see Insurance.) COD service is not available for international mail.

Merchandise Return Service

Merchandise return service is available to authorized parties through a special permit. The service enables one of your company's customers to return a parcel and have the postage paid by you. Under this arrangement, the company provides the customer with instructions and a special label to attach to the parcel if it must be returned. The customer applies the label to the parcel and deposits it at a post office or in a mailbox. Unless the label is provided, the customer must pay the required postage charges.

Certified Mail

Certified mail service (Form 3800; see Figure 4-18) provides the mailer with a receipt and a record of the delivery of the item mailed from the post office from which it is delivered. No record is kept at the post office at which the item is mailed. Certified mail is handled in the ordinary mails and is not covered by insurance. The matter mailed usually has no intrinsic value, with the sender wishing only to be sure that it has been sent to the correct point of receipt. If the item mailed does have intrinsic value, it should be sent via registered mail, *not* certified mail.

Certified mail may be sent special delivery if additional postage is paid. An additional fee is also charged if delivery is restricted (only to the person named in the address) or if a return receipt is requested by the mailer.

Certificate of Mailing

At a fee somewhat lower than that for certified mail, a certificate of mailing (Form 3817; see Figure 4-19) will furnish evidence of mailing only. No receipt is obtained upon delivery of mail to the addressee. The fee does not insure the article against loss or damage to the item mailed.

Return Receipt

When the sender wants evidence that the mail was delivered, he or she should request a return receipt at the time the article is mailed (Form 3811; see Figure 4-20). A return receipt can be purchased for mail that is sent COD or by Express Mail, is insured for more than $50, or is registered or certified. It identifies the article by number, the signer, and date of delivery. For an additional fee, the sender can get the addressee's correct address of delivery or can request restricted delivery service (see below).

Return receipt for merchandise service—another form of return receipt service, which provides a mailing receipt, return receipt, and record of delivery—is available for merchandise sent at first-class, priority, third-class, and fourth-class rates of postage.

Figure 4-18. Receipt and form for certified mail.

Z 011 264 729

**Receipt for
Certified Mail**

UNITED STATES
POSTAL SERVICE

No Insurance Coverage Provided
Do not use for International Mail
(See Reverse)

Sent to	
Street and No	
P O , State and ZIP Code	
Postage	$
Certified Fee	
Special Delivery Fee	
Restricted Delivery Fee	
Return Receipt Showing to Whom & Date Delivered	
Return Receipt Showing to Whom, Date, and Addressee's Address	
TOTAL Postage & Fees	$
Postmark or Date	

PS Form **3800**, March 1993

Fold at line over top of envelope to the
right of the return address

CERTIFIED

Z 011 264 729

MAIL

Courtesy of the United States Postal Service.

Restricted Delivery

Restricted delivery means that the sender's mail is delivered only to the addressee or to someone authorized in writing to receive mail for the addressee. Restricted delivery is offered in connection with return receipt service and is available only for registered mail, certified mail, COD mail, and mail insured for more than $50.

Restricted delivery mail addressed to officials of government agencies, mem-

Figure 4-19. Certificate of mailing.

| U.S. POSTAL SERVICE   **CERTIFICATE OF MAILING** | Affix fee here in stamps or meter postage and post mark. Inquire of Postmaster for current fee. |

MAY BE USED FOR DOMESTIC AND INTERNATIONAL MAIL, DOES NOT
PROVIDE FOR INSURANCE—POSTMASTER

Received From:

_____

_____

One piece of ordinary mail addressed to:

_____

_____

_____

PS Form 3817, Mar. 1989   ★U.S.GPO:1991-0-282-404/25747

Courtesy of the United States Postal Service.

bers of the legislative and judicial branches of federal and state government, members of the diplomatic corps, minors, and individuals under guardianship can be delivered to an agent without written authorization from the addressee.

Insurance

Protection against loss or damage to packages with contents valued in any amount up to $600 is available, with fees ranging from $.75 to $6.20 (Figure 4-21). The fee is based on the amount of insurance desired. Insurance can be purchased for third- and fourth-class mail, as well as for third- and fourth-class matter that is mailed at the priority mail or first-class mail rate. Insurance coverage up to $25,000 can be purchased on registered mail, the most secure service offered by the postal service. For articles insured for more than $50, a receipt of delivery is signed by the recipient and filed at the delivery post office.

Do not overinsure your packages since the amount of insurance coverage for loss will be the actual value, less depreciation. No payments are made for sentimental losses or for any expenses incurred as a result of the loss. For example, if you send a package containing a three-year-old computer that was originally purchased for $2,500, its actual value (due to depreciation) might only be $800. Even if you insured the computer for $2,500, if it were damaged or lost, the insurance would only pay the current value of $800.

(text continues on p. 63)

Figure 4-20. Domestic return receipt.

**Thank you for using
Return Receipt Service.**

SENDER:
- Complete items 1 and/or 2 for additional services.
- Complete items 3, and 4a & b.
- Print your name and address on the reverse of this form so that we can return this card to you.
- Attach this form to the front of the mailpiece, or on the back if space does not permit.
- Write "Return Receipt Requested" on the mailpiece next to the article number.

I also wish to receive the following services (for an extra fee):

1. ☐ Addressee's Address
2. ☐ Restricted Delivery

Consult postmaster for fee.

3. Article Addressed to:

4a. Article Number

4b. Service Type
☐ Registered   ☐ Insured
☐ Certified   ☐ COD
☐ Express Mail   ☐ Return Receipt for Merchandise

7. Date of Delivery

5. Signature (Addressee)

8. Addressee's Address (Only if requested and fee is paid)

6. Signature (Agent)

PS Form **3811**, October 1990   ☆U.S. GPO: 1990—273-861   **DOMESTIC RETURN RECEIPT**

Is your **RETURN ADDRESS** completed on the reverse side?

Courtesy of the United States Postal Service.

Figure 4-21.   Receipt for insured mail domestic–international.

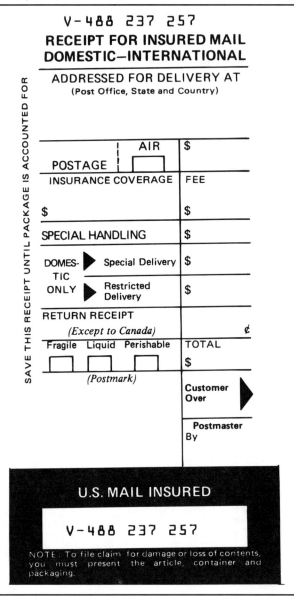

Courtesy of the United States Postal Service.

Registered Mail

The most secure option offered by the post office is registered mail (Form 3806; see Figure 4-22). Registered articles are placed under tight security from the point of mailing to the delivery office, providing added protection for valuable and important mail. Insurance may be purchased on domestic registered mail up to $25,000 at the option of the mailer. Return receipt and restricted delivery services are available for additional fees. Registered mail to Canada is subject to a $1,000 indemnity limit. For all other foreign countries, the indemnity is currently $32.35. First-class or priority mail postage is required on domestic registered mail.

There are special packaging requirements for registered mail. For example, you can't send a soft-sided package, or put tape over the edges, or reinforce an old box with tape. The box must be able to accept a postage ink stamp, and slick tape surfaces will not.

Special Delivery

Special delivery service, which can be obtained on all classes of mail except bulk third class, provides for delivery even on Sundays and holidays and beyond normal delivery hours. This delivery service is available to all customers served by city carriers and to other customers within a 1-mile radius of the delivery post office.

The purchase of special delivery does not always mean the article will be delivered by special messenger. Special delivery may be delivered by your regular carrier if the mail piece is available before the carrier departs for morning deliveries. Call your post office about the availability of special delivery service. Make sure the mailing is endorsed "Special Delivery."

Special Handling

Special handling service is available for third- and fourth-class mail only, including insured and COD mail. It provides preferential handling to the extent practical in dispatch and transportation but does not provide special delivery. Basically, this means that the post office will attempt to accelerate its normal delivery schedule for your package. It also does not mean special care of fragile items. Anything breakable should be packed with adequate cushioning and marked FRAGILE. The special handling fee must be paid on parcels that require special care, such as baby poultry or bees, except those sent at the first-class mail rate.

New Address Verification Card

To request the particulars of an individual's or company's change of address, one formerly used Form 3575A, New Address Verification Card. With the advent of the Freedom of Information Act, a letter may be written instead to the U.S. Postal Service asking for the new address. Figure 4-23 contains a sample suggestion

(text continues on p. 66)

Figure 4-22.   Form 3806, for registered mail.

REGISTERED NO.		POSTMARK

To Be Completed By Post Office

Reg. Fee $	Special $ Delivery
Handling $ Charge	Return $ Receipt
Postage $	Restricted $ Delivery
Received by	

Domestic Insurance
Is Limited To
$25,000; International
Indemnity Is Limited
(See Reverse)

To Be Completed By Customer (Please Print) All Entries Must Be in Ball Point or Typed

Customer Must Declare Full Value $	☐ With Postal Insurance
	☐ Without Postal Insurance

FROM

TO

PS Form **3806**, **RECEIPT FOR REGISTERED MAIL** *(Customer Copy)*
April 1991   *(See Information on Reverse)*

SAVE THIS RECEIPT FOR REGISTERED MAIL CLAIMS & INQUIRIES

DECLARATION OF VALUE – Mailers are Required to declare the Full value at the time of mailing on all registered mail articles, whether insurance is desired or not.

WITH POSTAL INSURANCE – Domestic postal insurance against loss or damage may be purchased by paying the appropriate fee. Domestic insurance on registered mail is limited to the lessor of (1) the value of the article at the time of mailing if lost or totally damaged, or (2) the cost of repairs. Consult your postmaster for additional details of insurance limits and coverage for domestic and international registered mail. See sections 149 and 911, Domestic Mail Manual for limitations of coverage.

WITHOUT POSTAL INSURANCE – An article may also be sent by registered mail without postal insurance by paying the appropriate fee. No indemnity will be paid for articles mailed without postal insurance coverage.

TO FILE INSURANCE CLAIM – Claim must be filed within 1 year from the date of mailing. Present this receipt. Claims for complete or partial loss of contents, damage or alleged rifling must be filed immediately. The article, container, and packaging must be presented when filing a complete or partial loss of contents or damage claim. Submit evidence of value or repair costs to substantiate your claim. Inquiries on registered mail claims should not be filed for at least 3 months after the date the original claim was filed.

INTERNATIONAL REGISTERED MAIL – Indemnity coverage for International Registered Mail is limited to the maximum set by the Convention of the Universal Postal Union. Consult postmaster and the International Mail Manual for limitations of coverage and individual country prohibitions and restrictions.

PS Form **3806,** April 1991 (Reverse)

Courtesy of the United States Postal Service.

Figure 4-23. Sample letter suggested by the USPS to ask for new address verification.

_____

Date

Postmaster
City, State (where person last resided)

Dear Postmaster:

In accordance with the Freedom of Information Act, I request to know the particulars of the latest change of address order given by:

_____
Name

_____
Street Address

_____
City   State   Zip

I understand that the $3.00 fee is to be paid before the records are searched and that this fee is not refunded if there is no record of a change of address.

Yours truly,

_____
Name

_____
Address

_____
City   State   Zip
- -
_____   No change of address on file

_____   Moved, left no address   Date_____

_____
Name

_____
NEW Street Number

_____
City   State   Zip

furnished by the USPS. Note that the bottom section should be included for return to you.

International Mail

Outgoing Mail

Airmail and surface mail can be sent to virtually all foreign countries in a variety of ways:

- *Letters, postcards, and letter packages:* Items of mail containing personal handwritten or typewritten communications.
- *Aerogrammes:* Air letter sheets that can be folded into the form of an envelope and sealed.
- *Printed matter:* Regular printed matter, books and sheet music, publishers' periodicals, catalogs, and directories.
- *Small packets:* Items of merchandise, commercial samples, or documents that do not have the character of current and personal correspondence.
- *Parcel post:* Packages or merchandise or other articles that are not required to be mailed at letter postage rates.
- *Express Mail International Service:* High-priority or other urgently needed items, including merchandise in many instances. These can be sent to more than 120 countries around the world via Postal Service Express Mail International Service.

All categories of international mail other than Express Mail may be sent either airmail or surface mail. However, all U.S.-originating letters and postcards intended for delivery in Canada or Mexico receive first-class mail treatment in the United States and airmail treatment in those two countries. Check with your post office for specific information about the country to which you are mailing.

A free publication, *International Postal Rates and Fees,* that is available at all post offices contains general mailing information and current postal rates and fees for postal services from the United States to more than 120 foreign countries.

Parcels and Publications Sent to Military Bases

Parcel airlift mail (PAL) and space-available mail (SAM) are for personal parcels and publications mailed to military personnel overseas at the third- and fourth-class rates.

Packages up to 30 pounds and 60 inches in combined length and girth may be sent by PAL. PAL mail is flown to the military mail dispatch center, where it becomes space-available mail for airlift overseas. The military mail dispatch center is a central receiving location for all overseas military bases. The actual shipment to the bases is usually handled by military transport, and therefore your mail must wait for a normally scheduled transport that has room on board for mail. You pay the regular parcel post rate to the military dispatch center, plus a fee from 35 cents to $1.40 for the air service, depending on the weight.

Parcels of any class that weigh up to 15 pounds and are not more than 60 inches in combined length and girth marked SAM are airlifted to military post offices outside the 48 contiguous states. The parcels are transported by surface in the United States and flown on a space-available basis from the United States to the overseas destination.

Express Mail Military Service is available to send urgent letters, documents, and packages to overseas military APO/FPO addresses. The postal service delivers to over 300 military post offices for $9.95 a half-pound.

Special International Mailing Services

Companies today use the entire world as their marketplace. Even if the company you work for is a small business, it may need to mail overseas. The USPS offers many ways to communicate internationally. Here are the services offered and how long they take to deliver:

- *INTELPOST:* 1 hour to next day. See the discussion earlier in this chapter under Electronic Mail Services of this fastest of all service for document delivery.

- *Express Mail International Service:* two to three days. Express Mail International delivers urgent letters, documents, and parcels to over 130 different countries, with two- to three-day delivery to major business centers. This service is especially economical with lighter-weight shipments. Your mail gets VIP treatment in all destination countries by going on an expedited basis.

- *International Priority Airmail (IPA):* presorted, three to six days; nonpresorted, four to seven days. This is for the company that has volume business mail to send abroad by air but not much money to spend on it. The solution is international priority airmail—airmail service with substantial savings compared to regular airmail rates. Mail pieces do not even have to be identical in size or weight. Letters, letter packages, small packets, and printed matter are accepted by the postal service. The postal service will provide free pickup in service areas around dozens of gateway cities.

- *Airmail:* four to seven days. For reliable, economical worldwide service, airmail is still one of the best ways to send letters, small packages, documents, and parcel post to virtually every country in the world.

- *International Surface Air Lift (ISAL):* seven to fourteen days. If the company has printed matter to send overseas—direct mail, catalogs, publications, brochures, periodicals—it may find itself in a dilemma: Surface mail takes time, and airmail takes money. The alternative is ISAL: fast, economical service for bulk printed matter. The company's mail goes overseas by air. It is then processed and delivered via surface mail by the official government postal service in the destination country. Minimum weight requirement is 50 pounds.

To save even more, deliver your mail directly to an ISAL gateway for a special discount. The postal service will give a direct-shipment discount when the company has large-volume shipments to an individual country (e.g., all to England, or all to France). Or send your printed mail to a single foreign address and get another discount.

- *M-Bag.* A way to get a discount on printed matter that is being sent to a single foreign address is to bag it, giving the company a reduced rate on airmail, ISAL, and surface mail based on the country of destination and weight of the contents. The postal service will supply special address tags and customs forms to ensure efficient handling. There is no limit on the number of sacks you can send.

- *Surface mail:* four to six weeks. When time is not an issue, the cheapest way to send mail to any country is surface mail. The postal service can get almost anything mailable to its destination in four to six weeks.

Extra Conveniences

If your company wants added security, speed, or efficiency for its foreign mailings or added convenience for its contacts and clients, it may want to take advantage of the following special options (the international version of postal service features you're already familiar with):

- *International Business Reply Service,* with your company billed only for the actual number of reply cards or envelopes returned from foreign countries.
- *Insurance* against loss, rifling, or damage to your parcel, with compensation based on the fee paid for the amount of insurance desired.
- *Registered mail* for additional protection and security for letter-class mail, small packets, and all other printed matter.
- *Return receipt* for mailer confirmation of delivery of insured or registered mail being offered for Express Mail International Service to certain countries, with receipts returned to senders by airmail.
- *Special delivery* for more expeditious delivery of letter-class mail, small packets, and printed matter when it reaches the addressee's post office.
- *Recorded delivery* for a mailing receipt for letter-class mail, small packets, printed matter (including M-Bags), or matter for the blind. Return receipts and restricted delivery service may be purchased for recorded delivery items to all countries with which restricted delivery agreements are in force.

Customs Inspection for Incoming Foreign Mail

All mail originating in foreign countries and United States overseas territories, other than the Commonwealth of Puerto Rico, is subject to U.S. Customs Service examination upon entering the United States. Many imported goods are subject to the payment of U.S. Customs duty. When dutiable merchandise enters by mail, the amount due is determined by the customs service but is collected by the postal service. When the duty is collected on behalf of the customs service, the postal service also collects a customs clearance and delivery fee on each dutiable item, to offset the cost of collection and remittance. For detailed customs information, write:

United States Customs Service
Treasury Department
1301 Constitution Ave., NW
Washington, DC 20229-0001

Alternatives to the USPS

Although documents, letters, and advertisements are usually shipped through the USPS, it is likely that your company will also use an alternative form of service—for example, United Parcel Service or air express services like Federal Express or Airborne Freight. Many airlines have an air freight express service that can transport a package from one city to another the same day. In addition, there are bus freight services, trucking freight shippers, and even couriers that can deliver packages in town the same day. Here's a quick overview of these delivery options.

United Parcel Service

When it comes to shipping parcels, many businesses turn to the United Parcel Service (UPS). UPS specializes in overnight shipping in addition to its regular package shipping service. Its freight charges are comparable to other carriers; prices vary depending on how far your package is being shipped and how much it weighs.

UPS distance charges are based on zones—both ground transportation zones and air freight zones. The ground transportation zones can also tell you approximately how many working days it will take for your package to arrive at its destination. You can determine the zone by looking up the zip code of the package's destination on a UPS zone chart (Figure 4-24).

There are several ways to ship via UPS:

1. Take your packages directly to the nearest UPS office. You can find the location by calling UPS at (800) PICK-UPS (742-5877).

2. Bring your package to one of the local UPS pickup stations, found at hardware stores, print shops, and office supply stores, in addition to chains of mailbox and packaging stores. Because each of these locations has a specific time when the UPS truck arrives to pick up packages, be sure you know when it is before you make the drop-off. You also may want to note that these local pickup stations as well as mailbox and packaging stores charge a sometimes hefty surcharge on top of the regular shipping costs.

3. Call UPS and ask to have your package picked up at your location. Normally UPS will schedule the package pickup for the next day. When calling, you

Figure 4-24. UPS zone chart.

UPS Zone Chart

Ground/UPS 3 Day Select℠/UPS 2nd Day Air®/UPS Next Day Air®

For shipments originating in ZIP Codes 300-01 to 303-99
Service to every address in all 50 states and Puerto Rico

To determine zone, take the first three digits of the consignee's
ZIP Code and refer to chart below.

ZIP Code Prefixes	Ground	3 Day Select	2nd Day Air	Next Day Air	ZIP Code Prefixes	Ground	3 Day Select	2nd Day Air	Next Day Air	ZIP Code Prefixes	Ground	3 Day Select	2nd Day Air	Next Day Air	ZIP Code Prefixes	Ground	3 Day Select	2nd Day Air	Next Day Air	ZIP Code Prefixes	Ground	3 Day Select	2nd Day Air	Next Day Air
004-005	5	35	12	22	293	2	32	12	22	397	3	33	12	22	640-649	5	35	12	22					
006-007	-	-	15	25	294-295	3	33	12	22	399	2	32	12	22	650-659	4	34	12	22					
008	-	-	**	**	296	2	32	12	22	400-402	4	34	12	22	660-690	5	35	12	22					
009	-	-	15	25	297	3	33	12	22	403-409	3	33	12	22	691-693	6	36	12	22					
010-041	5	35	12	22	298	2	32	12	22	410-412	4	34	12	22	700-729	4	34	12	22					
042-049	6	36	12	22	299	3	33	12	22	413-418	3	33	12	22	730-748	5	35	12	22					
050-089	5	35	12	22	300-312	2	-	12	22	420	4	34	12	22	749	4	34	12	22					
090-099	-	-	-	-	313-316	3	-	12	22	421-422	3	33	12	22	750-754	5	35	12	22					
100-149	5	35	12	22	317-319	2	-	12	22	423-424	4	34	12	22	755-756	4	34	12	22					
150-163	4	34	12	22	320-326	3	33	12	22	425-427	3	33	12	22	757-796	5	35	12	22					
164-165	5	35	12	22	327-339	4	34	12	22	430-483	4	34	12	22	797-799	6	36	12	22					
166	4	34	12	22	340-341	-	-	-	-	484-489	5	35	12	22	800-820	6	36	12	22					
167	5	35	12	22	342	4	34	12	22	490-492	4	34	12	22	821	7	37	12	22					
168	4	34	12	22	344	3	33	12	22	493-499	5	35	12	22	822-823	6	36	12	22					
169	5	35	12	22	346-349	4	34	12	22	500-525	5	35	12	22	824-825	7	37	12	22					
170-174	4	34	12	22	350-353	2	32	12	22	526	4	34	12	22	826-828	6	36	12	22					
175-198	5	35	12	22	354-355	3	33	12	22	527-564	5	35	12	22	829-834	7	37	12	22					
199	4	34	12	22	356-362	2	32	12	22	565-567	6	36	12	22	835-838	8	38	12	22					
200-218	4	34	12	22	363-367	3	33	12	22	570-571	5	35	12	22	840-864	7	37	12	22					
219	5	35	12	22	368	2	32	12	22	572	6	36	12	22	865-885	6	36	12	22					
220-241	4	34	12	22	369-372	3	33	12	22	573	5	35	12	22	889-893	7	37	12	22					
242-243	3	33	12	22	373-374	2	32	12	22	574-588	6	36	12	22	894-897	8	38	12	22					
244-245	4	34	12	22	375	4	34	12	22	590-592	7	37	12	22	898	7	37	12	22					
246-248	3	33	12	22	376	3	33	12	22	593	6	36	12	22	900-961	8	38	12	22					
249-268	4	34	12	22	377-379	2	32	12	22	594-598	7	37	12	22	962-966	-	-	-	-					
270-274	3	33	12	22	380-381	4	34	12	22	599	8	38	12	22	967-968	-	-	14	24					
275-279	4	34	12	22	382-385	3	33	12	22	600-609	4	34	12	22	969	-	-	**	**					
280-282	3	33	12	22	386-387	4	34	12	22	610-612	5	35	12	22	970-986	8	38	12	22					
283-285	4	34	12	22	388	3	33	12	22	613-634	4	34	12	22	987	-	-	-	-					
286	3	33	12	22	389-392	4	34	12	22	635	5	35	12	22	988-994	8	38	12	22					
287-289	2	32	12	22	393	3	33	12	22	636-639	4	34	12	22	995-999	-	-	*	*					
290-292	3	33	12	22	394-396	4	34	12	22															

* See reverse side for Alaska zones   ** See UPS International Air Service — Rate/Zone Chart

017232 REV. 2-93

Courtesy of United Parcel Service.

will need the weight and dimensions of each package, along with the delivery address, to give to the operator over the telephone. The operator will give you a price for the shipment, which you will have to pay by cash or check when the package is picked up. There is a small additional charge for the pickup service.

4. Register with UPS for regular weekday pickups. This is the ideal choice for the company that does a lot of shipping. To make the arrangement, meet with a UPS representative, register your company, and pay a small deposit, usually based on the company's normal expected monthly shipping bill. UPS will then provide a shipping kit that contains various supplies as well as a shipping register and a UPS shipper's number on a rubber stamp. With these materials you can prepare your own shipments for a pickup each day. In addition to the shipping charges, there is a small weekly pickup fee, paid whether you have any outgoing packages or not.

With the regular weekday pickup service, each package you ship must be registered on the shipper's pickup record (Figure 4-25). These two-part forms come with slips of carbon paper so you have a copy of all shipments. Each form must include the name of your company; the date; your UPS shipper's number; the name, address, city, state, and zip code of the package's destination; the package's weight; and the zone it will travel to.

UPS also offers an overnight shipping service and a two-day air service for both documents and packages. For documents, UPS provides next-day air and second-day air tracking labels and packaging envelopes (Figure 4-26). These tracking labels must include the package weight, as well as your UPS shipper's number.

UPS offers as well a variety of special services, such as package insurance, international shipments, COD services, and package tracking via bar code (Figure 4-27).

Air Express Services

Shipping services from companies like Federal Express, Airborne, and DHL focus on rapid delivery of packages and documents. They offer most of the same services as UPS does, including regular daily pickups, overnight shipment, package tracking, and so forth, but not every destination in the country may be available with each service. For example, it may be impossible to deliver an overnight letter to someone in a small town in Nevada via these services. However, air express companies generally provide reliable shipping to most cities and towns.

Unlike UPS, air express provides same-day pickup. If your company doesn't have an account with an air express service, it can pay by cash, check, or credit card. You can even have shipping charges paid by the receiver of the package if you have the receiver's permission and account number. In addition, most mailbox and shipping chain stores accept shipments for air express.

Federal Express has its own mail drop-off points and small booths or drop boxes in shopping-center parking lots scattered throughout most cities and towns. (See Figure 4-28 for a sample Federal Express shipping form.)

(text continues on p. 74)

Figure 4-25. UPS pickup record.

UPS COPY

United Parcel Service

PICKUP RECORD

DATE

REC'D FROM

PICKUP RECORD NO. 640528499

CHECK CODE 2

STAMP YOUR UPS SHIPPER NUMBER BELOW

ENTER EACH PACKAGE ON A SEPARATE LINE. IF RECORD IS VOIDED, PLEASE GIVE TO DRIVER.
INCREASE FRACTIONS OF A POUND TO NEXT FULL POUND.

REFERENCE #	NAME – STREET – CITY	STATE	ZIP CODE		TYPE SERVICE: GROUND (✓) RES DEL	GROUND (✓) GRND TRAC	GROUND ZONE IN STATE	GROUND ZONE OUT OF STATE	AIR ZONE	LBS	(✓) OS*	DECLARED VALUE** IF IN EXCESS OF $100.00	COD*** AMOUNT	(✓) CALL	(A)	FOR UPS OFFICE USE ONLY
1				1												
2				2												
3				3												
4				4												
5				5												
6				6												
7				7												
8				8												
9				9												
10				10												
11				11												
12				12												
13				13												
14				14												
15				15												

RECEIVED BY	PICKUP TIME	NO. PKGS.	NO. CALLS

* OS (Oversize) applied if less than 25 lbs. and more than 84 inches in length and girth combined.

** Unless a greater value is declared in writing on this receipt, the shipper hereby declares and agrees that the released value of each package or article not enclosed in a package covered by this receipt is $100, which is a reasonable value under the circumstances surrounding the transportation. The rules relating to liability established by the Warsaw Convention and any amendments thereto shall apply to the international carriage of any shipment hereunder insofar as the same is governed thereby. The entry of a C.O.D. amount is not a declaration of value. In addition, the maximum value for an air service package is $25,000 and the maximum carrier liability is $25,000. Claims not made to carrier within 9 months of the scheduled delivery date are waived.

*** All checks in payment of C.O.D.'s accepted at shipper's risk.

01120218 REV. 6-92 (800M BKS. 6-92)A

Courtesy of United Parcel Service.

Figure 4-26. UPS next day air and 2nd day air tracking labels.

TRACKING NUMBER

1Z 327 000 01 0335 1139

UPS Next Day Air.

12/92 S

 NEXT DAY AIR SHIPPER RECEIPT
1Z 327 000 01 0335 113 9
PLACE ON YOUR SHIPPING RECORD

NEXT DAY AIR SHIPPER RECEIPT
1Z 327 000 01 0335 113 9
PLACE ON YOUR SHIPPING RECORD

TRACKING NUMBER

1Z 327 000 02 0264 3261

UPS 2nd Day Air.

12/92 S

 2ND DAY AIR SHIPPER RECEIPT
1Z 327 000 02 0264 326 1
PLACE ON YOUR SHIPPING RECORD

2ND DAY AIR SHIPPER RECEIPT
1Z 327 000 02 0264 326 1
PLACE ON YOUR SHIPPING RECORD

Courtesy of United Parcel Service.

Figure 4-27.   UPS GroundTrac label.

Courtesy of United Parcel Service.

Other Shipping Services

Air Freight

For special situations, such as large packages or packages that must be delivered to another city the same day, air freight services are available from many airlines and specialty air freight companies. Some have special offices at the airport for same-day shipments. These shipments must usually be dropped off at the freight office and picked up at the destination freight office. The fees are much higher than other next-day air and two-day air shipments.

Bus Freight

Most passenger bus lines provide a freight service, often useful for moving packages to small towns that are not served by other shipping services. Packages are taken along with passenger baggage and unloaded at the bus station at the intended destination. The recipient must pick up the package at the station.

Trucking Freight

For large shipments and heavy or bulky packages, there are many trucking companies that specialize in hauling freight. These companies will load the shipment at your place of business, transport it to the destination, and unload it for

Figure 4-28. Federal Express shipping form.

Instructions

FedEx
Federal Express

SHIP DATE: 05OCT94
MAN-WGT: 1 LBS

FROM: Tim Allen (408)555-9442
The Windward Group
718 University Ave.
Suite 100
Los Gatos, CA 95030

SHIPPER'S FEDEX ACCOUNT NUMBER

TO: Gayle M. Christensen (901)555-1212
Fedex
2003 Corporate Avenue

Memphis, TN 38132-

REF:

DELIVERY ADDRESS BARCODE (FED-A-DEX)

CAD #   PRIORITY OVERNIGHT   THU

TRK # 006 2982 765   AA

38132-TN-US   SEA

DROP OFF   **83 BVU**

a fee that is usually competitive. Depending on what you are shipping and where it is going, coast-to-coast shipping can take anywhere from seven to twenty-one days.

Courier Services

If you need to ship a package across town within a few hours, your best bet is a courier service. These companies operate in most large towns and cities and provide pickup and delivery within a few hours. The prices for these services vary depending on the distance traveled and the weight and size of the package. Most of the time the charge is paid in advance by the sender. Courier services are bonded against theft or damage.

For documents and other small items, many taxi companies also provide a courier-type service. Check your telephone book for courier services or taxi services.

International Shipments

If you ship packages to another country, you can use most of the services already mentioned, including the USPS. If your international shipment must arrive within a day or two, an air express service or UPS may be your best choice.

Preparing international shipments is similar to preparing an ordinary domestic shipment; however, you must also provide customs documents and copies of any invoices in case a duty must be paid by the recipient of your package.

Chapter 5
Travel Arrangements

Today's Business Traveler

In today's competitive market, companies routinely buy and sell products and services both across the country and around the world. Because of this, business-related travel is common to every type and every size of company.

A small business just getting underway may have interest in local markets only; however, as the business grows and expands, a larger domestic market and possibly international markets will be of greater interest. Thus, as a business grows and an owner's needs increase, your secretarial duties will include keeping abreast of how to handle your employer's travel needs quickly and efficiently—no matter how far he or she goes.

Even if you work for a larger company that has an in-house travel department, it's useful to know the following procedures to troubleshoot for your boss when needed.

Getting the Trip Underway

Your main purpose in making travel arrangements is to get your boss to his or her destination and back home again as smoothly as possible; other considerations may be speed and cost. If you are a new secretary or new to a particular office, see what the policies and precedents for making travel arrangements are. You may find helpful information in the files; there may even be a step-by-step procedures manual to consult. If such information is not readily available, ask your boss whether to use a travel agency or to make the arrangements without an agent.

Whether you're going to do it yourself or are collecting information for the travel agent, be sure to determine the following basics:

- ☐ What is the purpose of the trip?
- ☐ What are the desired departure and return times and dates?
- ☐ What is the point-by-point itinerary?
- ☐ Will the boss be traveling alone, or will other staff members or family members be traveling along?

☐   What type of transportation does your boss desire? What is the best means of transportation available at that particular destination? If you're not sure, a travel agent may help you with some of this information even if arrangements are ultimately not made through the agency.

☐   What is the lodging facility closest to the activities of the trip? If your boss's appointments are scattered throughout the city, perhaps a downtown hotel or an airport hotel or motel would be preferred.

If your employer travels frequently, it might be wise to secure a copy of the *Official Airline Guide,* available in both domestic and international editions. It is obtainable from:

Official Airline Guides
2000 Clearwater Drive
Oak Brook, IL 60521

Another useful guide provides a complete description of many hotels and motels throughout the United States, as well as their toll-free 800 numbers. This is the *Hotel and Motel Red Book;* it can be ordered from:

American Hotel and Motel Association
888 Seventh Avenue
New York, NY 10019

If you make arrangements on your own, these guides let you call hotels toll-free to make reservations directly. And even if you do use an agency, the two publications might still be valuable because they provide information concerning each hotel and motel, including room rates, which will help you select a hotel best suited to your employer's needs and desires.

Doing It Yourself

Many employers ask secretaries to arrange travel services and not use a travel agent. If this is the case, first have your boss confirm basic departure and return times and dates and then proceed to make the reservations.

Hotel Reservations

If the meeting is in a major city, make the lodging reservations without delay because city hotels are often fully booked weeks in advance. State your employer's name, office or home address, telephone number, type of accommodation preferred (single room, two-bedroom suite, etc.), plus your own name as the contact person. Ask for written confirmation, which your boss should carry when traveling in case he or she arrives only to be told that no such reservation exists.

Some hotels also make car rental or limousine reservations. If your boss needs either of these, make a reservation now. Have the date and exact time of day the car or limousine is needed, and give that information to the hotel reservation person. Again, ask for written confirmation to be mailed or faxed to you, with the room reservation information.

Hotels hold room reservations only until a specific deadline, typically 6 P.M. You can extend the reservation beyond that time limit by guaranteeing payment, whether or not the boss arrives. To do this, you must give the hotel reservation person a credit card number. Remember that if the boss should change his or her mind about making the trip or staying at that hotel, the room charge will have to be paid anyway since you've guaranteed arrival. However, most hotels and motels will allow you to cancel a guaranteed reservation without charge if you cancel before 6:00 P.M. on the day of arrival.

What if you aren't able to make a reservation in the hotel of your boss's choice? You may be able to use a travel agency for this service alone. Large travel agencies often have a number of hotel and motel rooms blocked and held exclusively for them, a practice especially common at conventions. Select an agency that's very large, perhaps choosing on the basis of telephone classified ads if you don't have a personal recommendation. Call and explain your problem. The travel agent will usually be eager to assist you with the hope you'll eventually become a regular client.

All of this presumes you know which hotel to choose. If your boss is traveling to a city he or she has never visited before or is going to a convention that does not recommend a particular hotel, investigate your choices using the *Hotel and Motel Red Book*. You may also write to the convention bureau or chamber of commerce in that city, or secure a local newspaper. Much valuable information can be obtained from these sources. If your boss has a favorite hotel chain, you can call the national reservations center for the chain and find out if they have a hotel in the city your boss will be visiting. You can then make reservations using the national reservations center.

Travel Reservations

Airline

Call the preferred airline's reservation office by consulting your telephone directory for a toll-free 800 number. If you're unable to find one, call 800 telephone information: (800) 555-1212.

As soon as you're in touch with the airline, you can instantly make a reservation and usually secure a preferred seat and/or car reservations as well. Advise the reservations agent of the company's or employer's credit card number and whether the ticket and reservations information should be mailed or held for pickup.

Train

In days gone by, rail travel was the way to go: comfortable Pullman compartments and dining cars with fine food graciously served. But today, with time being money, more and more executives prefer air travel. Still, there are executives who either prefer not to fly or genuinely enjoy leisurely travel such as that provided by Amtrak. Railway travel is usually done when there is adequate time and easy access to rail terminals.

If your employer prefers rail travel, obtain a schedule for Amtrak trains, as well as for commuter lines and connecting lines from the nearest rail station. A call to Amtrak will answer your questions.

Using a Travel Agency

A good travel agency is invaluable to the busy secretary. Few other outside services provide more time-saving help. A competent agency can provide a host of services: recommend hotels and make reservations; make airline, ship, and rail reservations; take advantage of special fares you may not be aware of; issue tickets; make car rental reservations; assist in securing passports and visas; provide tickets to shows, the theater, sporting events, or a special event occurring in one or more of the cities on the itinerary; and mail all these tickets and reservation information directly to you.

Travel agencies charge your company no fee for making these reservations (their commissions are paid directly by the hotels and the airlines). A charge may be made for rail reservations unless the reservation is part of a prearranged package tour. Refunds for any unused tickets can also be obtained by the agency. In addition, a travel agency can often help solve problems that occur during your employer's stay. Even small agencies often have a toll-free 800 number, making it convenient for either you or the boss to call from anywhere.

After you've compiled an itinerary for your boss and know his or her exact travel needs and desires, a telephone call to a travel agency may be all that's needed. This will save you an incredible amount of time from the moment your employer leaves home or the office to the time of return.

Finding a Reputable Agent

To find a reputable travel agent, ask secretaries in other companies or your own company for a recommendation, or obtain a list of agencies from the professional organization:

American Society of Travel Agents
501 Fifth Avenue
New York, NY 10017

Many good and reputable agents do not belong to this society, so do not discount a recommended agency simply because it's not a member. If you need still further sources of agencies, consult your classified telephone directory. If you wish, ask if the agency can give you the name of one or more business clients as references.

Once you've found a good travel agent, use that same person whenever possible every time your employer travels. The agent will soon become familiar with your boss's travel habits and travel needs, making it easier to arrange trips. A rapport between you and that agent will be to your employer's advantage and perhaps to your own when vacation time comes for you.

Making the Arrangements

To establish a good relationship between you, your employer, and your travel agent, always have all the facts ready when you call. If you're not sure what your employer needs, you cannot expect the agent to know. But once you do have complete information, the agent can begin to find the best schedules, the best fares, and the best hotels and hotel rates.

The facts you should have ready for the agent include:

☐ Your name and the traveler's name

☐ The traveler's office address and office telephone number

☐ Date and time of departure and date and time of return

☐ The traveler's preferences: specific carrier, if desired; general time of departure, such as early morning or evening; general time of return; and type of service desired, such as first-class, coach, smoking or nonsmoking

☐ The traveler's home telephone number

☐ Your home telephone number (in case an emergency should arise, such as a change in return-flight time or a return-flight cancellation, and the boss needs to be notified while away)

Quickly and efficiently your travel agent will provide you with confirmation of your reservations, the advised check-in time, the travel time, and estimated time of arrival.

These services may be paid for with a credit card. The airline or rail tickets and reservation confirmation forms can be picked up by you or mailed, as you wish.

The Itinerary

An itinerary—that is, a written travel agenda—is useful to both the executive and the secretary who remains in the office. Quick reference to it can be made when questions arise. Perhaps the executive has forgotten the address or time for an appointment. Or perhaps the secretary, faced with a sudden emergency, needs to know exactly where the employer can be contacted.

Before preparing the written itinerary, confer with your boss, making notes of all activities on the trip. Show your employer a draft of the written schedule so that changes can be made or forgotten items added. Once the itinerary has been completed, it could be typed on small pocket-size cards or on plain paper. Figure 5-1 contains a sample itinerary.

Foreign Travel

If the boss's trip involves foreign travel, make plans well in advance because of the many details involved. He or she should be aware of both U.S. requirements regarding foreign travel and the requirements of the country or countries to be visited. There are many conditions imposed on business travelers that are different from those imposed on tourists.

For assistance in arranging a foreign business trip, you can contact:

Bureau of International Commerce
Department of Commerce
Washington, DC 20230

For Foreign Travel, Always Use a Travel Agent

Even if you do not use a travel agency to arrange domestic business trips, it's highly recommended that a reliable agency be used for foreign travel. To select a travel agency, solicit recommendations from coworkers or friends, consult the classified section of your telephone directory, or look for advertisements in the newspaper that indicate an agency not only is well versed in foreign travel rules and regulations but also specializes in individual itineraries rather than package tours.

The agency will handle all of the complicated details involved in foreign travel. Its expertise will be invaluable to you, and at no cost to your company since the travel agent's fee will be paid by the airlines and hotels.

The agency will handle all arrangements for transportation, lodging, car rentals, even sightseeing excursions. It will furnish accurate information as to documents needed for each particular country—passport, health certificates, police certificates, visas, and so forth—and exactly how to obtain each. The agency will handle all checks or arrange for letters of credit as your employer prefers; it will even secure a small amount of currency in the denominations of the country visited so that the boss won't arrive with U.S. currency only.

Visas and Passports

Most U.S. citizens need a passport to leave the United States and to reenter it. A passport is not required by U.S. laws for travel to North America, South America, Central America, or adjacent islands (except for Cuba). Nevertheless, citizenship documentation is required—a birth certificate will do—and the traveler should

Figure 5-1. Sample itinerary.

Philip Smith	**Itinerary**	**June 1, 1995**

Monday, June 1 (Dallas to New York)

8:00 A.M.   Leave Dallas residence by limousine for airport. (Limousine reservation attached)

9:00 A.M.   Leave DFW Airport on American Airlines Flight 122, Seat 1B. Includes lunch. (Ticket attached)

12:40 A.M.   Arrive New York, JFK Airport. Limousine to Americana Hotel. (Limousine reservation attached)

2:30 P.M.   Don Daley, president of Bryant Industries, will provide car for trip to his office, World Trade Center II, Suite 1000. (Bryant Industries file in briefcase)

Tuesday, June 2

9:00 A.M.   Appointment with Henderson, Smith & Jackson, Empire State Building, Suite 8000.

10:30 A.M.   Appointment with Mary Louise Henderson. (Henderson, Smith & Jackson file in briefcase)

2:00 P.M.   Appointment with August Terrell, your hotel; meet in lobby. (Terrell Corporation file in briefcase)

7:00 P.M.   Dinner, Don Daley's home. (5203 Legendary Lane, New York; Telephone 212-555-6120)

Wednesday, June 3

7:45 A.M.   Leave hotel by limousine for airport. (Reservation attached)

9:45 A.M.   Leave JFK Airport on American Airlines Flight 292, Seat 12A. Includes breakfast. (Ticket attached)

11:05 A.M.   Arrive Dallas. Limousine to office. (Limousine reservation attached)

---

always carry personal identification, such as a driver's license or an employee ID card.

In addition to a passport, many countries require a visa to enter the country. Usually the visa must be obtained in advance and can't be purchased at the border or point of entry. Visas are issued by the individual embassies and consulates of various countries. Sometimes there is a small fee charged, and some countries issue visas for free. Since the requirements can and do change often, even if you have obtained a visa in advance of a trip, double-check before you leave to make sure the visa is still valid.

To find out more about passports and visas, use the telephone directory or call telephone information. Some telephone directories list the numbers under "United States Government, Passport Information" or "Government Offices—County—Passport Acceptance Office." Call the county in which the prospective traveler lives.

If a passport is needed, apply at a passport agent's office or go to a clerk of a federal court, a clerk of a state court of record, a judge or clerk of a probate court, or a designated postal clerk.

Passport agencies are located in the following cities:

Boston, MA 02203
Chicago, IL 60604
Honolulu, HI 96850
Los Angeles, CA 90261
Miami, FL 33130
New Orleans, LA 70130
New York, NY 10020
Philadelphia, PA 19106
San Francisco, CA 94102
Seattle, WA 98174
Stamford, CT 06901
Washington, DC 20524

Required Immunizations and Vaccinations

Anyone traveling to a foreign country must have up-to-date information concerning required immunizations. A pamphlet titled *Health Information for International Travel* can be obtained by writing to:

U.S. Department of Health and Human Services
Public Health Service
Centers for Disease Control
Bureau of Epidemiology
Atlanta, GA 30333

Ask for HHS Publication No. (CDC) 81-8280. This publication may also be obtained from the Superintendent of Documents, Washington, DC 20402. Another source for this information is local travel agents. Travel agents will gladly help you with all your business and personal travel needs. Usually their services are free, as they are paid a commission by airlines, car rental companies, and other travel-related businesses.

Customs

When returning from foreign countries, the traveler must declare certain items acquired abroad to determine whether a tax is owed. Travelers returning home to the United States are allowed certain exemptions, which help cover the inevitable souvenirs. Articles totaling $300 (fair retail value in the country where purchased) are duty free, except for cigarettes, cigars, and liquor.

Be aware: Travelers should not try to understate the value of an article or misrepresent the nature of any article. To do so could result in the seizure and forfeiture of the item, and the tax will still be assessed. If a traveler has doubt as to whether to declare an item, he or she should declare it and then ask the customs inspector about it.

Complete and detailed pamphlets concerning customs regulations are available from a district director of customs in the following cities:

Anchorage	New Orleans
Baltimore	New York City
Boston	Nogales (AZ)
Bridgeport (CT)	Ogdensburg (NY)
Buffalo	Pembina (ND)
Charleston (SC)	Philadelphia
Chicago	Port Arthur (TX)
Cleveland	Portland (ME)
Dallas–Fort Worth	Portland (OR)
Detroit	Providence
Duluth	St. Albans (VT)
El Paso	St. Louis
Great Falls (MT)	St. Thomas (VI)
Honolulu	San Diego
Laredo (TX)	San Francisco
San Pedro (CA)	San Juan (PR)
Los Angeles	Savannah (GA)
Miami	Seattle
Milwaukee	Tampa
Minneapolis	Washington, DC
Mobile	Wilmington (NC)

Languages Spoken in Foreign Countries

The average businessperson will sometimes be aware of the language spoken in some countries of the world, but not in others. The following chart indicates the official language(s) spoken in that country:

Country	Official Language(s)	Country	Official Language(s)
Afghanistan	Afghan, Persian, Pashto	Bahamas	English
		Bahrain	Arabic
Algeria	Arabic	Barbados	English
Angola	Portuguese	Belgium	Dutch, French, German
Argentina	Spanish		
Australia	English	Belize	English

Country	Official Language(s)	Country	Official Language(s)
Bermuda	English	Israel	Arabic, Hebrew
Bolivia	Spanish	Italy	Italian
Bosnia and Hercegovina	Bosnian	Ivory Coast	French
		Jamaica	English
Botswana	English	Japan	Japanese
Brazil	Portuguese	Jordan	Arabic
Bulgaria	Bulgarian	Kenya	English, Swahili
Burma	Burmese	Korea	Korean
Canada	English, French	Kuwait	Arabic
Chad	French	Lebanon	Arabic
Chile	Spanish	Lesotho	English, Sesotho
China, People's Republic of	Chinese (Mandarin)	Liberia	English
		Libya	Arabic
Colombia	Spanish	Macedonia	Macedonian, Albanian
Congo	French		
Croatia	Croatian	Madagascar	French, Malagasy
Cuba	Spanish	Malawi	English
Denmark	Danish	Malaysia	Malay
Dominica	English	Mali	French
Dominican Republic	Spanish	Malta	English, Maltese
		Mauritania	Arabic, French
Ecuador	Spanish	Mexico	Spanish
Egypt	Arabic	Monaco	French
El Salvador	Spanish	Morocco	Arabic
England	English	Mozambique	Portuguese
Ethiopia	Amharic	Nepal	Nepali
Fiji	English	Netherlands	Dutch
Finland	Finnish, Swedish	New Zealand	English
France	French	Nicaragua	Spanish
Germany	German	Nigeria	English
Ghana	English	Norway	Norwegian
Great Britain	English	Oman	Arabic
Greece	Greek	Pakistan	Urdu
Grenada	English	Panama	Spanish
Guatemala	Spanish	Paraguay	Spanish
Guyana	English	Peru	Spanish, Quechua
Haiti	French	Philippines	English, Pilipino, Spanish
Honduras	Spanish		
Iceland	Icelandic	Poland	Polish
India	English, Hindi	Portugal	Portuguese
Indonesia	Indonesian	Trinidad and Tobago	English
Iran	Persian		
Iraq	Arabic	Tunisia	Arabic
Ireland	English, Irish	Turkey	Turkish

Country	Official Language(s)	Country	Official Language(s)
Uganda	English	Yemen	Arabic
Ukraine	Russian	Yugoslavia	Serbo-Croatian
Uruguay	Spanish	Zaire	French
Vatican City State	Italian	Zambia	English
Venezuela	Spanish	Zimbabwe	English
Western Samoa	English, Samoan		

Chapter 6

Keeping Accurate Records

A Critical Duty

Keeping accurate records and maintaining an up-to-date filing system are important responsibilities for most secretaries. Any filing system ever conceived requires the person maintaining it to approach the duty with a sense of pride. He or she must be confident that any file can be retrieved quickly, perhaps even as the employer is speaking on the telephone.

Most firms today, even small businesses, store their letters and documents in their computers or word processing equipment and automatically maintain them there or on disk. (See Chapter 10, Database Management Systems.) However, as secretaries know only too well, even with computers the amount of paper correspondence and documents to be saved seems to grow daily.

Large companies often have a central file department, where all papers are kept by competent file clerks. Other companies maintain files by division, and small companies may have only a few file cabinets for their entire operation; in these cases, it's the secretary who is usually responsible for record keeping and maintenance. But no matter what your usual duties, you should be familiar with the various filing systems used in both small and large offices.

Getting Ready

It's often tempting, especially at the end of the day, simply to throw a file in its own folder. Don't. Filing is an important duty, no matter how tedious it seems. Instead of trying to get rid of that piece of paper as quickly as possible, approach it with these questions always in mind: Where could I easily find this tomorrow (or next week, or next year)? What's in this letter or document that would cause me to recall where I'm placing it in the file now?

Follow this checklist before you start to file:

☐ Prepare the papers by separating personal correspondence from business correspondence and documents.

☐ Check all stapled papers to be sure that only papers belonging together have been stapled together.

☐ Remove all paper clips: They not only crowd the file but also can catch papers that should not have been clipped to them.

☐ Mend any torn papers with tape.

☐ Underline in bright pencil or with a marking pen the name or subject under which the paper is to be filed.

On the file folders, use staggered tabs or one-position tabs. The straight-line tab, all in the center or in the far right position on the edge of the folder, is often preferred.

When various sets of files are used, it's wise to tab each set with a different color label. For example: white for correspondence, blue for subject files, green for case files, and so forth. Each category has its own color for quick recognition.

On labels, type the name of the folder on the first line beginning two or three spaces from the left edge; use initial caps and lowercase letters, and abbreviate freely; leave two spaces between name and any number.

Basic Filing Systems

Common or basic filing systems that might be used in a business office include the following: alphabetical, subject, geographical, numeric, and combination subject (though the office would probably be a very large one with many technical files to utilize the last). About 90 percent of offices use the alphabetical system.

Two less-used systems are the decimal filing system and the group name system (sometimes called the phonetic filing system). The decimal system is used primarily in libraries, being based on the Dewey decimal classification system. The material being filed must be organized under ten or fewer main headings numbered 000 to 900. In turn, each main heading is divided into ten or fewer subheadings numbered from 10 to 90 and preceded by the correct hundreds digit. Each subheading may then be subdivided into ten or few further headings numbered from 1 to 9, preceded by the correct hundreds and tens digits.

The group name or phonetic system is used when there are a great many names involved, as in census surveys. Names that sound alike but are spelled differently are grouped together according to pronunciation rather than spelling: Allan, Allen, Allyn; Nielsen, Neilson, Nealson; Schneider, Snider, Snyder.

Alphabetical System

The alphabetical system is the most widely used filing method because it's the most efficient and least complicated. Material is filed alphabetically according to name. No cross-indexing is necessary. A label should be typed for each name and applied to the tab on each folder.

Papers are placed in the folder in chronological order, with the most current date in front. The folders are filed behind alphabet guides (obtainable in any office supply store). When there is heavy correspondence with one client, several folders may be needed to hold all current material. In this case it's a good practice to separate the material into time periods: one folder for the year 1993, another for the year 1994, and another for 1995. If several projects have been handled for that customer, one folder may be labeled FLORIDA, another NORTH DAKOTA, another MICHIGAN, and so on.

If only the current year's files are kept handy (previous years' files are stored elsewhere), it's useful for at least the first few weeks of the new year to have the old year's files and the new year's files placed back to back or side by side. Of course, a different year will be on each file tab, perhaps a different color as well—red for 1994, for example, and yellow for 1995.

Subject System

This classification is used when papers are called for by subject rather than by a person's or a company's name. Subject classification may be needed when dealing with, say, advertising, brand name products, or materials of all kinds.

You should be thoroughly familiar with the papers flowing through the office and across your desk before attempting to set up this kind of system. The list of subjects must be comprehensive, as simple as possible, and in alphabetical order or by number code. The alphabetical list is usually preferred so a cross-index is not necessary. Papers in the subject folder are arranged chronologically, always with the latest date in front.

Subject Index

While an index of files is not required for a small filing system, it's imperative for large companies. And since most small businesses hope to grow, it's a good practice to maintain one from the first. The subject index will prevent the filing of material under a new heading when a folder has already been set up for that subject, perhaps under a different title. It also permits a person other than the secretary to trace information in the file.

A card is made for each subject heading or subheading. Each subheading shows the main heading under which it is filed. Cross-reference cards are made if the subject is complex. The employer may indicate on the paper where he or she wants it to be filed, while the secretary may have formerly filed that subject under another heading. A cross-reference enables both to find the paper later. The index cards are filed alphabetically.

How to Alphabetize for Filing and Indexing

Individual or Personal Names

The names of people are alphabetized by their surname. When surnames are the same, the position is naturally determined by the letters that follow:

Smith, Mary B.
Smith, Ned
Smithson, John

When two or more similar names are of unequal length, file the shorter name first:

Smith, M.
Smith, Mary
Smith, Mary C.
Smith, Mary Charlene

Individual surnames with prefixes are alphabetized as each is written and are considered to be one word, whether or not they are written as one word:

Mason, Tim
McFarland, John
Merrill, Jane
Vane, K.
Van Houton, Mae
Vargas, Louise

A religious title or foreign title is alphabetized when it is followed by a first name only:

Brother Thomas
Burton, Francis (Rev.)
Friar Tuck
Queen Elizabeth
Sister Mary Rose
Tilton, Sarah (S.S.J.)

Company or Business Names

Words joined by a hyphen are treated as one word. However, if the hyphen is used instead of a comma in a firm name, the individual parts of the name are treated as separate words and therefore the name is indexed by the first word alone. The second name of the hyphenate is used only when needed, similar to a given name:

Johnson, Samuel
Johnson-Smith & Company
Johnson, Steven
Johnson, Victor

Whether a company name is composed of a compound word or is spelled as two words, it is alphabetized as if it were one word:

New Deal Loan Company of America
Newdeal Marine Works
Suncity Shipbuilding Corporation
Sun City Tannery

The exception is when a company name contains the name of a person. In this case, alphabetize by using the surname, followed by first name, then middle initial or middle name if any. The exception is the names of schools. These are alphabetized as written, as are other organizations, businesses, or institutions:

Name:	*Filed as:*
American Petroleum Co.	American Petroleum Co.
Mary Brown Cafe	Brown, Mary Cafe
John Dillard Company	Dillard, John Company
Dillard Stores	Dillard Stores
Joyce Kilmer High School	Joyce Kilmer High School
May's Floral Center	May's Floral Center
John C. Wilson Realty	Wilson, John C. Realty
Wilson Realty Company	Wilson Realty Company

Single letters used as words are treated as words and arranged alphabetically, preceding word names:

BB Shop
BBB Service Company
Bakery Heaven
Brighton Clothes Company

When two or more similar company or business names are of unequal length, file the shorter name first:

National Bank
National Bank of Commerce
Bronson Club
Bronson Club of New York City

Miscellaneous

Abbreviations are alphabetized as if spelled in full:

Name:	*Filed as:*
St. Luke's Church	Saint Luke's Church
Jas. Smith	Smith, James
Chas. Williams	Williams, Charles

Designations following names are alphabetized according to natural order of age:

Smith, James III
Smith, James, 2d
Smith, James, Jr.
Smith, James, Sr.

Articles, prepositions, conjunctions, and the ampersand are disregarded in alphabetizing:

Thomas & Anderson, Inc.
Thomas, Brown R.
Washington Bank, The
Workshop for the Blind

When words end in *s*, the *s* is considered part of the name:

Name: *Filed as:*

Jim's Bait Store   Jim's Bait Store

If a name contains a number, do not put it in "numerical order" with other numbered names. Alphabetize it as if the number were spelled out:

1020 Building Corporation (one thousand twenty)
13 Park Avenue Studio (thirteen)
21 Club (twenty-one)

Titles are disregarded:

Jones, R. L. (Dr.)
Simms, Carlotta (Countess)
Smith, Nancy (Miss)

Exception: If a firm name starts with a title, the title is considered to be the first word:

Queen Mary Boat Company
Sir John Thomas Cigar Company
Viceroy of India Silk Company

File Cabinets

A standard file cabinet has four drawers that accommodate material written on 8½-inch by 11-inch typing or computer paper. An office with many legal-sized papers (8½ inch by 13 or 14 inch) will need a wider cabinet made specifically for these.

Your file cabinet should be near your desk since you will go to it frequently throughout the workday. Label each drawer of the cabinet either horizontally (left to right) or vertically (top to bottom). If an alphabetical system is used, the top drawer might be labeled "A–G," the second drawer "H–M," and so forth.

Many secretarial desks have a built-in file drawer, handy for files used often, for you can reach for them quickly without having to leave your desk to go to the larger cabinet.

Section Two

Office Equipment and Computers

Modern office technology has revolutionized the way secretaries work.

Chapter 7
Office Machines

Typewriters

For years electric typewriters accomplished much of what is now done with computers and word processors. For some applications, such as typing an address on an envelope or a mailing label, a typewriter is still the simplest office tool available. And now the merging of electric typewriters with dedicated word processors has produced a machine that will do everything a sophisticated computer will do, and at much less expense.

Almost all models of electric typewriters have advanced word processing features built in. At the heart of them is a powerful microprocessor based on the technology found in early personal computers (PCs). Although this technology is outdated for today's PCs, it is perfectly capable of managing a word processing typewriter, allowing it to do everything from the ordinary to the truly extraordinary.

Here are just a few of the many new features of today's electronic typewriters:

- Word erase for simple corrections.
- Spell checkers, comparing every word you type with the words in a built-in electronic dictionary.
- Display screen.
- Advanced revision features combined with an optional capacity for unlimited storage using diskettes.
- Capacity to store and merge mail with telephone lists with other documents.
- Background print feature to allow you to print documents while you create or revise other documents.
- Upgradeability—one of the most useful features of all.

Whether you're looking at an electronic typewriter as the sole typing tool for a small office or as a supplement to a larger office's PC, consider getting an upgradeable machine. Office needs change frequently, and what might not be quite right for you now could be a necessity in the near future. With upgradeability, you could move from a one-line display to twenty-five lines on the screen, or you could double your storage memory from fifteen pages to thirty pages or more.

Because much of the correspondence and many of the documents you create tend to be repetitive, having a typewriter with some memory can greatly automate this task. For example, you can store commonly used addresses for typing envelopes or even a form letter such as a "thank you" letter. These documents can be stored in the typewriter's memory or on a diskette. Later you can recall and customize it for a particular person or company.

On a word processing typewriter (see Figure 7-1), you can automatically move to any position on the page and correct characters or whole words at a touch. The typewriter's cursor keys give you the same flexibility of movement on paper that you would have on a word processor's display. The Word Tab and Line Find functions can be used in combination with the cursor keys; whether you want to move across an area of blank space, jump from word to word, or locate your last line of typed text, there is a convenient way to do it.

To make your written letters and documents works of art, there are also fast and easy ways to add interest and emphasis to a page: a Bold function, automatic underlining, and more. Both pitch and impression can be set to match ribbon and paper thickness automatically. A programmable paper-feed function takes you to your customary top writing line and saves you the trouble of positioning the paper. On some advanced models, an adjustable keyboard lets you select from three typing positions the one that suits you best. Automatic correction cleanly removes or covers up typing errors. The Relocate feature automatically puts you

Figure 7-1. A Xerox electronic typewriter.

Photo courtesy of the Xerox Corporation.

back in position to continue typing after you make a correction. And alternate language keyboards allow you to type in many languages, such as French and Spanish.

In selecting a typewriter that's just right for your office, you should consider the following word processing features:

- [ ] *CRT display,* with or without brightness and contrast adjustment.
- [ ] *Menu display,* either text or icons.
- [ ] *MS-DOS compatibility,* to allow for transfer with computers.
- [ ] *Keyboard type and design*—number of keys, special keys.
- [ ] *Memory*—the amount in kilobytes.
- [ ] *Online help*—the ability to get help via a CRT screen or display.
- [ ] *Double-column printing capability*—prints two or more columns on the page.
- [ ] *Hyphenation*—automatic insertion of hyphens.
- [ ] *Insert/delete/overwrite*—special editing techniques.
- [ ] *Block moves/copy/delete*—additional editing techniques.
- [ ] *Global search and replace*—allows replacement of words or phrases throughout the document.
- [ ] *Automatic word wrap*—moves words that do not fit down to the next line.
- [ ] *Headers and footers*—automatic insertion of text at top or bottom of page (e.g., page numbers).
- [ ] *Auto page numbering*—calculates and puts page number on page.
- [ ] *Auto pagination*—determines where the page will break before you print.
- [ ] *Paper size adjustment*—allows for a variety of different sizes of paper.
- [ ] *Save/retrieve documents*—storage of documents in memory or disk.
- [ ] *Grammar checking*—looks for incorrect grammar usage.
- [ ] *Spell checker*—looks for misspelled words.
- [ ] *Word count*—automatic counting of the number of words in a document.
- [ ] *Redundancy check*—looks for words typed twice in a row.
- [ ] *Thesaurus*—an online database of synonyms.
- [ ] *Paragraph/line indent*—special function for indentation.
- [ ] *Decimal tab*—keeps decimals lined up when printing a column of numbers.
- [ ] *Tab settings*—insertion of tabs across the page.
- [ ] *Justification*—centering, as well as right, left, and full justification.
- [ ] *Underlining*—allows for underlining a word.
- [ ] *Bold typing*—makes type darker for emphasis.
- [ ] *Super- and subscript*—allows for typing special characters for formulas.
- [ ] *Line/word/letter correction*—will remove typing mistakes.

Copy Machines

Another essential office tool is the copy machine. Although the advent of word processing typewriters and personal computers has reduced reliance on copiers to some extent, because you can make additional paper copies by printing out duplicates, many documents that do not originate from your word processor or PC require copies.

Many small businesses use a local print shop for copies; however, considering the amount of time lost going back and forth to the shop and the convenience and relative cheapness of owning a personal copier, purchasing or leasing a copier for the business may be a good idea.

Copiers and laser printers function similarly (see Figure 7-2). They are often referred to as "nonimpact printing." Rather than have a hammer strike a ribbon to produce type on the page, copiers use a photographic process involving static electricity.

When you place a document to be copied inside a copier machine, a very strong light is projected on the original. The image of the original is then projected to an electrically sensitive rotating drum. The dark and light areas of the original affect the electric charge on the print drum. After being exposed to the original, the copier drum turns through a powder called **toner,** which sticks to the electrically charged areas. The drum then comes into contact with a fresh piece of copier paper, transferring the toner to the paper, thus creating a copy.

More advanced copiers magnify the projection of the light from the original to the copier drum, thus enlarging or reducing the size of the reproduction. Many copiers now use microprocessors to store images and to automate many of the functions, such as sorting, collating, and making two-sided copies. With the use of multicolor toners, color copies can be produced. Other copiers have automatic document feeders, copier paper trays, sorters, and even built-in staplers. The choice of features makes for a wide range of prices.

How to Select a Copier

When selecting a new machine for your office, consider these six main factors:

- ☐ *Features.* What features do you really need?
- ☐ *Reliability.* How much reliability do you demand?
- ☐ *Cost.* What is the price of the copier, and are there any hidden costs?
- ☐ *Service/maintenance.* Who will maintain or repair your copier?
- ☐ *Warranty.* What does the warranty cover, and for how long?
- ☐ *Productivity.* Will this copier improve productivity in your office?

For some companies even copiers stripped of all features are too large. These companies may want to consider the smallest of models, or minicopiers, the most inexpensive way to acquire the convenience of a copy machine. Minicopiers are

(text continues on p. 103)

Figure 7-2. A copier is an essential office tool in the modern office.

Figure 7-3. A printing calculator.

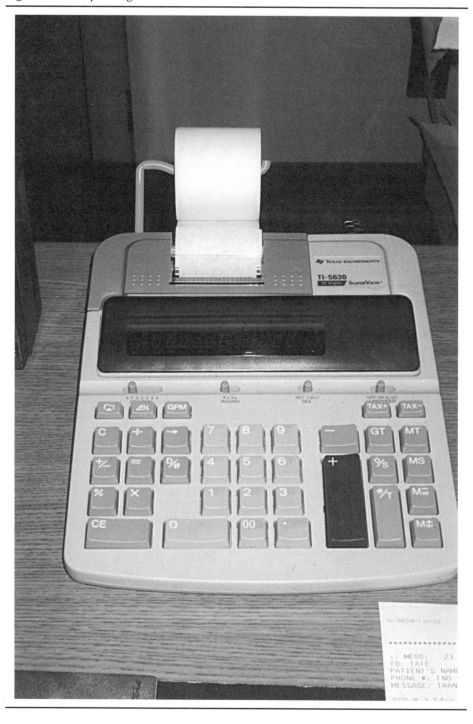

so small they don't even have paper trays and require the insertion of a single sheet of copier paper for each copy made. They use disposable toner cartridges (readily available at office supply stores) and replacement drums. They usually require little to no maintenance, and although it is possible to get paper jams just as in the larger machines, they are easily cleared.

One of the major drawbacks to minicopiers is the cost of the replacement cartridges. While a low-cost minicopier can be purchased for under $500, a replacement cartridge, good for anywhere from 1,000 to 5,000 copies, depending on the model, can cost $75 or more. One alternative to purchasing a replacement cartridge is to have the cartridge refilled with toner, accomplished by a company that specializes in this service. The cost can be half the price of a new cartridge. You send your empty cartridge to one of these organizations, which evaluates and then refills it. Sometimes a cartridge cannot be refilled due to damage, such as scratches on the copier drum.

Calculators

Small electronic calculators have been around since the late 1960s and are now required in almost every business, large or small. They are useful for working with budgets, accounting, and other number-intensive business tasks. For larger projects, a spreadsheet on a personal computer is a better choice.

Calculators come in a variety of sizes and designs. Some have large LED (light-emitting-diode) screens that can be used in dim light situations and others use LCD (liquid-crystal-display) screens that require good lighting to see. Some use solar power, while others use batteries or AC power from the wall outlet. Some are very small so they can be carried with you, while others are designed for desktop use. Some also have built-in printers (see Figure 7-3).

Besides being able to add, subtract, multiply, and divide, many calculators also have the ability to use fixed or floating point decimals, programmable function keys, memory keys, and special keys to perform square roots.

Many calculators are produced for specific applications. Here is a list of some of the many special application calculators available:

- Scientific calculator
- Programmable calculator
- Graphing calculator
- Financial calculator
- Travel organizer
- Statistical calculator

Chapter 8

Telecommunications Equipment

New developments in telecommunications equipment are changing the way all businesses, large and small, communicate. Telephone, computer, fax machine, cellular phone, pager—each now plays a vital role in the success or failure of the company you work for. As a frequent user and a potential purchaser of such equipment for the company, you should be aware of all the latest features and benefits.

Telephones

Telephone service has come a long way since the late 1800s, when it was invented. In the early days, telephone service was primitive and selective. Not everyone had a telephone, nor could you call everyone, everywhere. Only towns that put up the poles and ran the wires had service, and even then many people had to share a telephone line.

Today telephone service is taken for granted. Businesses use voice mail and computerized answering machines to take messages, to network computers across town or across the country, and to send fax transmissions to offices around the world. Let's start with the basic business services that allow you to call across the street.

PBX

You may have seen in old movies a switchboard operator struggling with a tangle of wires and plugs. Today's larger businesses have replaced the switchboard operator with a PBX (private branch exchange) system. Ideal for a company with many employees and individual phone extensions, a PBX is a computerized telephone management system. It allows a single telephone number for a business to be accessed at the same time by numerous outside callers. As each call is received, it is automatically routed to the appropriate extension via a touch-tone phone or with the help of a receptionist/operator.

Multiline Telephones

In a small business, a multiline telephone system is often the preferred choice. This allows you to answer an incoming call from anywhere in the office and to route it to another telephone at the touch of a button. If one line is being used, you can access another line to make an outgoing call.

Other Business Telephones

A wide variety of other business telephones available combine telephone service with computer operations. Many of these more sophisticated telephones are equipped with special features, such as buttons and lights to designate different lines. More modern telephones use computer-like LED (light emitting diode) displays to designate and select lines, as well as indicate the number dialed. Others are programmable to store frequently called numbers in the telephone's memory. Some have speaker telephones built in to free up one's hands while talking. Still others have automatic redialing, intercom capabilities, and built-in answering machines.

Voice Mail and Answering Machines

When you're away from your desk and no one else can cover your telephone, it's important that you use an answering machine or computerized voice mail system. You don't want to miss critical calls for your boss or yourself; in addition, customers now expect the use of such devices, no matter what size company you work for.

Many different types of answering machines are available. Some use audiotapes to play an outgoing message and to record incoming messages. Others record messages digitally using built-in computer memory. Even the most inexpensive answering machine can automatically record the date and time of the call, as well as retrieve messages from remote locations. This last is an essential feature to look for, especially if your boss is frequently away from the office. He or she doesn't have to wait to make contact with you to collect messages but can call in any time from home or on the road. By using a code combination from a touch-tone telephone, the boss can listen to messages and even record a new outgoing message.

Computerized voice mail systems, often used in larger companies, usually consist of a computer system along with a modem connected to the telephone line. These systems accept incoming calls and route them to various voice mail boxes for each employee. All messages are stored in the computer's memory or on hard drive. The use of a touch-tone telephone is usually required to access voice mail boxes and to leave and retrieve messages.

Special Telephone Services

Many telephone companies have a variety of special services that enhance the performance of your business telephone system, no matter which model you have. These services may vary from one part of the country to another. Here is a description of some of the more common services available.

- *Call waiting,* useful for individuals and for small businesses that have only one incoming telephone line. When you're on one call, you are alerted by a tone that another incoming call is waiting. If you wish, you can put the current call on hold and switch to answer the new incoming call.
- *Select call waiting,* which permits only the calls the user has programmed into the telephone to beep you in the call-waiting mode.
- *Call forwarding,* which allows you to redirect calls intended for your telephone to another telephone of your choice—ideal when you or the boss must spend extended time at another location.
- *Select call forwarding,* which enables you to program your telephone with a list of only those people you want to be able to contact you at the forwarding number.
- *Three-way conferencing,* which allows you to call more than one person at a time.
- *Calling number ID,* which allows you to see on a visual display the name and number of the person calling. Calling number ID lets you use your telephone like a pocket pager, enabling you to decide whether to take the call, return it later, or ignore it.
- *Busy number redial,* which continues to dial a busy number automatically until the line is free. The telephone then alerts you when the line is ringing.
- *Selective call acceptance,* by which you program your telephone with a list of only those people you want to contact you. When a person on that list calls, the call rings your telephone. No other calls are allowed to get through.
- *Voice message,* by which callers leave a message, which you retrieve later, just like an answering machine. Voice message is similar to voice mail; however, no special equipment is required at a user's location.

Long-Distance Services

Since the break-up of AT&T, there have been many choices for long-distance service. Besides AT&T, MCI, and SPRINT, a host of smaller, regional long-distance companies market themselves to specific parts of the country. These services may or may not have their own long-distance networks. In many cases they purchase blocks of long-distance time from a common telephone carrier and then resell that time to small businesses and individuals.

Toll-Free Numbers

One long-distance service can benefit your company's customers: an 800 number, often called a "watts" line. As the owner of an 800 number, your company pays for all incoming long-distance charges. A toll-free number is an expense, true, but it's more than just a convenience for your distant customers; it can be a selling point in whether your company makes the first sale at all.

900 Numbers

The 900 prefix is often associated with information lines that require the caller to pay a per-minute fee for the time on the call. This fee is charged to the caller's telephone bill and paid to the owner of the 900 number. Some small businesses involved in mail order have tried using 900 numbers, but often it is reserved for technical help, not for customers who want to order a product.

Teleconferences

One way to reduce travel costs associated with meetings is to use a teleconference. Teleconferences can be scheduled in advance with a long-distance carrier. With a reservation, you can link up different callers from around the country at the same time.

There are two basic ways to conduct a teleconference. In the first, each caller dials a special telephone number at a designated time and is connected to the group teleconference one by one. The second uses an operator, who calls and connects each individual to the teleconference. The cost of the teleconference includes a setup fee and an hourly fee for each caller, along with the long-distance charges for each individual.

Cellular Telephones

One of the most versatile ways your boss can communicate while away from the office is a cellular telephone. Cellular telephones use radio frequencies to communicate with a cellular telephone network consisting of various microwave radio towers spaced throughout a city or region. These are called *cells*. When a call is being made, the telephone first establishes a radio link with one of the cellular transmission towers. The cell then connects the telephone with the regular telephone system to make the call. Calls are received in much the same manner.

There are many different types of cellular phones. Transportables come with a battery and carrying case. Other handheld models consist of just a handset. Various attachments allow a cellular telephone to be used inside a car. For example, power can be provided from the car's cigarette lighter, and an external antenna can be connected to increase the telephone's range. Some have a hands-free feature, which allows a speaker and microphone to be connected inside a car. Most cellular telephones also have memory for storing frequently called numbers.

Fees

Cellular service requires payment of a flat monthly fee, plus a per-minute charge that can be expensive. Often a telephone is provided as part of the basic package if your company agrees to a specific service contract of one to three years.

This is the basic arrangement, but of course even here there are special services—each at a price.

Special Services

Personal communications services combine the power of a home or business telephone with the mobility offered by a cellular phone. The boss's home or business telephone is replaced by a cellular-ready portable telephone. When he or she uses the telephone around the home or office, the usual rate applies. Then if the boss wants to take the telephone along in the car, his or her telephone service will follow—the ability to both make and take calls. The rates paid while using the mobile service are different from those paid while using it in a fixed location.

Another innovation, cellular data services, combines the power of computer communications with a cellular modem. By having a cellular modem installed inside a portable computer, you can connect your boss's computer with various networks and databases while he or she is on the road. Some systems even allow for a regular telephone handset to be plugged into the computer in order to use cellular voice service.

Finally there are miniature computers called PDAs (personal data assistants), also equipped with cellular modems. Most PDAs do not use a traditional typewriter-style keyboard for input. Instead they use a touch screen and a pen interface to access various menu choices. To enter text information or graphics, simply write or draw on the small screen. Built-in handwriting recognition software translates handwriting into computer text, where it can be stored in the PDA's memory or later transferred to an office computer.

Pagers

Pagers have become an important business communication tool. The caller dials the pager's telephone number and then enters his or her telephone number or even a voice message. The owner of the pager is then notified by the pager's beeping or vibrating; information about the call is displayed on the LCD display screen (see Figure 8-1). The owner of the pager can then go to the nearest telephone to return the call.

Pagers are very useful when your boss must be away from the office for extended periods of time. When there is an important call from a business associate or client, the pager can be used to pass on the caller's number. Most pagers

Figure 8-1. A small vibrating pocket pager.

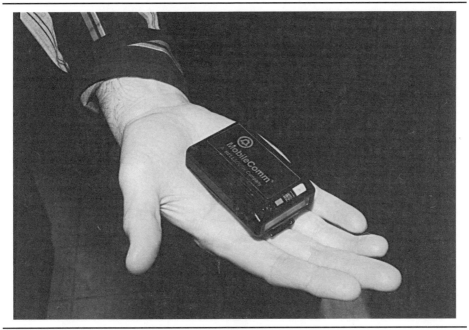

function within the range of a city or a specific region. However, some systems using satellite communications can page a person anywhere in the country with just one call.

Facsimile Machines

The following information was furnished by AT&T General Business Systems, which retains the copyright. The information is concise and useful for any secretary, especially if you're purchasing the company's or the department's first fax machine.

Choosing a Fax That Suits Your Needs

The fax revolution continues to spread to U.S. offices and homes, with more than 5 million machines in use and 900 million messages sent annually. The challenge lies in choosing the right machine (or machines) from the more than 200 models on the market.

Today's facsimile machines are faster and more versatile than ever; there are even products available that tie your fax machine to your office telephone's voice messaging system. Those products make it as easy to check for fax messages when you're out of the office as it is to check for voice messages. In addition, a new business phone with fax capabilities, recently introduced by AT&T, could make desktop faxes as much a desktop staple as personal computers. This is an exciting alternative to installing a dedicated fax phone line when the company's fax usage is high.

How to Select a Fax Machine

Selecting a machine begins with a clear understanding of how it is going to be used. Some of the factors to consider include:

1. What type of documents will you send and receive?
2. How many pages will each document have?
3. How many locations will you send the same document to?
4. Do you frequently send illustrations, photographs, or sketches?
5. Are company employees often on the road? Would it be useful for them to be able to reroute fax messages to another fax machine, at any time of day or night?
6. Does your company need more than one fax machine?
7. Would it be more convenient—and more efficient—if employees could send and receive faxes right at their desks, while at the same time transacting other business?

Low- and High-Volume Usage

Fax machines cost from several hundred dollars for basic, no-frills machines up to thousands of dollars for more sophisticated models and plain-paper faxes (see Figure 8-2). However, if you opt for a basic machine for the company or department, consider that usage often grows dramatically as employees become accustomed to the convenience of sending and receiving fax messages.

If you anticipate high usage, consider these factors:

■ *Paper capacity.* Most fax machines use thermal paper, a glossy paper that comes in rolls ranging from 66 to 328 feet. Each foot equals approximately one page. If you receive lots of fax messages, choose a machine that can accommodate the larger rolls.

■ *Plain versus thermal paper.* Plain-paper fax machines cost more than those that use thermal paper and have more moving parts that can malfunction. Many users reconcile a preference for plain paper with the cost benefits of thermal fax machines by copying thermal fax messages on plain bond paper as they come in. But whatever your choice, use only the paper the manufacturer recommends. Improperly coated paper—usually the cheaper brands available—can damage your fax machine.

■ *Document feeder.* Document feeders can hold up to 50 pages at a time; however, approximately 60 percent of all fax messages transmitted today are three pages or less. If your company is small or you're buying only for your own department, a ten-page document feeder may be adequate for most of your needs.

Figure 8-2. A plain-paper fax machine.

- *Usage.* If your business sends or receives photos, illustrations, or graphics, consider purchasing a fax machine with grayscale (halftone) capability, which translates pictures into between eight and sixty-four shades of gray.

- *Resolution.* Most faxes have a normal resolution (picture sharpness) appropriate for most business correspondence and simple line drawings. If your business requires a sharper image, higher resolutions are available. Remember, however, that the machines at both ends of the transmission must have that capability.

- *Broadcasting.* If you send daily reports to satellite locations, broadcasting capability can be an important time saver. Broadcasting stores pages in the fax machine's memory, for transmission to the locations you specify.

- *Automatic dialing.* This is another time saver that lets you store frequently called fax numbers in the machine's memory bank. The numbers can be dialed at the touch of a button—individually or in groups.

- *Delayed send.* This money-saving feature lets you program a document for transmission at a specific time, for example, during off-peak hours, to take advantage of lower calling rates. It's also valuable to companies doing business overseas that want to schedule delivery during business hours in another time zone.

- *Polling.* Polling lets your machine retrieve documents stored in another fax machine's memory. If collecting sales figures from branch offices is a routine part of your business day, polling lets you retrieve the data whenever it's convenient for you, via their fax machines.

Making Your Decision

Like any piece of high-tech equipment, fax machines have movable parts that may require attention at some point. Ask about the length of warranty and the availability of a maintenance contract. While at the dealer, try the machine to ensure it performs as advertised. Many stores, like the AT&T Phone Centers, have fax machines set up so customers can have hands-on experience.

Whatever your business, there's a fax machine (or combination of fax machines) to meet your company's needs. The key lies in doing your purchasing homework up front—building features, options, quality, and service into your buying decision.

In addition to the above information supplied by AT&T, you should also know that there are fax modems available for personal computer systems. A fax modem will connect your computer to the phone lines to send and receive data and allow your computer to send and receive faxes.

To send a fax, you first compose the document on the computer electronically. Then, without having to print out the document and take it to a fax machine, you access the software that comes with the fax modem and transmit the document, just as a regular fax machine does. Incoming faxes are stored in your computer's memory like a graphic. You can read the fax using the software or print it out with your printer. (See also Chapter 11, Computer Communications.)

Chapter 9

Computer Systems

Office Computers

Companies of all sizes routinely use personal or desktop computers in the office. Computers allow employees to be more productive by automating many repetitive tasks, such as word processing, billing, and filing. When an office has even only one computer, the secretary may be its most frequent user. You may also be the person who investigates the different types of hardware and software and recommends which PC the office should buy.

Computers available for business uses range from powerful mainframes and minicomputers, to networked systems, to the personal computers (PCs) many people have in their homes. For most small businesses, personal or desktop computers are often used. These come in a wide variety of different configurations in both IBM compatible and Apple Macintosh.

When most people use a PC, what they really are using is a computer system. The computer itself may be no larger than a single integrated circuit chip soldered to a circuit board inside the computer's case. However, the user interfaces with a variety of other elements that together make up the computer system. These elements, called **peripheral devices,** include the keyboard, monitor, mouse, disk drives, and printer.

A true computer system usually consists of five elements:

1. An *input device,* such as a keyboard or mouse, that allows you to communicate with the computer.
2. An *output device,* such as a monitor or a printer, that allows the computer to communicate back with you.
3. A *processor* that allows for the manipulation of your data.
4. A *storage system,* such as a floppy disk drive or hard disk drive, that allows you to save your work electronically.
5. *Software* that provides instructions for the computer in the form of programs.

Hardware

How to operate your computer and what type of work it can perform depend on how your system unit is equipped. The system unit from the outside is just a case to house the electronic components. Most people refer to the system unit as "the computer" since it is the part of the system that handles all the processing jobs. There are a variety of different computer designs, such as the desktop system that sits on a desk, the floor-standing tower system, and the portable or laptop computer (see Figures 9-1 through 9-3).

All computers have a power switch on the system unit, located on the front of the case or on the back. Depending on which brand of computer you use, on front there will also probably be **disk drives** mounted inside the system unit. One type of disk drive may be a floppy disk in either 5¼-inch or 3½-inch format. Another type of disk drive is a hard disk drive, which can be mounted inside the system unit or contained in its own case and connected via a cable. The hard disk drive is capable of storing the same information as many floppy disks, depending on its size rating.

Each disk drive is given a letter, number, or name so that it's easy to load and save information to or from a particular drive location. On IBM-compatible computers, the first diskette drive is called drive A, the second diskette drive is called drive B, and the hard drive is called drive C. On Apple Macintosh computers, the drives are given names or labels. The same is true for computers such as the Commodore Amiga. You can name your hard drive something like "My Hard Drive" so it will be easy to find when saving or loading data.

PCs are usually designed to be expandable. For this reason, it's possible to

Figure 9-1.   A desktop computer system.

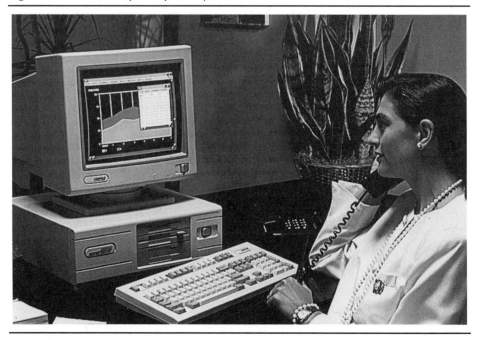

Figure 9-2. A personal computer in the "tower" configuration.

Figure 9-3. A laptop portable computer.

remove the case should you need to get inside to install a new component. Many people are afraid to open the computer case, yet the more familiar you are with your computer, the better able you will be to troubleshoot little problems that arise from time to time. If you work for a small business, your boss is the person who probably bought the computer. Ask permission to open the case (or let the boss do so and look over his or her shoulder). Computer repairs and upgrades are simple skills to acquire yet they are invaluable, especially in terms of time saved. Once a small company begins to rely on a computer to run its day-to-day business, the whole company can come to a screeching halt if the computer goes down.

Inside the system unit of a typical IBM compatible you will see a metal box, which is the computer's power supply. This **transformer** converts the power from the wall into electricity that can be used by the computer. You'll see the disk drives and hard disk drive that are mounted inside the case. And you'll see the **mother board,** which occupies most of the inside of the computer. This large circuit board contains various chips and your processor. On the mother board, you will see various slots for plug-in expansion boards. For example, if you want to use a monitor or a printer with your computer, you may need to plug an interface card into one of these slots so that the device can communicate with the computer.

Expansion boards are available for a variety of different purposes. They easily plug into the mother board expansion slots so you can add a device such as a monitor or CD-ROM. The expansion slots in the mother board provide a common electronic signal called a **bus.** A bus allows electronic signals to be passed from one part of the PC to another.

Some expansion boards have a plug at one end where you can attach a device such as a disk drive or printer. These are called **ports.** Some ports are located on expansion boards, and some are connected directly to the mother board. The two most common ports are the **parallel** port, used primarily for printers, and the **serial port,** primarily used to connect modems for telecommunications.

Looking at the back of a typical PC (see Figure 9-4), you will see a parallel port for the printer, a serial port for the modem, another serial port for the mouse, and a video port for the monitor.

On the back of an Apple Macintosh, you will see the same ports with different types of connectors (see Figure 9-5). There are a printer port, a modem port,

Figure 9-4. The rear of an IBM PC-compatible tower computer showing the communications and peripheral ports.

a port for an extra disk drive, an SCSI (small computer system interface) port for connecting an SCSI hard disk drive, an Apple BUS port for connecting a mouse or track ball, and additional ports for a speaker or microphone.

The term *expansion board* may appear to mean that all such boards are only options. However, there are several such expansion boards found in almost all IBM-compatible models, such as the **disk controller,** connected to the floppy disk drives and hard disk drive and used to manage communication with these devices, and the **display adapter,** which converts the computer's instructions into pictures on your monitor screen.

Other key components in your computer are the **memory chips** and the **processor chip.** The amount of memory your computer has determines the amount of workspace available for data. For example, if you are working with a large word processing document or a large accounting program with a lot of data, you might eventually see messages on your monitor screen that the computer is running low or is out of memory. Most computers allow for upgrading the amount of memory. For most IBM compatibles and Apple Macintosh computers, you can add to the computer's memory by plugging in additional **SIMM** (single in-line memory module) **chips,** rectangular circuit boards that contain additional RAM (random access memory) chips, which are what provides your computer's mem-

Figure 9-5. The rear of a Macintosh Quadra computer showing the communications and peripheral ports.

ory. SIMMs can be plugged into the SIMMs slots on the mother board of your computer to increase system memory. Your computer will likely have between four and eight SIMMs slots. Adding eight 1-megabyte SIMMs chips will increase your system memory to 8 megs. Adding eight 4-meg SIMMs chips would increase the memory to a whopping 32 megs.

Computer performance and speed are determined mainly by the type of processor chip included with your computer. Apple computers were originally built around a processor called the 6802. With the introduction of the Apple Macintosh, a more powerful 68000 chip was used. Since then, the 68010, 68020, 68030, and 68040 processor chips have been used. For IBM compatibles, a different type of chip was used. In early PCs, the 8086 was used, followed by the 8088. Then came the 80286, 80386, and the 80486. Eventually for both Macintosh and IBM compatibles, you will see chips as high as 68050 and 80586 and beyond. When people talk about processing power, most often they just talk about the last three letters of the chip—for instance, a "486" or an "030."

Depending on the particular application, a **math co-processor** may also be installed in your computer. This is actually another processor, which helps with complicated mathematical functions. If your computer is equipped with one, it will allow it to handle complex spreadsheets and computer-aided design applications faster than normal. Some processors, such as the 80486 and the 68040, have a built-in math co-processor in the main chip. Others, like the 80386 or 80286, must use an 80287 or 80387 math co-processor. Still others, like the 68030 chip used in older Macintosh computers, must use a 68882 math co-processor. If your computer does not have a math co-processor and you find yourself doing a lot of mathematical formulas or graphics-intensive applications on your PC, you can purchase one as an addition to your system.

Another performance enhancement enjoyed by many PC users is an **internal cache,** an extra bit of memory built into your processor that allows it to store certain instructions internally rather than using your computer's normal memory. This saves time and greatly increases speed. Some computers have up to a 256 K (256,000 bytes of information) cache.

Also important in evaluating speed and performance is the **clock speed** of your processor. Clock speed is the speed at which messages from the computer processor travel to other parts of the computer, such as the disk drives, hard drive, monitor, printer, and so on. Many early model PCs had clock speeds of 4 to 8 megahertz (MHz). Current models equipped with clock-doubler chips can go up to 66 MHz and beyond.

The key point to remember when you're choosing a company computer is that better speed and performance usually translate into greater productivity. Therefore, an investment in a good computer system can help you do more in less time. In many cases, it isn't always necessary to replace the company's existing computer system. You may be able to add more memory and an add-on accelerator card that will equip your PC with the latest processor, math co-processor, and internal cache. This would plug into one of the expansion slots on the mother board of your PC.

Memory

Computer memory is often very confusing to new computer users because it implies that the computer will remember your data automatically. However, if you create a document with a word processor but don't save it and then turn off your computer, that document will be lost. Unfortunately most computer users learn this lesson the hard way. Long-term storage of data is handled by the disk drives and hard disk drive, not by the computer's memory.

Your computer's memory is that area where programs and data are temporarily copied from a diskette or hard disk drive so that you can use them. Moving programs and data into memory is called **loading,** or on some systems **opening.** It is just like taking a document out of a file cabinet and putting it on your desk. Unlike this analogy, however, when a computer loads a program or a document into memory, it only takes a copy, leaving the original intact on the disk. You can modify the original by saving your latest work with the same name as the original. Or you can retain the original and keep a new version by saving the new version with a slightly different name.

RAM (random-access memory) is the SIMMs chips we discussed earlier and is the area of memory where your programs and data are loaded. Memory is measured in terms of bits, bytes, kilobytes, megabytes, and gigabytes.

Electronically, the RAM in your computer is made up of lots of little electric switches that are turned on or off. For programming purposes, *on* is given a numerical value of 1, and *off* is given the numerical value of 0. Therefore, programs and data are represented as lots of 1s and 0s. Each character in the alphabet is represented by a special code made up of 1s and 0s. The same is true for numbers and graphics on your monitor. Some computers use an 8-bit system. That means that it takes a combination of eight 1s and 0s to form each character or graphic. Other more advanced graphics computers use 24-bit systems, and still other computers are using 32-bit systems. New advances will soon incorporate 64-bit systems. For an 8-bit system, each group of eight 1s and 0s is called a **byte**, and 1,024 bytes equals a kilobyte, 1,024 kilobytes equals a megabyte, and a gigabyte is 1,000 megabytes.

Most computers are standardly equipped with at least 1 megabyte of memory. However, this is usually not enough to handle today's modern operating systems and applications software. For many applications 4 megs is the recommended minimum, and 8 to 32 megs is common.

For Apple Macintosh computers, the basic memory limitation is 8 megs, but the latest operating system will allow computers equipped with a 68030 processor chip or better to access 32-bit memory models. This allows for accessing greater amounts of memory.

For IBM compatibles, the same is true, although an 80386 or better processor and special operating system extensions are required in order to access over 8 megs. For IBM compatibles using DOS, there are three types of memory available. When DOS was originally written, it was created with a basic memory limit of 640 K. This is called **conventional memory.** Since most modern computers are now equipped with at least 1 megabyte of memory, the extra 384 (640 + 384 =

1,024, or 1 meg) is called **extended memory.** Memory beyond 1 megabyte is called **expanded memory.**

Most programs written for DOS use conventional memory. To maximize the available memory for these programs, certain accessory programs (such as device drivers for your mouse or CD-ROM drive) can be loaded into extended memory. In order to use extended memory or expanded memory, you must use an extended memory manager or an expanded memory manager. For more information on how to maximize your system performance and to gain access to the most possible memory, consult your DOS reference manual.

Another way some computers access even greater amounts of memory is to use **virtual memory.** Computers equipped with at least an 80386 processor or a 68030 processor can use part of the computer's hard drive as if it were extra RAM. This is called virtual memory. Virtual memory is slower than RAM memory and is used primarily when multiple programs are loaded and running at the same time. The program not being accessed by a user can be temporarily swapped to virtual memory.

ROM (read-only memory) is another type of memory that is built into the computer and cannot be changed by programs. ROM chips contain a permanent set of instructions that support the overall operation of the computer. Essentially they function automatically and require little attention from most computer users.

Input Devices

In order to use computers, you need some way to communicate with them. This process is known as **input.** There are many types of input devices; probably the most common is a keyboard. By simply typing on a typewriter-like keyboard, information is sent to the computer for processing. In order to see what it is you have typed, most computers use a **monitor** or **video display.** As characters are typed on the keyboard, they appear on the monitor screen.

One of the most familiar devices for input are game controllers such as **joysticks.** These devices allow a game player to communicate information to a computer, informing it of key decisions necessary to play a game. A similar device is a **mouse,** a hand controller that is used in some software applications and operating systems for a variety of different computers (see Figure 9-6). A mouse is used to select menu choices and to move a **cursor,** or pointer, around on the monitor screen. A mouse consists of a rubber ball inside a plastic housing. By moving the mouse over a surface such as a desktop or a mouse pad, the ball moves, providing input to the computer to move a pointer on the display screen. Similar to a mouse is a **track ball.** Many small portable computers use track balls since the operator may be using the computer where there is no desktop available for a mouse.

You can also communicate with a computer monitor screen by pointing with a device called a **light pen.** The light pen forms an electrical connection that sends information to the computer depending on where you touch the monitor. Light pens have led to a whole new user interface called a **pen interface,** which allows you to write information and create drawings just as you would on paper

Figure 9-6.   A mouse and track ball hand controller.

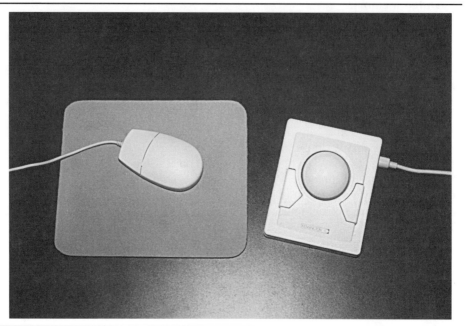

using your own handwriting. The pen is placed on a special computer tablet in order to write or draw. Powerful handwriting recognition software compares your writing with characters it understands or those you teach it. The software then translates the proper character as input for the computer. The pen interface is used for small personal communications devices such as those offered by Apple and Microsoft.

If you shop at a large supermarket, you're already familiar with another form of input: the **bar code.** The bar code is printed on most retail products available today. Made up of wide and narrow bars with the spaces between them, the code represents inventory and pricing information about a particular product. An input device called a **bar-code reader** or **scanner** uses a light or a laser to input the code. Special bar-code interpretation software inside the computer then translates the code into data.

Another useful form of input designed originally for disabled individuals is **voice recognition.** Voice recognition and natural language speech systems interpret the human voice into signals that a computer can understand as input. Voice recognition systems are now popular and can be used to select menu items in software and, in some cases, even to create text for a word processing document or spreadsheet.

For graphic artists and designers and others who need to input precise drawings, a special drawing device called a **graphics tablet** is available. A graphics tablet consists of a plastic board containing a grid of fine electrical wires. A special drawing pen is used to draw. When the pen comes into contact with the grid of wires, information on the location of the pen is sent to the computer in order to create a graphics image on a monitor screen.

Another input tool used by graphic artists is the **scanner.** There are various models available. Some you hold in your hand; other desktop models operate much like a copy machine. With the desktop version, you place an original document into the scanner, and the scanner copies an image of the document or graphic into the computer's memory. When the document is text, special optical character recognition software is often used. This software takes the images input from a scanner and compares them against various text styles in memory. It then translates the scanner image into text for your word processor.

Output Devices

When you work with a computer, most of your attention will be focused on output devices. This is where you can see the results of your work. The most common output devices found on computer systems are the monitor and the printer. Both output devices are available in many different models.

The Monitor

Early PCs used television sets as their display system, but they were difficult to read and commonly caused eyestrain. Today there are several different types of monitors to fit various needs. Monitors can operate in several different modes depending on what must be displayed. The biggest difference depends on whether the monitor displays text or graphics.

When displaying text, only letters, numbers, punctuation, and symbols can be shown on the monitor. These characters are part of the **character set** that is built into the computer memory just like the letter keys on a typewriter. The screen is divided into segments where these characters can be displayed. Most monitors display eighty columns of characters across the screen and twenty-five rows from top to bottom.

The graphics mode is designed for displaying pictures and illustrations, in both color and black and white. To display a graphic, the computer displays an array of tiny dots called **pixels** anywhere on the screen, not just in the predetermined segments as is the case with text mode. With your monitor in the graphics mode, you can draw pictures and type text and display them both on the same screen.

While the graphics mode is more versatile, it is much slower than text mode. In the past, a good typist could out-type the computer when the monitor was in the graphics mode. However, the newest monitors and PCs can use the graphics mode very effectively. In fact, there is a trend toward graphics-based software using a **graphical user interface** (GUI). This is common with the Apple Macintosh operating system, Microsoft Windows for the PC, and Amiga DOS. With programs written for these operating systems, you can type text and insert graphics at the same time. Along with this innovation comes a variety of font choices for your type. Your text can assume a variety of shapes and sizes.

The monitor itself also offers you several choices. Some models for the Apple Macintosh, such as the Classic or earlier Mac Plus and SE class, have built-in black-and-white monitors. Other models, such as the Mac II, LC, IICi, IIFX, IISI, and Quadra, have external color monitors, with varying resolution and number of colors. In the PC-compatible world, early users had a choice between monochrome and CGA (color graphics adapter) systems. The monochrome systems displayed black-and-white text, while the CGA systems could produce up to sixteen colors. Other color modes and displays soon appeared, such as EGA (enhanced graphics adapter) and VGA (video graphics array). Each offered more colors and high resolution.

Laptop and portable computers utilize another display technology. Some use an LED (light-emitting diode) system, while others use an LCD (liquid crystal display). For working in low-light conditions, many portables are equipped with backlit displays. The majority of laptop and portable displays are in black and white, amber and white, or red and white. Recent advanced systems utilize color displays.

The Printer

Along with video display monitors, the other most popular form of output for a computer system is a **printer.** Printers produce a hard-copy paper version of what is on your display screen. There are several different types of printers available.

Dot Matrix

Dot-matrix printers are the most popular because they are inexpensive, fast, and versatile. The dot-matrix printer creates characters on the page by combining tiny dots just like the pixels on a video display. The print head uses a group of tiny pins (usually nine to twenty-four in number) that press through an inked ribbon to make a mark on the paper. Depending on which of the pins are extended, different characters are printed. Dot-matrix printers can produce fairly attractive output but not as good as traditional typewriter-quality text.

Daisy Wheel

A daisy-wheel printer can produce traditional typewriter-quality printing, often called **letter quality.** A daisy-wheel printer uses a method similar to a typewriter, except that its letter keys are arranged on a wheel that revolves and comes into contact with an inked ribbon.

Ink Jet

Ink jet printers produce letter-quality output by spraying ink through a series of tiny nozzles onto the paper to form each letter.

Laser

Perhaps the most successful and popular method of producing letter-quality text is with a laser printer. Although laser printers are more expensive than the other choices, their quality and speed have made them popular among all types of computer users. Laser printers function similarly to copying machines. A graphics image of the computer output is sent to the laser printer, which also has a computer processor. The laser printer then uses a laser to display an image on an electrically charged drum surface. Once the charged surface comes into contact with a powdered or liquid toner, the toner sticks in the image areas and falls off the nonimage areas. When paper comes into contact with the drum, the toner is transferred to the paper, producing an image.

Color Printing

Recent advances in color printing have resulted in dot-matrix printers that use multicolored ribbons, color laser printers, and color photographic devices for producing color output.

Other Output Devices

Another device for reproducing computer output is a **pen plotter,** which draws the computer output using a group of multicolored pens. This is often used in architectural and design offices. In addition, there are a variety of other devices for utilizing computer output, among them, sound from your computer speakers, voice synthesizers, communications output to modems, and control of electrical devices.

Storage Devices

The ability to store, search for, and retrieve specific information from permanent data storage media is ideal for helping secretaries organize the department or company—and keep it organized. Using the computer's electronic filing system, you should see a great time savings for yourself, as well as an increase in your productivity and efficiency in day-to-day business activities.

A computer stores your work in two areas, one temporary and one permanent. The temporary storage is your computer's memory, its RAM. We've already discussed computer memory, but it's important to remember that information stored in RAM is stored only as long as the computer is turned on. One common storage device used by many computers is a **RAM disk,** a segment of the computer's memory set aside to act and respond as if it were a disk drive. Information you store on the RAM disk is kept there for convenience while working. If you turn off the computer, the RAM disk contents will also be lost.

The Hard Drive

The main permanent storage device is the computer's **hard drive** (sometimes called a **fixed disk**), which can be either internal (mounted inside the computer case) or external (in its own case connected to the computer via a cable). Some computers are not equipped with hard drives, though most new systems are. A hard drive is actually a stack of disks coated with a magnetic coating similar to audio- or videotape. Information is saved on a hard drive much the same way a song is recorded on audiotape. The computer's electronic signals are recorded on the magnetic hard drive disk, and when you want the information back, the hard drive "plays back" those signals. Saving information on a hard drive is called **writing** to the drive; playing information back is called **reading.** It is also possible to erase information on a drive; this is called **deleting.**

Disk storage capacity is measured in units called **bytes.** A byte is made up of 8 bits of information. A thousand bytes is a kilobyte, or K for short. Hard drives can store millions of bytes. Typically hard drives store anywhere from 20 megabytes to 2,000 megabytes (called 2 gigabytes).

The Floppy Disk

Another form of permanent storage is a **floppy disk** (see Figure 9-7). A floppy disk or diskette is used in a floppy disk drive. Disks come in several varieties:

Figure 9-7. A floppy diskette and microdisk.

3½-inch, 5¼-inch, and 8-inch disks, with the first two being the most common. The 3½-inch and the 5¼-inch disks are sometimes affectionately called by their description: **stiffies** and **floppies,** respectively. Although the 5¼-inch disk is flexible, avoid bending it; otherwise, the stored data may be damaged. The 3½-inch disk is housed inside a rigid case.

Floppies store far less than hard drives. A 5¼-inch double-density diskette can store 360 K (360,000 bytes). A high-density version of the same diskette can store 1.2 megs (1,200,000 bytes). For 3½-inch diskettes, a double-density version can store 720 K (720,000 bytes), and the high-density version can store 1.44 megs (1,440,000 bytes). Improvements in disk-drive storage capabilities have increased storage capacities up to 2.88 meg on some specially formatted 3½-inch diskettes, but this is still much less than the hard drive.

On a 5¼-inch floppy disk, the central open slot is where the read/write head of the disk drive contacts the spinning disk. Never touch this area, or you could damage the magnetic information stored there. On the side edge of the diskette is a **write-protect** notch. This can be covered with tape to prevent accidentally writing data to the disk. In this way, archive files can be protected when working with them.

On a 3½-inch diskette is a sliding door that protects the read/write slot. And instead of a write-protect notch, there is a small hole with a sliding piece of plastic. When the hole is open, your data are write-protected. When the hole is closed by the piece of plastic, you can write information on the disk and thus modify your existing data files.

Since the data and programs you use on floppy disks must be protected, an understanding of how to care for disks is very important. Here's a rundown of how to handle them:

☐ Always keep disks in a cover or jacket when not in use, and store them so they'll be protected. For example, keep them away from food or drinks.

☐ Always store disks upright in a closed container.

☐ Avoid extreme temperatures and humidity.

☐ Keep disks away from magnets, such as those in stereo speakers or the telephone.

☐ Label your diskettes so you'll know what they contain, but never write on them with a ballpoint pen or pencil. Instead, fill out a label before sticking it on the diskette.

☐ Always insert diskettes label side up, with the read/write slot going into the disk drive first.

☐ Never touch the exposed area of the disk.

☐ Never clean disks with a solvent, such as alcohol.

☐ Never insert or remove a diskette while the disk-drive indicator light is on.

If your computer is equipped with a hard drive, it too requires special care. Unlike a floppy disk, a hard drive cannot be removed from the computer or case.

It is specially mounted and sealed to protect it from most general abuse; however, it is still subject to wear. Most hard drive specifications include the **search time,** or how fast the drive can locate a file, along with something called the **mean time** between failures, an estimate of how long you can use your hard drive before it will fail. Most hard drives are specified at 50,000 hours mean time between failures.

Making Backups

When your hard drive fails, you could lose all your data. Since your hard drive is like a very large filing cabinet filled with important and often confidential data about the business you work for, protecting that information is very important. Therefore, you should back up your hard drive frequently by making copies of all data onto a set of floppies. This may take some time, though there are special software programs that can make it easier. Also, there are some programs and special service companies that will take the information on your hard drive and give you a copy on diskette or another hard drive.

One specialized storage medium is available solely for the purpose of making backups. Tape backup drives use a cartridge tape or 8-mm tape (similar to 8-mm videotape) to back up your hard drive and all your data. A tape backup drive is much slower than a hard drive or even a floppy drive, so it's very useful for normal day-to-day use as a storage medium. However, special software combined with a tape backup drive can automatically back up your data periodically so you'll also be protected in the event of hard drive failure.

Other Special Storage Media

A cross between a floppy disk and a hard drive, **removable cartridge drives** are popular in many businesses. A removable cartridge drive acts like a hard drive, although it's somewhat slower in terms of reading and writing data; however, like a floppy disk, a removable cartridge can be taken from the drive and replaced with another. This offers great flexibility: When one cartridge is filled up, it can be replaced by another. It's like having a completely new hard drive. The removable cartridges are contained in a special housing that protects the sensitive media inside. Since these cartridges can store as much as 90 megabytes or more of programs and data, they must be handled very carefully and stored in a cool, protected environment.

Another increasingly popular data storage medium is a **CD-ROM.** This system uses a compact disk to store computer data. Approximately 600 megabytes can be stored on one CD-ROM, the equivalent of more than 1,500 floppy disks. However, a CD-ROM does not allow you to modify and save data back on it. Thus you can read data from it but cannot write data to it.

Optical disks are similar to CD-ROMs. They use a disk similar to a compact or laser disk, but unlike CD-ROMs, you can write information on optical disks. These disks use laser technology to read and write data to and from the disk.

Formatting

When you want to save something onto a disk, it's important that your software know where on the disk those particular data are to be saved. Thus, there must be some type of format that assigns particular locations and creates a table of contents. This is the purpose of the special software procedure called **formatting:** to create the available locations for saving data and to create a space for a table of contents. Formatting is also sometimes called **initializing.** When you purchase a disk from the store, in most cases it will not be formatted; you will format the disk yourself.

Data are recorded on the disk surface in concentric circles. As the disk turns inside the disk drive, information can be saved on each circle, called a **track.** Each track is divided into **sectors,** and each sector can hold a specific number of bytes.

Floppy disks must be formatted according to a specific standard that correlates to the capabilities of your disk drive. For instance, some disk drives can read 720 K MS-DOS diskettes or 1.44 meg MS-DOS diskettes. Others can only read 360 K floppies or 1.2 meg floppies. On Apple Macintosh computers, disk drives are capable of reading 400 K, 800 K, or 1.44 meg diskettes. In order to format a diskette in the 1.2 meg range and beyond, you must purchase **high-density diskettes,** which allow for storing more information.

How you format a diskette the first time you use it varies depending on the type of computer you use and your operating system. For example, with an IBM-compatible machine running MS-DOS, you type the following at the DOS prompt, "Format A:" You then insert a blank diskette in the disk drive and press Return on the keyboard. For an IBM-compatible machine running the OS/2 operating system, you click your mouse pointer or the Drives icon in the System Info file, select the format size wanted, and then insert the blank diskette into the drive.

Formatting a disk with a Macintosh computer is somewhat simpler. The first time you use a blank disk, the computer's operating system automatically asks if you want to format the disk using a pop-up menu. If you click your mouse pointer on "format" or "initialize," your diskette will automatically be formatted.

Software

An integral part of your computer system is the software. Computers are powerful tools that can be very complicated to communicate with directly. To simplify your interactions with the computer, the software programs were written to provide the computer with instructions.

Operating Systems

The most basic of the software programs available for business applications is your computer's operating system, such as MS-DOS and Windows, OS/2, Macintosh System, UNIX, or Amiga DOS. An **operating system** is a collection of programs that perform essential functions, for example, managing the keyboard, monitor, printer, and memory; starting other programs like a word processor; and saving, deleting, copying, or renaming files.

The standard operating system for IBM PC compatibles is also perhaps the most popular. It's called **DOS,** short for "disk operating system," and is sometimes referred to as PC-DOS or MS-DOS. Most of the communication with DOS takes place in the form of commands typed on the keyboard. If your computer is equipped with DOS as an operating system, your DOS manual will list all the DOS commands and the exact format required.

Windows is an increasingly popular user interface that is an extension of DOS. Rather than you having to type in commands to load, save, delete, and so forth, Windows uses a GUI featuring icons or symbolic pictures and graphical windows. A Windows user uses a mouse to point and click on icons to run programs and select menu choices. Windows is available only for MS-DOS compatible computers and requires DOS in order to operate.

Another popular operating system for IBM compatibles is OS/2. OS/2 (Operating System Two) was created as a DOS replacement. It too uses a GUI featuring icons or pictures along with the use of a mouse to select icons or choices from pop-up menus. OS/2 is more powerful than DOS in that it will access more memory and run programs faster. In fact, it can run several programs at the same time—a feature called **multitasking.** OS/2 will run most DOS and Windows applications along with applications written especially for OS/2.

UNIX is a third operating system for IBM compatibles. It was written in the 1970s for use in minicomputers. Like OS/2, UNIX is multitasking and is also a multiuser system. A computer with UNIX as its operating system can allow you to attach terminals to the computer and locate the terminals in different locations around the office. UNIX operates somewhat like DOS in that special commands are used to communicate with the computer, but the actual commands and terminology are different. Therefore, DOS programs will not run directly under UNIX.

The Apple Macintosh uses its own special operating system. The Macintosh system features icons and windows and pull-down menus. A mouse is used to select programs, data files, and menu choices. Commodore's Amiga computer system also uses a GUI very similar to OS/2, Windows, and the Apple Macintosh. The trend in operating systems is an improved graphical user interface that makes using a computer an intuitive experience.

Applications Software

In addition to your computer's operating system, there are many other software programs available for particular applications. These programs, often called **applications software,** are your primary tools in a business computing environment. They are designed to accomplish specific tasks or applications such as word processing, database management, or accounting.

Most applications software comes with reference manuals and even special templates for the keyboard. Some have online help and tutorials to help you learn how to use them. Most applications software is contained on diskettes. If your computer is equipped with a hard drive, you install the applications software on your hard drive to make it easier and faster to access. To install, you copy the program from the diskettes to the hard drive. The exact way you install an application is discussed in the first few pages of the manual. The installation process will allow you to customize the software to your particular computer configuration. In this way, the software will know what type of printer you are using, what type of monitor, and where you want to save the data files it creates.

Following is a list of major categories of applications software that may be useful for your company:

Accounting	Optical character recognition
Charting/graphing	Personal organizers
Clip art	Personal productivity
Communications	Programming tools
Computer-aided design (CAD)	Project managers
Database management	Security
Desktop presentation	Software emulators
Desktop publishing	Software instruction
Drawing	Specialty printing
Educational programs	Spelling checkers
Electronic mail	Spreadsheets
Grammar checkers	Statistics
Graphics	Style checkers
Integrated software	Utility programs
Multimedia	Virus detection
Music composition	Word processing

Chapter 10

Database Management Systems

Creating and Using a Database

Database management systems are efficient tools for organizing and processing large amounts of information, for example, your company's accounting work, inventory, customer records, and mailing lists. **Data** refers to individual items of information such as a customer's name, address, or phone number. A **database** is a collection of data, such as a mailing list. A **database management system** is computer software that allows you to store and manage the data in your database.

Although the various database programs available are different, the key to all of them is the way you organize your data. Let's say you want to keep a list of the company's customers. You might start with their names, addresses, and telephone numbers. With this list, you can easily look up telephone numbers or print out mailing labels to send holiday greetings. But what if you wanted to know which customers purchased a particular product or service from the company or how much they spent? To do this, you would have to keep additional information about each customer.

Fields, Records, and Files

To begin creating your database, you need to define its structure. Most database management systems provide a screen that prompts you through this procedure. "To define the structure" means to determine the **fields** that go into your database. A field is a single category of information. Thus, the fields in an address database might include customer name, street address, city, state, zip code, and telephone number (Figure 10-1). Each of the fields needs to be defined individually and to be given a name. You must also tell the database whether the field will contain text information or numbers and what the maximum number of characters per field is.

Once all of your fields are determined, the next step is to enter information

Figure 10-1. One "record" in a HyperCard database program from Apple Computer appears as a 3 x 5 card. By clicking on the "Find" button, other information in the database can be located. By clicking on the telephone icon, the number is automatically dialed by the computer's modem.

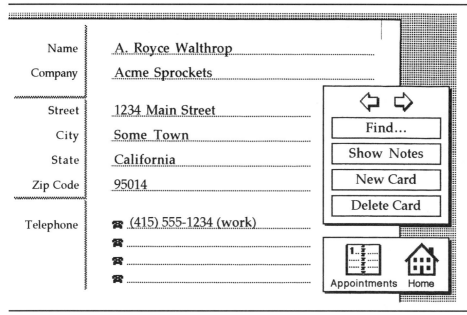

or data into your database. A **record** is a single entry of information. Thus, in a mailing list database, a single record is one person's name, address, city, state, and zip code (Figure 10-2). Most database management programs have enough room for thousands of records to be entered into the database, limited only by the amount of disk storage space available on your computer. You may view the data in your database by looking at individual records one at a time, or by displaying a table showing your data arranged in rows and columns (Figure 10-3). To assist you in entering records, database management software programs provide a data entry form, although many programs allow you to design your own form. With the data entry display form on the screen, you only have to fill in the blanks. When one record is entered into the system, the program will display a new blank form.

Adding new records or updating previous records is relatively simple with most database programs. New records can be added to the end of your file of records. Changes to existing records can be made by accessing a record, erasing the current information, and then typing the update in its place.

Figure 10-2.   One "record" in a database, containing name and address information for one individual.

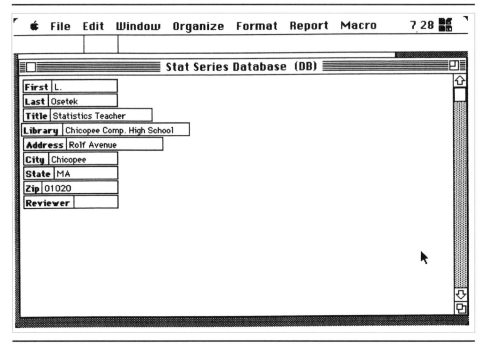

Screen shot reprinted with permission from Microsoft Corporation.

Sorting and Searching

Sorting the Data

Once you've added some records, you can begin tapping the power of the database management software. One of the first things you may want to do is to sort the database. Indexing and sorting capabilities allow you to rearrange all the records in a meaningful order. Let's say you want to sort the records alphabetically by last name. In this case, the "last name" field would be the **key** or **primary field**—the field that determines the sort order. The first name may be the **secondary field,** the field that determines the sort order in a case where two last names are identical.

Another use for your database is to extract information that meets a specific criterion, whether narrow or broad. You can choose simple criteria, such as displaying the address of a person named John Doe or locating the records for all persons who reside in the state of Texas. You can also use complex criteria. For

Figure 10-3. "List view" in a database shows multiple records on a single screen.

First	Last	Title	Library	Address
L.	Osetek	Statistics Teacher	Chicopee Comp. High School	Rolf Avenue
Allen	Gagnon	Statistics Teacher	Holyoke High School	500 Beech Str
James	Lonczak	Statistics Teacher	Ludlow Sr. High School	500 Chapin Str
Maureen	Pooler	Math Dept. Chairperson	Armory Street Elem. School	426 Armory S
Nancy	Korol	Mathy Dept. Chairperson'	Van Sickle Middle School	1170 Carew St
J.	Bianchi	Statistics Teacher	Pittsfield High School	300 East Stree
David	Lemere	Math Dept. Chairperson	Ralph Mahar Reg. Jr/Sr High School	South Main Str
Robert	Blanchard	Statistics Teacher	St. Bernards High School	45 Harvard St
W.	Masuck	Mathy Dept. Chairperson	Blackstone Millville Jr./Sr. High	175 Lincoln St.
James	Allen	Statistics Teacher	Tantasqua Reg. Sr. High School	319 Brookfield
Thomas	Obrien	Math Dept. Chairperson	North High School	150 Harrington
J.	Yurkinas	Math Dept. Chairperson	Worcester East Middle School	420 Grafton
George	Delaney	Math Dept. Chairperson	Worcester Academy	81 Providence
Judith	Lawson	Math Dept. Chairperson	Holy Name Ctl. Cath. High School	144 Granite St
Brian	Hastings	Statistics Teacher	Holliston High School	Hollis Street
Joseph	Cincota	Math Dept. Chairperson	Fowler Middle School	Summer Street
P.	Hebert	Math Dept. Chairperson	Maynard High School	Great Road

The window title bar reads: **Stat Series Database (DB)**. Menu bar: File Edit Window Organize Format Report Macro 7.27

Screen shot reprinted with permission from Microsoft Corporation.

example, in an accounts database, you may want a list of all persons within the 214 area code who have unpaid account balances as of September 1.

One advanced feature found on some database programs is the ability to perform mathematical functions. By creating a field that contains numerical information, a report can calculate totals for that field. This feature comes in handy when using a database program for keeping track of financial records.

Database management software handles all these tasks easily. You tell the database what type of information you need; the database extracts and displays only those records that meet your requirements. This process of extracting information is also called **querying the database:** You ask the database questions, and it gives you the answers.

Conducting a Search

The fastest way to find specific information in a database is to conduct a **search.** Most database management programs have a search feature that can be accessed via a keyboard command or a pull-down menu. When the command Search is selected, you are asked to type in comparison information. The program then searches the database for any records containing the comparison information and displays any that do.

To find more complex associations between your data, record selection rules—often called **arguments**—are used. These special commands combine the power of sorting with searching to find records that match a certain combination of criteria. Let's say you wanted a list of people who live in a certain state and have purchased a product or service from you but spent under $100 on it. Many database management programs use Boolean logic to narrow down the selection. This involves the use of *and, or, not, less than, more than, equal to, not equal to, blank, not blank,* and so forth. For example, our record selection argument might be listed as following:

> State Field Contains: Texas
> Purchase Field Contains: Not Blank
> Purchase Amount Field Contains: <$100

To create a record selection, most database management programs use a menu system that allows a user to type in comparison information (arguments) and to select from various choices to combine arguments (Figure 10–4).

Printing the Information

Finally, a database management program organizes and prints the information you've selected in the form that you need it. Printed output from a database is referred to as a **report.** A report may be a list of names, a customer invoice, or a monthly statement. In any case, most database management programs allow you to design your reports to include as much or as little information as you want in a layout that suits your needs.

Some programs are designed to display and print data on specific forms such as insurance forms, tax forms, and other business forms. Many office forms suppliers have a list of forms and compatible database software.

Types of Databases

As a secretary, you'll probably most often see two basic types of databases: the **file manager** and the **relational database.** The file manager is the simpler type of database, acting much like a regular filing cabinet. You use it when you need to organize a single group of information, such as a name and address file or a telephone record. Some database management applications are mainly designed for use with file manager software.

Other programs allow you to create a more complex type of database—a relational database. This type of system relates information in one database file to information in another by tying together key fields, such

Figure 10-4. A record selection screen in Microsoft Works database. A user selects a field from the list on the left and a selection rule from the list on the right.

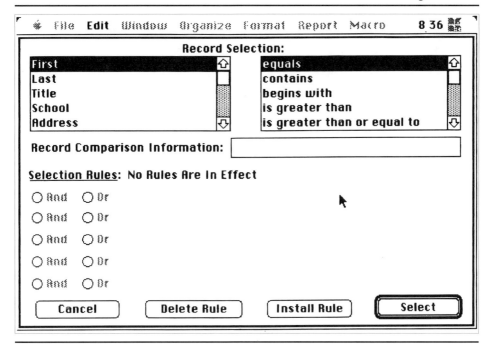

Screen shot reprinted with permission from Microsoft Corporation.

as a customer ID number. Suppose you had two databases: a customer address database and a customer order database. These two databases are linked by one common field: a customer ID number. When you type the customer ID number into an order, the order database retrieves the name and address of a customer from the address database. Thus, you would not have to type in the customer's name and address each time you completed a new order, saving you time and energy and reducing the opportunity for mistakes.

Applications

In general, software applications that allow you to develop only file-manager type databases are less expensive and easier to learn and to use than relational databases. Here is a list of some common file managers and relational database programs.

File Managers	*Relational Databases*
Microsoft File	dBASE
Windows Card File	FoxBASE +
My Mailing List	Paradox
Borland's Reflex	R:BASE
Microsoft Works Database	FileMaker Pro

Chapter 11

Computer Communications

Connecting With Other Computers

Using a personal computer on the job can lead to substantial improvements in your productivity and organization. Being able to connect with other computers to share information or perhaps to share a printer can produce even more surprising results. There are two ways to connect computers together: telecommunications and networking.

Telecommunications involves connecting computers via telephone lines, accomplished with a hardware device called a **modem.** The computer that receives calls from other computers and stores information that can be retrieved is often called the **host computer.** Other computers that access the host computer are called **remote computers.** These terms are used as a way to distinguish the two computers when they are connected.

Networking involves linking computers together using special coaxial cable within an office or office building complex. Each computer connected to the network can communicate with any other computer on the network. This allows for sharing of files and printers and intra-office electronic mail. Usually one computer is set up to provide storage for important data files and programs. This computer is called the **server,** because it provides access to needed resources whenever a computer user on the network needs them.

Modems

There are two general types of modems: **internal** and **external** (Figure 11-1). External modems connect to your computer through one cable and to a telephone line through another cable. An internal modem is inserted inside the computer into an expansion slot. It does not require a cable to connect it to the computer, but you still must connect it to the telephone line.

The purpose of a modem is to convert data to a form that can be sent over telephone lines. At the other end, another modem receives the transmission and converts it back into data that a computer can understand.

Figure 11-1. An internal modem and an external modem.

Modem performance is measured in the number of bits of data that can be transmitted per second, called the **baud rate.** Early modems communicated with a baud rate of 300 bps (bits per second). These were followed by 1,200-baud and 2,400-baud modems. The newest modems can communicate from 9,600 baud up to 19,200 baud.

Communications Software

In order to use a modem with your computer, you must have a telecommunications software program. There are many available. Some provide only telecommunications features, while others include telecommunications as part of word processing or integrated software. There are also many **shareware** and other free or almost-free telecommunications programs available from local computer user groups and local bulletin boards.

A telecommunications program will let your computer communicate with the modem to perform such functions as dialing or answering the telephone, establishing links with another computer, and automatically checking for errors in data transmissions.

Most communications programs allow the user to select a **communications protocol,** a set of rules and procedures used for transmitting data between two computers (see Figure 11-2). In most cases, the protocol you use will be determined by the host computer you want to connect to. Whatever protocol and settings the host computer is using, you must also use. Here is a list of some of the special settings that are possible:

Start bit	Data encryption
Stop bit	Simplex
Asynchronous	Half-duplex
Synchronous	Full-duplex
Parity	

Each of these technical terms describes how information is transmitted from one computer to another. Some systems send more information at a time than others, and some have special error-checking ability. The key to successful computer communications is to make sure your settings are the same as the computer you want to communicate with.

If you are connecting to an existing host computer to access information it contains, you should find out in advance what settings the host is using and set your communications software accordingly. Each of these protocols and settings can enhance your ability to communicate quickly and error free with another computer.

One of the main reasons to connect two computers is to transfer files. You might want to send someone a word processing document or a spreadsheet so he or she can review it, or you might want to get a similar document from this person's computer. Most communications software has various commands that

Figure 11-2. Configuring communications software is as easy as clicking your mouse on the correct protocol settings.

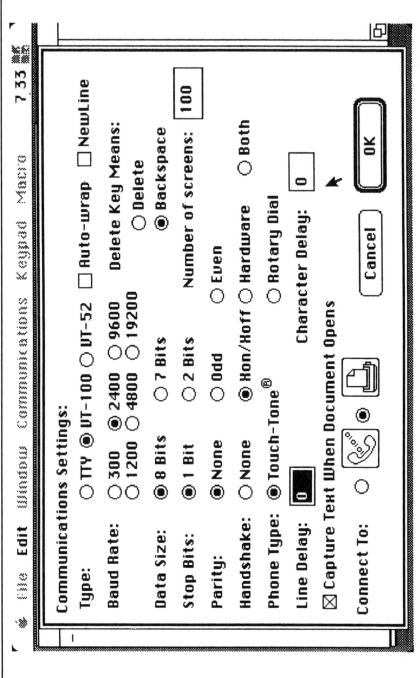

allow you to send or receive a file. When you send a file to another computer, it is called **uploading.** When you receive a file, it is called **downloading.**

Online Databases

Another main reason for computer communications is to access online databases, sometimes called **videotext services.** You can send and receive messages, get late-breaking news or stock quotes, make airline reservations, order merchandise, download software, or search databases of information. Some of the most popular services are CompuServe, Prodigy, Dow Jones News Retrieval, America Online, GEnie, and MCI Mail. Each of these services charges monthly fees along with additional fees to access certain services. Commercial online databases may be valuable to your company; you may be able to find a variety of useful business-related facts, research, mailing lists, and sources of government help.

In addition, there are a number of professional research databases for all kinds of information. With these services, you can search for information using key words, and then download copies of articles that contain those key words. These services are usually more expensive and are commonly used by lawyers and doctors.

Bulletin Boards

Another useful purpose for computer communications is the **bulletin board system** (BBS). A BBS has a message base where you can read messages and leave them for other people. Most BBSs also have a library of public domain shareware software, which you can copy to your computer. BBSs are usually run by computer hobbyists, and there are thousands of systems around the country. Many are free; some charge a nominal fee.

Many businesses set up their own BBS in order to link workers who are on the road with the mail office. In this way, a roving salesperson can communicate with managers and other personnel to place orders, receive instructions, send and receive messages.

Networking

Yet another useful purpose for computer communications is the linking of computers together within a single office or office building; this is known as **networking.** Networking requires two main components: special network hardware and network software. Together this system is known as a **local area network** (LAN).

Networks are useful for sharing data, storing large amounts of information, and sharing expensive equipment such as laser printers. With a network you can run multiuser programs such as database and order-entry and accounting systems. Each worker in the office using a computer connected to the network can add or retrieve information or share common peripherals such as the printer or hard drive.

The Physical Setup

The physical setup of a network is called its **topology.** The best-known topologies are named roughly for their descriptions: **ring, star,** and **bus.** A ring topology contains computers and devices set in a closed loop. In a star topology, computers and devices are connected to a central computer like spokes on a wheel. A bus topology connects the devices in a line with additions put at the end. In addition, you can connect various smaller networks together.

In a small business, a network may just be two computers linked together to share a printer. In small networks like this, each computer has equal status so that everyone can access disk drives of other computers or the printer. This is called a **peer-to-peer** network. In larger businesses, there may be a central dedicated computer with a large-capacity disk drive to which all the other computers are connected. The central computer is known as a **file server,** and the other remote computers are called **nodes.**

A popular network type used in many businesses is the **token ring** network. Each time a node has a message for the network, it waits for a turn on the network. From the network's point of view, it passes control from one node to another at almost the speed of light. This method is called **token passing.** All the messages move in a circle around the network.

Hardware and Software

Network hardware usually consists of a network interface card along with special cables to link the computers together. Some computers have built-in network interfaces, such as Macintosh computers with their Appletalk networking capability. All that is needed in these cases is cabling to link the computers.

To manage the network, special LAN software is required. This software keeps up with the sending and delivering of information and manages use of the printer and other common peripherals.

Every user on a network has a password. You can connect to the network by typing in your name and your password. Once you are on, you have access to the extra disk drives and printers. You can run programs stored on other computers and access data files. In some cases, you can prevent other users from having access to certain confidential files stored on a particular computer. For instance, accounting records or personal data can be locked so that a special password is required for access.

Electronic Mail

In addition to sharing data and peripheral devices, one common application for networks and computer communications is **electronic mail,** the passing of memos in an electronic form. Rather than print out the document, you send it to a user on the network as e-mail. E-mail can be sent to computers at remote sites via online database services such as CompuServe and Prodigy. In fact, e-mail can be sent to people who don't even use computers. Some companies such as MCI Mail will accept e-mail messages and transmit them to a center in a city or town close to the delivery address; there they are printed out on paper and sent via the post office or telegram.

Chapter 12

Computerized Spreadsheet Software

What Is a Spreadsheet?

Many secretaries use computerized spreadsheet software to handle accounting chores, assist with budgets, and for similar tasks. Spreadsheet software takes the place of the columnar pad that was so popular in the past. A columnar pad is divided into columns across the top and rows that run down the side. The rows and columns intersect at a small box. Altogether, there are hundreds of these little boxes on each page.

An electronic spreadsheet is a large grid of columns and rows. Where a column and row intersect is called a **cell.** Each cell has a unique **address.** Most spreadsheets label columns using letters and rows using numbers. Therefore, the cell at the intersection of column C and row 5 is cell C5.

The largest spreadsheet can contain millions of cells depending on the memory size of the computer running the software. However, most of the applications you'll be working with use only 500 to 1,000 cells (Figure 12-1).

Navigating Around a Spreadsheet

When you are using a spreadsheet, one cell is always **active**—that is, ready for you to input data. This cell is designated by a cell pointer, highlighted area, or flashing cursor. To make another cell active, you use the arrow keys, numeric keypad, or mouse to move to another location. Due to the limits on screen size, only a small group of cells can be displayed at any one time. If you wish to view additional cells, use a mouse or the arrow keys to move even farther on the spreadsheet.

Navigating around on a spreadsheet is much like looking through a window. Moving the window around to view additional cells is called **scrolling.** There are also special commands that will take you to predefined locations on a spreadsheet, such as the bottom or top.

To make using a spreadsheet as simple as possible, most spreadsheet software programs have some type of control panel. Some have the control panel at

Figure 12-1. An electronic spreadsheet software screen.

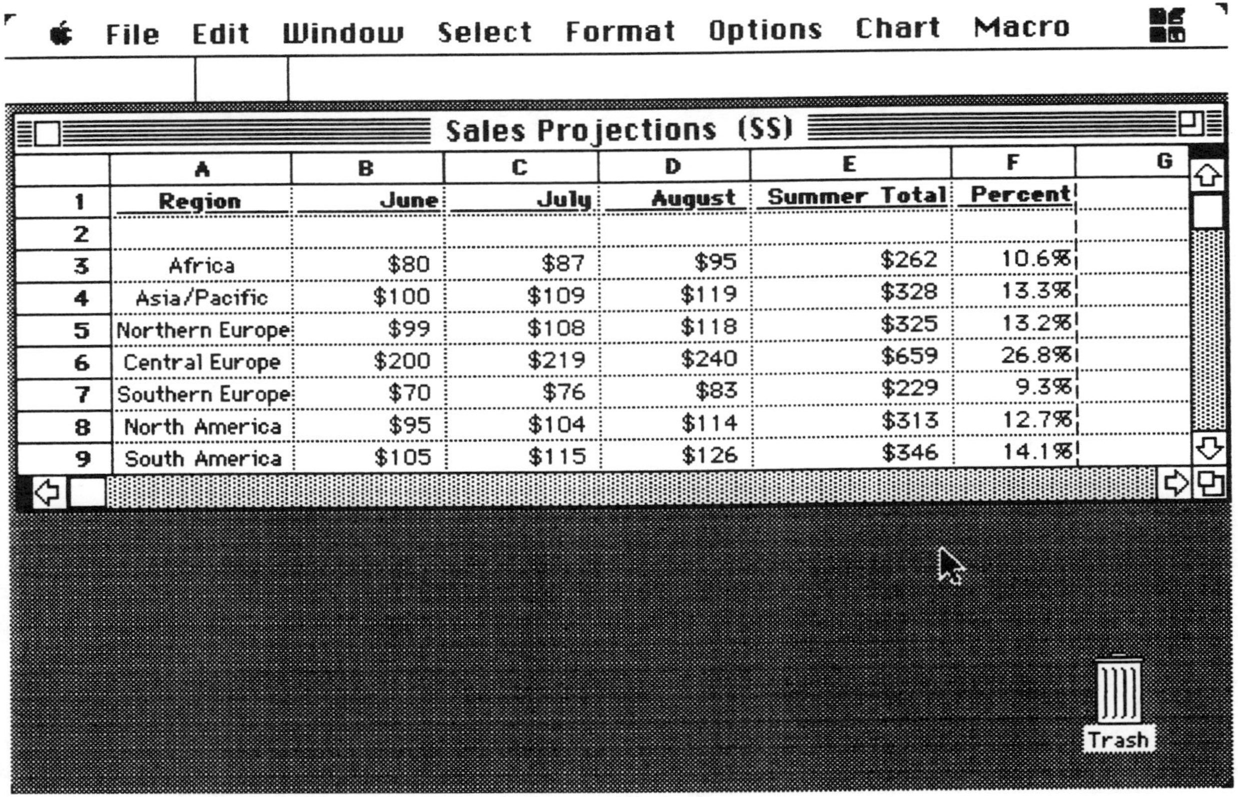
File Edit Window Select Format Options Chart Macro
Sales Projections (SS)
Trash

	A	B	C	D	E	F	G
1	Region	June	July	August	Summer Total	Percent	
2							
3	Africa	$80	$87	$95	$262	10.6%	
4	Asia/Pacific	$100	$109	$119	$328	13.3%	
5	Northern Europe	$99	$108	$118	$325	13.2%	
6	Central Europe	$200	$219	$240	$659	26.8%	
7	Southern Europe	$70	$76	$83	$229	9.3%	
8	North America	$95	$104	$114	$313	12.7%	
9	South America	$105	$115	$126	$346	14.1%	

Screen shot reprinted with permission from Microsoft Corporation.

the bottom of the screen, and others have it at the top. The control panel displays information about the active cell and a space where a user can type information into the active cell. In addition, it displays menus for activities such as saving, printing, and loading, as well as a list of special built-in functions in some cases. To select a choice, you move the cursor around using the arrow keys, numeric keypad, or mouse to highlight your choice and then press Enter/Return or click the mouse.

Spreadsheet Data

Cell Entries

Any entry into a cell can be one of three possible things: a label, number, or formula. A **label** is a word used to describe information in your spreadsheet. For example, you might want to calculate a budget for office expenses. Therefore, you would create a list of those expenses: paper, pens, computer supplies, stamps, and so forth. These words describe the numbers in another column or row, which is why they're called labels.

The actual expenses for the office supplies are the **numbers.** In order to add up a total of all the expenses at the bottom of the list, you need to enter a **formula,** a combination of cell addresses connected by mathematical symbols—for instance, A1 + A2 + A3.

To enter a label, number, or formula into a cell, place the cursor on the cell you want to make active. Then begin typing. As you type, the information you enter will be displayed in the control panel. When you are ready to put that information in the active cell, you either click the mouse or touch Return/Enter on the keyboard.

Formulas

A formula will work correctly only with numbers. Therefore, in order for a spreadsheet to distinguish labels, numbers, and formulas, most spreadsheet software programs use special predefined characters so that a user can specify the difference. For example, if the first character you type in a cell is a number, the spreadsheet will assume that entry is a number. If the first character you type is a letter, the spreadsheet will assume the entry is a label. And if you type in a special software-defined character such as "=" or "@," the spreadsheet will assume your entry is a formula.

Spreadsheet formulas can get complicated. Formulas can link information from one area to another so that totals from one group or section can be added to an overall summary. For example, an accounting system could be set up that allows you to enter expenses into various accounts. One formula would calculate the total expenses for each account; another would be used to link the total of a particular account to an overall profit-and-loss statement.

The simplest formula is one that moves the data from one cell to another. If you entered the following formula in cell A1—"=Sum(A2)"—whatever amount appeared in cell A2 would automatically also appear in A1.

The use of parentheses is an important aspect of formulas. For example, a formula such as "=Sum(A1:A10)" would provide a total of all the numbers in cells A1 through A10. When combined with other mathematical symbols for division, multiplication, and subtraction, a formula containing multiple sets of nested parentheses could be created—for example, "Sum(((A1:A10) * A20) − A30)." In order to create a formula correctly, you must know the order in which the mathematical operations will be performed by the computer. The natural order is to perform any calculation involving exponents first, followed by multiplication and division, and then addition and subtraction.

For example, to solve the formula "Sum((2^2 × 10) + ((144/12) − (5+6)))," you first square the 2 to get 4, and then multiply by 10 to get 40. Next you divide 144 by 12 to get 12. Then do the addition and subtraction, starting inside the parentheses: 5 plus 6 equals 11, and 12 minus 11 equals 1. To finish, 40 plus 1 equals 41.

Whenever a continuous group of cells is involved in a formula such as a row or column or block of numbers, rather than type in each individual cell address, a **range** is specified instead. For example, A1:A10 specifies a range of cells from cell A1 to cell A10 and all cells in between. A range can be as small as two cells or as large as the entire spreadsheet. It can be a row, a column, part of a row or column, or a block of several rows and columns. Most often a range is specified by identifying the beginning cell, followed by a colon or periods, followed by the ending cell.

Automatic Recalculations

One of the nice features of a spreadsheet is the ability to recalculate formulas automatically if you change any of the numbers in the cells included in the formula. If you have formulas that link various columns, rows, or sections, changing one number in a cell can cause numbers to change throughout the entire spreadsheet as each formula automatically recalculates. This recalculation feature is extremely useful for performing a "what-if" analysis.

If you want to see the effect of a change on one particular area on a spreadsheet, enter the new number and see what it does to the overall total. This feature allows you to build what are sometimes called **spreadsheet templates.** For example, if you created a spreadsheet to keep track of petty cash or a project budget, once you create the spreadsheet and the formulas, you can go back and change the labels and the numbers and have a whole new spreadsheet with a lot less work. By saving the new spreadsheet with a new name, both the old version and the new version will be stored for future use.

Functions

Spreadsheets have a variety of built-in functions that can replace complicated formulas. One of the simplest is the **sum function.** It allows you to calculate the total of a range of cells. Functions are identified by first typing either "=" or "@" depending on the particular software and then the function name. This lets the software know that the entry is a function, and not a label. Some mouse-based spreadsheet programs allow users to select functions from a pull-down menu.

Functions are available for many different mathematical, statistical, and financial formulas.

Editing Spreadsheets

Copying Feature

Another feature that can save you much secretarial time is the spreadsheet's ability to copy labels, numbers, and formulas from one location to another. For example, you might want to list your petty cash expenses by months, with each month in a separate column. Rather than re-creating the labels and formula for each month, you could copy the entire first month's information and paste it into the next column or the next group of columns. The spreadsheet software automatically compensates for the differences in cell labels from column to column and row to row and adjusts the new column so that the formula calculates the numbers in the new column, not in the original month column. The commands for selecting, copying, and pasting can all be found in the control panel of the spreadsheet.

Arranging Layout

Arranging your layout to look the way you want is another useful feature of an electronic spreadsheet. You can change the contents of any cell; add or delete rows or columns; and copy, cut, and paste data from one cell, row, column, or block to another similar area.

Editing Commands

Most spreadsheets have editing commands listed in their control panels. The simplest editing feature is to access the contents of a single cell and to alter the data there. When you make a cell active by selecting it with the cursor or mouse, its contents appear listed in the control panel. There you can insert text, type in completely new text, change a number—or do anything else.

You create new cells by inserting a new row or column. The Insert command or Create New Column or Row command allows you to do this easily. You select a column to the left of where you want to insert a new column and then select the Insert command from the control panel. For inserting rows, you select the row just above where you want to insert a new row. Pointing to the very top of a column or the extreme left of a row with a mouse will allow you to select it. If you do not have a mouse, position your cursor at the top of a column or on the cell on the far left of a row, and choose Select from your control panel menu. Then move your cursor to highlight the row or column.

To delete a row or column, select the entire column or row and choose Delete from the control panel menu.

Whenever you insert or delete a row, it's important to note that some cells and formulas will move in the spreadsheet to a new cell address. Most spreadsheets automatically adjust to compensate for these moves so that you don't have to go back and make changes. Therefore, if you have a formula that adds up the total of a column of ten cells and you insert five new rows in the middle, the formula will automatically be changed to add up a total of fifteen cells instead.

Formatting features help align the numbers and text to make your spreadsheet look good when printed out on paper. Formatting commands, found in the control panel, allow you to justify the text in a document, center text or numbers, or make them flush left or flush right. You can format individual cells or rows to specify how many decimal points will be displayed or to create dates, dollar signs, commas, percentages, and scientific notations. You can change the width of a cell or column in order to display more information, such as a long label or a very large number. Some of the newest spreadsheets allow you to change the spacing of rows, the typeface style, and even the type size of your text and numbers.

Other Spreadsheet Functions

Saving and Printing

Once you get your spreadsheet looking the way you want, you may print it or save it. Printing and saving are commands you can select from the control panel. If you select Save, you'll be asked where you want to save your spreadsheet and to give it a name. You choose the disk drive where you want to save the file—a floppy disk or a hard drive—and then type in the name. Whenever you work with a spreadsheet that has been saved previously and you wish to save it again, it will automatically be saved under the same name on the same disk. If you want to save two or more different versions of a spreadsheet, you will need to change the name slightly. This can be accomplished by selecting Save As from the control panel or by selecting No when asked if you want to save the file with the same name.

When you wish to print a spreadsheet, you'll be given an opportunity to determine how much of your spreadsheet you want printed, whether you want a header or footer, if you want borders or a grid, column and row numbers, and so forth. Some spreadsheets display a menu asking if you want to print the spreadsheet to a printer or to a file. Printing to a file is a way of saving a spreadsheet on a diskette or hard drive so that it can later be incorporated into another program such as a word processor.

Multitasking

Many of the newest spreadsheets allow you to share information from a spreadsheet with another program such as a word processor by copying data from the spreadsheet, and then accessing the word processor to paste the data. This operation requires running both a spreadsheet and a word processor at the same time, a feature called **multitasking.**

Online Help

Many spreadsheets are equipped with online help features, which provide detailed explanations of spreadsheet commands, functions, and procedures. These online help files can be accessed while you are in the middle of working on a spreadsheet by choosing Help from the spreadsheet's control panel and selecting the topic you need help on.

Templates

To help get you started, many spreadsheets have built-in **templates,** prebuilt spreadsheet models for common applications in business such as budgets and financial analysis. By loading a template, you can edit the spreadsheet to customize it to your particular business. This can be a great time savings.

Spreadsheet Macros

Spreadsheet macros are another great time saver. As you may already know from your word processing work, a **macro** is a way to minimize repetitive keystrokes. You can create a macro by selecting Macro from your spreadsheet's control panel. You will then be asked to type in the keystrokes you want to record. Once these are recorded, you'll be asked to assign a simple keyboard command to trigger the macro. Many spreadsheets come with built-in macros that you can customize and access with special keyboard commands.

Spreadsheet Software

There is a wide variety of spreadsheets available for both IBM compatibles and Apple Macintosh computers. Here is a partial list of some of the most popular programs available.

For IBM PC Compatibles	*For Macintosh Computers*
Excel	Wingz
Lotus 1-2-3	Excel
Quattro	Multiplan
Supercalc	Full Impact
VP-Planner	Lotus 1-2-3

Chapter 13

Data Security

Information = Profit

Information about your company is valuable not only to it but also to others. Such information includes confidential records such as bank transactions or corporate credit card numbers. It also includes paper or computer files about customers, new products, sales strategies, and so on. Consider how damaging it would be if such records were lost or destroyed or if they were stolen by a competitor. That's why data security is critical to protect computer information from theft, misuse, and disaster.

The misuse of computer information ranges from unauthorized use of computer time to criminal acts like sabotage; it all falls under one general category many people call "computer crime." Surveys show that over half of the government departments and industrial organizations in the United States have experienced some form of computer crime. Because of this growing epidemic, it's important that you understand the different types of computer crime in order to protect yourself and your company's information.

Computer Crime

Determining What Is a Crime

There are different degrees of computer crime, from breaking into other people's computers in order to steal or sabotage data, to making illegal copies of software to give to a friend. All of it is wrong.

Probably the most often-committed offense is theft of computer time. It ranges from the innocent borrowing of someone's computer without permission to the theft of expensive computer time from a business for personal use and gain. Theft of computer time—especially involving large computers, such as one running an office network—can easily translate into a theft of money. Besides the theft of time, unauthorized use of a computer also involves unnecessary wear and tear on the equipment and software.

The best way to judge whether a personal activity might be considered a criminal act is to compare it with the use of a company vehicle. Would it be wrong to borrow a company car or truck without asking? Would it be wrong to fill up one's personal car with gas and charge it to the corporate account? We know your answer is, "Yes; it would be wrong," so keep this comparison in mind when using business computer equipment and software yourself and when overseeing others' use of it.

Threats From Outside

Today's companies are using computer communications in ever-increasing ways—and these same applications are in the hands of criminals. Working from the privacy of their own homes, would-be criminals often gain access to an organization's computer for the purpose of stealing or altering information. This electronic trespassing or vandalism has several variations, which are referred to by their own slang terms:

- *Hacking.* Breaking into computer systems to gain access to restricted or private information.
- *Freaking.* The defrauding of a telephone company using stolen long-distance access codes or credit cards.
- *Crashing.* Breaking into a computer system in order to shut it down or turn it off.
- *Trashing.* The altering or erasing of a computer's data files.

Threats From Inside

One of the most serious threats to the security of business data comes from insiders: those working within a company who decide to misuse computer or data files as a form of vengeance or for financial gain. This type of computer crime is extremely harmful, since it may involve information worth thousands and thousands of dollars. If a computer crime happens in your company, any insider could be a suspect. However, there are certain individuals who are likely to be investigated first:

- *Disgruntled employees* may often take their vengeance out on the computer system in the form of sabotage.
- A *competitor* or an *employee who has recently quit or been terminated* may be responsible for theft of computer data or software.
- *Outside users* of a computer system via a communications system may attempt authorized sale of information, such as customer lists.
- *Computer programmers* may attempt to take their programs with them or to create hidden embezzlement schemes.
- *Computer operators* may alter or erase data on purpose.
- *Computer system engineers* may attempt to alter security information or passwords.

Software Piracy

Software piracy is another major computer crime problem. Individuals are sometimes allowed to make copies of their programs for protection purposes, but the sale and/or the distribution of those copies to friends and other computer users is a violation of federal copyright laws.

With the growing concern over the copying problem, many software publishers have been forced to devise elaborate copy protection schemes. Piracy may not affect your own company directly, but the cost of combating piracy is eventually passed along to you as the consumer.

Apprehending Criminals

Computer criminals have often been hard to apprehend due to a lack of understanding on the part of law enforcement agencies and the judicial system. However, things are beginning to change. Many states are leading the way with special legislation aimed at stopping software piracy. Other new laws make it a crime to trespass electronically on a computer system even if there is no damage or theft. And many cities are establishing special police units to combat computer crime.

Protecting Your Company's Data

Audit Logs

In order to protect your company's data from these human threats, there are steps you can take. Audit logs are a record of who has been using a computer system. As a user logs onto a computer, it records the time, the name of the user, the files that person accesses, and when the person logs off. The computer then keeps the data in a special security file.

In some cases an audit log can tell whether files have been altered. The use of audit logs is usually provided as part of security password software that can be installed on individual computers. If a computer crime occurs, the log can furnish the authorities with evidence they might need to prosecute.

Call-back Modems

A way many computer systems equipped with communications protect themselves is the use of call-back modems. When calling up the system from a remote location, a user logs on and types in his or her name, password, and the telephone number at the calling location. The system then hangs up. After verifying the name and password, it calls the remote user back.

Coding

Special data encryption techniques code your data files and your communications automatically. Someone who is attempting to intercept and manipulate the information would receive a file that looks like random symbols, thus preventing use of the data.

Computer Viruses

One type of computer crime that is a big concern to even the smallest business is the computer virus. A **virus** is a program developed by a computer vandal who finds pleasure in creating havoc. This program "infects" other programs, causing them to malfunction or to fail completely. Viruses are passed from computer to computer via communications services and by copying diskettes and files from one computer to another. Some viruses will display only messages; others can damage your hard drive and the files stored there. Some virus programs even try to extort money from victims in order to receive a software antidote.

To combat the rapidly growing virus problem, there are a variety of virus protection software programs available on the market. The key to selecting one of these programs is to purchase the most current edition and then update it from time to time. Most virus protection programs are designed to look for and destroy viruses that are known at the time the program was written. As new viruses appear, an older virus protection program may fail to detect them.

Acts of Nature

Mother Nature can be an enormous threat, even causing a computer system to fail and lose data permanently. Floods, lightning, tornadoes, hurricanes, and fires could completely destroy your office computer and all your data files, resulting in the failure of the business and loss of everyone's job, since business records, client lists, accounting records, and much more would all be lost.

Electrical surges or voltage spikes can damage the computer's important electronic components. These surges can also disrupt and scramble data storage media like the hard drive. A complete power outage can shut down a computer system, causing loss of all data in the memory.

Mechanical Problems

Mechanical problems can cause storage mediums such as the hard drive to fail, resulting in the loss of all data stored there. Sudden changes in temperature or humidity, or bumping or dropping a computer system when the hard drive is operating, can result in what's called a **head crash**—or hard drive failure. Floppy disks can be damaged by a variety of accidents, ranging from spilled drinks to exposure to magnets located in telephones and speakers.

A Security Checklist

Following is a variety of ways to protect your company's data and make it more secure from both human and natural threats. Some of these methods you may wish to use for your own computer. If you have office management responsibilities, you may also want to make changes for your entire department or company.

☐ Investigate theft prevention devices, which can lock a computer to a desktop.

☐ Install small cooling fans inside the computer system to help control high temperatures. They will add to the life of your system.

☐ Prevent electrical noise and power surges from damaging your computer system through the use of surge suppressors. A surge suppressor plugs into the wall, and the computer system plugs into it for power.

☐ Get even more security with a device known as an **uninterruptible power supply.** It will power your computer system for a limited period of time in the event of a power outage. Then if an outage does occur, you'd have ample warning to save your data.

☐ Make a backup copy of all data stored. The methods to back up your data range from printing out your files on paper, to using a tape backup system, to making an extra copy of your data files on a backup diskette.

☐ Always remember basic handling and storage rules for floppy disks and floppy disk drives (see Chapter 9).

Coping With Disaster

It is a good idea to insure your company's computer system and software. If you work in a small company, you may want to check with your boss to see if he or she has this insurance. But in the case of a disaster, getting reimbursed for the cost of the equipment can't ever replace the valuable data that the business relies on.

Most large organizations have disaster plans that shift data processing jobs from one location to another and protect data by storing them in two or more different locations. A small business should also have a disaster plan just in case. As secretary, you can get the ball rolling.

A good disaster plan should consider the following points:

☐ Is backup computer equipment available?
☐ Are backup software and data files available?
☐ What should employees do in the event of a disaster?
☐ What projects and tasks have priority?
☐ Are essential business supplies available?

Taking the time to create a disaster plan and to inform all employees in the company is essential. If the company is very small, even having an extra computer system, software, and supplies at someone's house may be a good start. It's like an extra insurance policy, and it may help all of you keep your jobs should disaster strike.

Chapter 14

Keyboarding Skills

Keyboards

Whether you use a computer, a dedicated word processor, or a typewriter, you are using a keyboard. There are many differences in keyboards depending on the particular system you use. There are also differences in typing on each. For instance, computers and word processors require greater sensitivity than the heavy stroking of a regular manual typewriter.

No matter what keyboard you use, basic typing skills are a must. If your typing skills are not up to the level you feel are necessary for your job, computer programs such as *Mavis Davis Teaches Typing* can help. If you don't use a computer, there are various touch-typing books that can provide assistance.

Since computer keyboards are the ones growing fastest in importance, the focus of this chapter will be on them. In many cases, electronic typewriter keyboards now have many of the same functions, and we will compare these at the conclusion of the chapter.

Common Keyboards

The most common keyboard layout is the QWERTY keyboard. It gets its name from the first five alphabetical keys on the top left-hand corner of the keyboard. This is the same style used on typewriters in the United States. An alternative keyboard layout is the Dvorak keyboard. It places the keys in different locations on the keyboard and is said to be faster and easier to use once you learn to touch-type with this layout. However, most people learn touch-typing with a QWERTY-style keyboard.

Keyboard Features

If you examine a typewriter and a computer keyboard side by side, you'll find many similarities. For instance, you'll see on each the normal alphanumeric keys, along with a space bar, an Enter or Return key, Tab keys, Shift keys, Caps Lock, and Backspace. The alphanumeric keys can be used to type letters or numbers. Typing a Shift along with a letter or number key produces an uppercase letter or, in the case of numbers, a special symbol. If you want to type all uppercase letters, you select the Caps Lock key once rather than holding down the Shift key. Touch the Caps Lock key again, and it toggles back off.

On both a typewriter and a computer keyboard, the Tab key moves your next keyboard entry to the next tab stop. However, with a computerized word processor or a modern electronic typewriter, tabs are no longer set mechanically. Instead, you use special software commands, menu or ruler choices, or a special key on the keyboard to set tabs and release them.

The space bar adds spaces between words or characters, and it can insert spaces between words and characters typed previously. The Enter or Return key on a computer keyboard may look similar to the carriage return found on a typewriter, but it is used much differently. On some typewriters, you type a Return at the end of a line in order to begin a new line of type. However, with a word processing computer or modern electronic memory typewriter, a special feature, called **word wrapping,** is standard. This automatically moves your text to the next line when it will not fit at the end of the previous line. The Enter or Return key is used only to skip lines, such as when starting a new paragraph.

Function Keys

Because of the increased functionality of a computer over a standard typewriter, a variety of extra keys have been added to computer keyboards to use with word processing software, electronic spreadsheets, and database applications. Early computer systems had just a few extra keys, but most modern keyboards have many special-purpose keys.

Numeric Keypad

The numeric keypad is a set of number keys just like those you might find on a calculator. In fact, it is often used for computerized accounting and electronic spreadsheet applications. Many computer systems have built-in calculator software that can be called up on the monitor screen, allowing the user to make quick calculations and then return to another application to insert the result. The numeric keypad is also sometimes used for navigational purposes in some software applications. For example, if you wanted to move a pointer up on the screen, you would hit the number 8 key. If you wanted to move down, you would hit the number 2 key. To go left, hit 4. And, to go right, hit 6.

The numeric keypad includes several mathematical function keys as well, such as +, −, *, . , / , and =. The "+" key is used for addition, "−" for subtraction, "*" for multiplication, "." for decimals, "/" for division, and "=" for equals or totals. There's also usually an extra Enter key, which is used similarly to the Total key on a calculator. In addition, you may find a Num Lock key or a Clear key. The Num Lock key, which stands for "number lock," toggles the numeric keypad so that it can be used to navigate or to type numbers. When the Num Lock is on, the numbers are entered when typed. The Clear key will clear entries during calculations when there is a mistake or when you want to perform a new calculation.

Navigation Keys

Along with the numeric keypad's navigational features, there are special-purpose navigation keys on many keyboards. Most have some form of arrow keys, allowing you to move a pointer on the screen up, down, left, or right. Other navigational keys include the Home, Page Up, Page Down, Insert, and Delete keys. These may also have special functionality in certain applications. For example, in some word processing programs, pressing the Home key will take you to the beginning of your document. In a spreadsheet program, pressing Home will take you to the top left-most cell, A1, sometimes called the **home cell.** The Page Up and Page Down keys in a word processing application will cause your document to scroll up or down one page at a time. The Insert key is useful in some older-style DOS-based word processors for editing and inserting text in the middle of an existing sentence. The Delete key works similarly to a Backspace key; it can also be used to eliminate entire blocks of text that have been previously selected.

Special Function Keys

The special function keys found on many computer keyboards are usually labeled F1 through F10 or F12, though some keyboards have fewer. Located across the top of the keyboard or along the left side, special function keys are used in many applications to allow easy menu selection or to perform common tasks like saving documents, loading documents, printing, and editing. In addition to assigning one command to a particular function key, additional commands are available by pressing Shift or the Alt key along with a function key. Without the guidance of the software, these keys have little purpose. However, when specially programmed by a particular software application, they can have a multitude of uses.

There is no real standardized method for assigning commands to particular keys, though F1 is often the Help key. To find out the assignments, check the manual for the software you're using. Some software publishers and other third-party vendors make keyboard templates available that connect to the top of your keyboard. These quick reference templates list the commands for each function key, as well as other special key combinations.

Special Command Keys

The special command keys found on most computer keyboards include keys like Alt, Control, and Escape. The Escape key is often used to back out of a series of menu choices or to leave a program. The Alt and Control keys are often used on computers without special function keys. By pressing the Alt or Control key and another designated key, a variety of commands, such as printing or saving, can be given from the keyboard. For keyboards with special function keys, using the Alt or Control keys in combination with the special function keys provides access to additional commands.

IBM Compatibles versus Macintosh

Perhaps the greatest differences between computer keyboards are those between IBM-compatible and Macintosh computers. Most of the keys we have been describing are common to IBM compatibles. Macintosh computers, due to their use of a mouse, usually have fewer keys because many of the commands are accessed from a pull-down menu and selected by clicking on a mouse.

Using a mouse is also now common with most IBM compatibles; however, keyboard designs have been slow to change. Macintosh computer keyboards rarely have special function keys. Commands can still be typed from the keyboard: the Open-Apple Command key, the Option key, and the Control key are used in combination with another keystroke. For example, pressing the Open-Apple Command key along with the S key will save a document. A list of these keyboard commands is available in the software manual, as well as in the pull-down menus.

Many of the Macintosh command key combinations have been standardized and are the same from one program to the next.

Macros

In addition to using special function and command keys to access specific commands from the keyboard, users can define their own keyboard commands with the help of special keyboard shortcut software. There are a variety of these accessory programs available for both IBM compatibles and Macintosh computers. These programs allow a user to assign a particular series of commands or keystrokes to a single multikey combination. For example, we use Option-C as a user-assigned command to bring up the calculator automatically. And we use Option-D to type today's date automatically.

Another similar keyboard shortcut tool, available in many software applications on both IBM and Macintosh, is the **macro.** A macro can be used to record a long series of keystrokes and menu choices. The recording of these keystrokes and commands can be saved and given a name. In addition, a user-definable key combination can be assigned to call up and play the recorded macro automatically.

The Mouse

Both IBM compatibles and Macintosh computers now use a mouse as an addition to the computer keyboard. A mouse is a hand controller that contains a small, round ball connected to a series of sensors. When you move the mouse around on your desk, the ball inside rolls, and the sensors translate this into movement of a pointer on the monitor screen. Thus, if you pick up the mouse and move it in the air, it does not affect the monitor screen at all.

Today it's impossible to discuss keyboarding skills without also discussing the use of a mouse. Most people use a mouse in conjunction with a mouse pad, a piece of foam rubber that gives the mouse extra traction. The amount of movement on the screen that a mouse can produce can be controlled by the computer's operating system. On IBM-compatible Windows-based systems, the mouse control is found in the Main Group folder. With Macintosh computers, the mouse control is found in the control panel under the Apple pull-down menu option.

As an alternative to a mouse, track balls are available. They are almost like a mouse turned upside down. By rolling the ball with your fingers, you can move a pointer on the screen. Track balls are now common with small laptop computers where operating conditions make it difficult to access a mouse.

Using Typewriters

Modern electronic typewriter keyboards provide many of the same features to be found on IBM compatibles and Macintosh computers. In addition to the common keys such as Tab, Space, Shift, Backspace, and Return are special navigation, special function, and command keys. Depending on whether a typewriter has memory capability, the number of special keys will vary. They also vary greatly by manufacturer. However, even the most modest electronic typewriters now have some small amount of memory available and thus several additional keys for editing.

Common keyboard layouts include correction keys for correcting a character, word, or line, along with navigational keys for moving around within a document. Typewriters with built-in spelling checkers usually have a key for turning this feature on or off. Special formatting keys can justify text in several different ways. A special command or code key is often used to access additional formatting commands as well as special symbols.

Chapter 15
Word Processing

A Boon for Secretaries

The use of word processing can greatly improve any secretary's overall productivity. Even if you don't use a computer, most typewriters now have some form of word processing built in. And although there are great differences between word processing typewriters and word processing software for microcomputers, almost all allow you to create documents, edit and format these documents, and print them. Other features include spelling checkers, style and grammar checkers, mail-merge features, and the ability to store documents electronically.

The most common word processors found in businesses are microcomputers equipped with word processing software. The word processing software, usually stored on a diskette, can be installed on your computer's hard drive for easy access. When the word processing program is run by the computer, the computer becomes an intelligent typewriter with the ability to create, edit, format, and store documents.

Creating Documents

In order to get started using a word processor, you must first create a fresh blank document. This is like loading a sheet of paper into a typewriter. Some word processors require the user to create a new document and to name it. However, most allow you to wait until you save the document for the first time before assigning it a name.

Typing

Once a new document has been created, you can begin typing and entering data. Some types of word processors, such as those for the Macintosh or Windows environment, allow you to begin typing immediately. Other systems, such as those written for MS-DOS, may require you to toggle into "edit mode" before typing can begin.

As you type on the keyboard, the letters and words appear on the display screen. The text or data you type are stored in the computer's memory temporarily, until the document is saved or discarded or the power is turned off.

Positioning

On the screen a pointer called a cursor shows where text will appear when typed. Cursors can take many forms: a vertical line, an underscore, or a rectangle. They may also flash on and off. It all depends on the particular word processor or software used.

You can move the cursor from one character to another, up or down, or left and right in order to make corrections, edit, or format the text. To move the cursor, some word processors employ the arrow keys on the computer keyboard. On keyboards that don't have arrow keys, special combinations involving the number keys on the numeric keypad or two or more keys pressed simultaneously will also move the cursor. Some word processing software programs, such as those written for DOS and Apple II systems, allow the use of special function keys on the keyboard or special key combinations to jump to the top or bottom of the page.

If you have word processing software written for the Windows and Macintosh environments, you can use a mouse to move around your document. By moving the mouse, a pointer moves on the screen. When you click the mouse, the cursor jumps to that location. If you want to change a word a few lines up from where you're currently typing, move the mouse up to that line; click; delete the incorrect word; and retype a new word in its place.

As you continue typing, you'll notice one of the main differences between word processors and typewriters when you reach the end of a line of text. On a typewriter, you type a carriage return and start a new line. Other more advanced systems with built-in computer memory automatically move a word that will not fit down to start the next line. This is a feature common to all word processors called **word wrap.** Thus, when typing on a word processor, you never have to type a carriage return unless you want to begin a new paragraph.

Editing Documents

For secretaries, one of the best time-saving features of word processors is the ability to make changes very easily, without retyping the entire document. Many secretaries start a document by typing without regard to format or the look of the finished document. They then come back, make revisions, and change the format. By coming back to spell-check, proof, and make corrections, they can remove most typos and sentence structure problems prior to printing out a copy of the document on paper.

Typing Over and Inserting

For some word processors, such as those that are DOS based, a user must first select the proper editing mode in order to make revisions. This is done by typing a special function key or a key combination. One editing function is the type-over mode that allows a user to type over mistakes. New characters appear on the screen in place of existing characters. If new characters or words must be inserted instead, an insert mode is available. When the insert mode is activated, new characters appear when typed, and all characters and words to the right of the cursor move to the right to make room.

Word processors written for Windows and Macintosh are always in insert mode by default. The user does not have to type any special function keys or key combinations to turn on insert mode.

Deleting Text

To delete text from a document, several choices are available. The simplest method is similar to the Backspace key on a typewriter. Some keyboards have Backspace keys, and others have a key marked Delete. Both work just like a Backspace key on a typewriter.

When you type the Backspace or Delete key, the cursor moves to the left one space and erases the character that was displayed there. Some word processors require you to move the cursor to highlight the specific character to be deleted and then to type the Delete key. When a Delete key is not available, a special key combination such as Control + D is used.

Undeleting

In case you inadvertently delete something you did not mean to, most word processors have an Undelete function. This can be accessed via a special function key or key combination or, in the case of Windows and Macintosh, a pull-down menu choice. When you delete text, it's stored in a temporary buffer memory. The buffer stores the last thing you deleted, such as a word, sentence, paragraph, or even whole pages. Hit the Undelete function, and your text is restored.

Cutting and Pasting

Moving text from one location to another is one more useful feature of word processors. For Windows and Macintosh environments, just click and drag the mouse to highlight a block of text such as a sentence, paragraph, or group of paragraphs. Once the text is highlighted, select Cut or Copy from a pull-down menu to put the text (or a copy of it) into the temporary memory buffer. Next, use the mouse to navigate through the document to the location where the text should be inserted. By clicking the mouse on this location and selecting Paste from the pull-down menu, you remove the text from the memory buffer and insert it into the new location. Thus, moving text from one location to another is called "cutting and pasting."

In DOS-based environments, the same procedure of moving blocks of text from one location to another is done without the mouse. Usually these word processors have a command that allows you to mark the beginning and end of the text to be moved. The text is highlighted as it's marked, so you can see exactly which text has been selected. After the text has been highlighted, it can be deleted or copied into the temporary memory buffer. If you want to insert that text into a new location, mark the new location with a special command, and the text will be inserted.

Searching

Most word processors provide the ability to search for and find a particular string of characters or words anywhere in a document. This feature comes in handy for finding names in a mailing list or other specific information from a document. Some word processors call this a Search function, others a Find function.

In order to search an entire document, position the cursor at the beginning of the document. On DOS-based word processors, the Search command is selected using a special function key. On Windows- and Macintosh-based word processors, a Search or Find function is available as a pull-down menu. Once Search has been selected, you'll be asked to type in the characters or words you want to find.

Searching and Replacing

A related function is Search and Replace. Many users save time by using Search and Replace like a macro. If these users frequently have to type a long, complicated word or phrase in a document, they will type substitute characters instead, such as "xxx." Since "xxx" would normally not appear in a document, the user can later access the Search and Replace function. This function then finds "xxx" and allows the user to type in a replacement string—the long, complicated word or phrase.

To search and replace a word or phrase every time, no matter how often it's scattered throughout a document, a global Search and Replace is used. This function automatically finds and replaces text in every location where it appears in a document.

Formatting Documents

Many users of word processors start by typing in text and later go back to make adjustments to the way the document will look when printed on paper. This is a process known as **formatting.** There are many different ways to format a document, for example, by changing the margins, the line spacing, or the type style and size of the characters.

Line Formatting

Margins

All word processors allow you to set the left and right margins. Most often a ruler is used to show where on a piece of paper the text will be positioned when printed. With DOS-based word processors, the margins and tabs can be set and changed within a document by using special function key commands. For Windows and Macintosh, margins are set by moving a margin guide, and tabs are positioned by moving a tab guide, both with the mouse.

Line Spacing

With a special command, DOS-based word processors set line spacing to single spaced, double spaced, or triple spaced. A hidden command marker is embedded in the text to designate that the following text has the particular spacing characteristics. This hidden command does not print, but it can be seen when editing. If you want to change the line spacing further in the document, use the Spacing command to set your choice and another embedded hidden command is inserted.

For the Windows and Macintosh environments, the spacing is changed by selecting a choice from the ruler or ribbon bar. There are icon choices for single spaced, double spaced, and triple spaced. They can be selected at any time when entering text; the text entered after the selection will be spaced according to your choice. You can also alter the spacing of already existing text by first highlighting the text with a mouse or pointer, and then selecting your line spacing choice from the ruler.

Tabs

Word processing programs let you set tabs and can be programmed to indent a specified number of spaces at the beginning of a new paragraph automatically. For DOS-based word processors, special key commands are used to set tabs and indentions. Windows- and Macintosh-based word processors use pointers, which can be placed on the ruler at various points to determine tab stops and indentions.

Justification

The remaining line-formatting option is justification. Any block of text can be aligned flush with the left margin or the right margin. Another choice is full justification, which aligns the text flush with both the left and the right margin, like typesetting in a book. This is done by adding spaces between the words of each line. A fourth option is centered justification, used to center titles and other text in the middle of a line.

With DOS-based word processors, you select your justification option via a keyboard command. In some cases the justification choice may be designated by characters inserted into the document that do not appear when printed on paper. In addition, the text on the monitor screen may not reflect the justification choice.

For Windows- and Macintosh-based word processors, select your justification option from the ruler or pull-down menu with the mouse or pointer. A previously written block of text may be justified by first highlighting the block with the mouse, and then selecting the justification choice from the ruler or pull-down menu.

Character Formatting

Another major document-formatting tool is the character format. Text can be printed in a variety of different styles, such as underlined, bold, and italics. In addition, the characters themselves can be printed in many different sizes and typefaces called **fonts.**

Often word processing programs come with a limited number of fonts and font sizes already installed. Additional fonts can be purchased as software to increase your number of choices. Some fonts are used to display text on the screen, and others are used by the printer. Some printers will print only fonts that are installed in the printer hardware.

DOS-based word processors use keyboard commands to insert embedded nonprinting commands into the text; these embedded commands then select various formatting options for the printed text. This means that often the chosen format doesn't appear on the monitor screen and can be judged only once it's actually printed on paper.

Windows and Macintosh word processors use pull-down menus to select font style choices, which appear on the monitor screen almost the way they'll appear printed on paper. The font and size of existing text can be changed by highlighting the text with the mouse or pointer and then selecting the font choice from the pull-down menu.

Page Formatting

Additional formatting options are available for entire documents and sections of a document. For example, the page format determines the top, bottom, left, and right margins for all text on a page. In addition, headers and footers can be inserted on each page for page numbers, the date, or the name of a document.

Printing Documents

Once a document has been created and formatted, getting that document printed on paper is the ultimate goal for most word processor users. The Print function allows you to specify additional information about the way the document should appear on paper—for example, which pages of the document are to be printed, whether the printing itself should be draft mode or letter quality, how many copies should be made, and whether the paper will be tractor fed or friction fed.

Most of the newest word processors have a preview feature, which displays on the monitor the overall layout of the printed document on the paper. In this way, you can see the formatting options before time and paper are wasted printing an incorrect document.

Before printing any document, it's important that you first save the document on a diskette or the computer's hard drive. Since printing involves a hardware connection between two different devices, occasionally there are problems that cause a computer to "hang up" on the printer. If you have not saved your document, you could lose it if this happens.

Some of the biggest problems for many word processing users are printer related. The printer might print something you didn't intend, or perhaps it might not print at all. In order for the computer to communicate with a printer, print driver software is required. This software is usually supplied with the printer but can also be found included with some word processing software. It's important that you specify the type of printer you are using and how it's connected to the computer. For Macintosh and Windows word processors, this can be done from the pull-down menus; for DOS-based word processors, it might require a special embedded printing command that is done once, when you first install a new printer. Check the reference manuals for your operating system, your word processing software, and your printer.

Saving and Loading Documents

One of the main benefits of using a word processor is the ability to save your documents electronically and to retrieve them to use again. In this way, common business documents such as letters, invoices, and contracts can be created once, saved, and then customized as needed. This feature eliminates having to re-create a letter or document every time it is needed.

Saving

Saving a document is an electronic way of recording the data on a floppy disk or on the computer's hard drive. Before you can save a document, you'll be asked to name the document and to designate where you want to save it. Some word processors limit the number of characters that can be used in a name, so many people resort to using codes that can be easily remembered, such as M92695 for "memo written on 9-26-1995." Other word processors will allow longer names.

If your computer is equipped with multiple disk drives and a hard disk drive, you must specify which drive you want to save the document on. One good rule of thumb is to save your data on floppy disks rather than on your hard drive since the storage space on the hard drive is limited. Another good practice is to save your documents twice, on two different diskettes. In this way if something happens to one of the diskettes, you'll have a backup copy for protection.

Loading

Loading or opening a document that has been previously saved involves specifying the name of the document you want to open and telling the computer which disk drive it is saved on. When a document is loaded from a disk into the computer's memory, only a copy of the document is loaded. The original saved version is still stored on the disk. If you make changes to the document and save it again using the same name, only the most recent version will be saved on the diskette. The original version is wiped out, and the new version is saved in its place. To save both versions of a document, you need to alter the name of the new version. Even if you change just one letter or character in the name, the new version will be saved in a different space, and the original version will still be intact on the disk.

Fortunately, most word processors have a built-in protection that warns you when an original version of a document is about to be "overwritten," as it's called. The word processor tells you that a previous version of the same document already exists and asks you to confirm that you really want to wipe out the old version. Other word processors use Update, Replace, or Revise commands to wipe out or protect your original version of a document.

Advanced Word Processing Features

Many word processors have advanced features that may be of use to you in your job. For example, if you create long manuscripts or reports, such features such as indexing, sorting, footnote tracking, automatic hyphenation, and tables may be of help. Check the manual for your word processing software if you wish to employ these powerful tools.

Checkers

Spelling checkers automatically look for spelling errors. Grammar and style checkers analyze the mechanics of your writing. Thesaurus programs can provide synonyms for words used in your document.

Just because you use a spelling, grammar, or style checker to analyze a document, it doesn't mean that you shouldn't proofread the material, too. Many times a word or phrase that appears correct to the computer is not correct in a given context.

Mail Merging

One of the most useful business-related features, **mail merging** allows you to create a single form letter and to merge it with a list of names and information to create individualized letters. For example, you might want to send a personal letter to customers telling each one about your company's new product or service. First you create a document containing the names and addresses of your customers. Then you create a form letter with special symbols or commands inserted where the customer's name and address and the greeting would normally go. These special symbols or commands are determined by your particular word processing software. These commands link the form letter with your address list, so that when you print out the form letter, it automatically picks up elements of the list such as name and address and positions them in the proper place. The result is individualized letters by the dozens or even hundreds, but you typed only one. The exact procedures for creating a mail merge vary; the software manual outlines the steps for your particular program.

Macros

Many word processors utilize macros to help customize and shorten repetitive processes. A macro is a way of recording a series of keystrokes or commands and recalling them by using a single keystroke or key combination. For example, you might have to type a long medical term repeatedly throughout a document. Rather than type it over and over, you might create a macro that with just a two-key combination automatically types the longer word.

Macros can also be created for a series of command choices from a menu, such as those required to select special formatting. Word processors such as Microsoft Word call these special formatting macros **style sheets.** Style sheets can be very helpful when the format changes often within a document. By highlighting a particular block of text, you can assign a name to this style, and it will be assigned a place on the ruler or pull-down menu, where it can be easily selected in the future.

Popular Word Processing Software

Here is a partial list of popular word processing software available for IBM compatibles and Macintosh computers.

IBM-Compatible Software	*Macintosh Software*
Microsoft Word	Microsoft Word
WordPerfect	MacWrite
Ami Pro	WordPerfect
DisplayWrite	Write Now

Chapter 16

Glossary of Computer Terms

access   To get to, to bring up and display, as "to access a file" or "to access a menu." In computer terminology, *access* is a verb.

alphanumeric   Refers to any combination of the letters of the alphabet and the ten digits. Contraction of "alphabet" and "numeric."

append   To add to the end of existing text or an existing file.

Apple, Inc.   A major developer of microcomputers that chose to use a different type of microprocessor chip from those found in IBM machines and their compatibles. Software designed for Apple computers will not work on IBM machines, and vice versa.

applications   *See* applications software.

applications software   An organized collection of computer programs that provides powerful tools for performing a variety of tasks in a specific area—for example, word processors, spreadsheets, and database management systems.

argument   Additional information added to a command to define the scope of an operation. In a spreadsheet, an argument tells a function values to use in a calculation. *Compare* parameter.

ASCII (pronounced "ask-ee")   Abbreviation for American Standard Code Information Interchange. ASCII is the most widely used code for the representation of alphanumeric information.

AT   Model of the IBM personal computer that first appeared in August 1984 and used the Intel 80286 microprocessor chip.

backslash   The "\" character; represents the root directory in DOS paths and serves as a separator between elements of a path name.

back up   To copy the information stored on the hard disk onto another medium, such as a set of floppy diskettes; usually done as a safeguard against malfunction of the hard disk. Used as both a noun and a verb.

batch files   *See* batch processing files.

batch processing files   A file containing DOS instructions to be performed automatically or with little input from the user.

BBS   Bulletin board system.

binary   A system of counting using only two digits, 1 and 0.

bit   Short for "binary digit"; the smallest unit of information.

block   In word processing, text that is highlighted and treated as a unit.

boot   To start a computer and its operating system software. From the phrase "lift by your own bootstraps."

bulletin board system (BBS)   An electronic "meeting place" for computer users and enthusiasts. Messages may be exchanged and software downloaded to your own computer.

bus   *See* data bus.

bus topology   A network arrangement connecting computers together along a common set of electrical conductors so that each can communicate with the others. *Compare* ring topology; star topology.

byte   The common unit of measurement, equivalent to about one character of data. There are 8 bits in a byte.

CAD   *See* computer-aided design.

CD-ROM   Compact disk read-only memory. An advanced storage medium capable of holding up to 550 megabytes of data.

cell   In spreadsheets, the intersection of a row and column. A cell may contain a value, a label, or a formula.

cell address   The identification of a spreadsheet cell by its row and column coordinates.

central processing unit (CPU)   A term often used interchangeably with the microprocessor of a personal computer.

CGA   *See* color graphics adapter.

character   A single letter, number, or symbol (including a "space"). Sometimes used interchangeably with byte.

character set   The 255 letters, numbers, and symbols available for use by personal computers and printers.

character string   A group of alphanumeric characters treated as one unit. A text string can be a single character, several characters, or many words.

chip   A small electronic component that contains microscopic electronic circuits.

circuit board   A nonconductive surface on which electronic paths or circuits are imprinted.

clone   Informal term for a compatible computer.

color graphics adapter (CGA)   Common type of display adapter, allowing up to sixteen colors to be used at once. At best, the resolution available is only fair.

column   In spreadsheets, the vertical divisions of the worksheet. On a computer monitor, one character space; most monitors display eighty columns. *Compare* row.

command   An instruction that controls the activity of a computer system, normally entered by the user through the keyboard.

compatible   A computer that is functionally identical to a competitor in appearance, operation, or both; clone.

computer-aided design (CAD)   Software application commonly used by engineers, designers, and architects to simplify their work.

copy   A frequently used operation to duplicate text, data, or a file without disturbing the original. *Compare* move.

CPU   *See* central processing unit.

cursor   Most often a blinking bar of light indicating where text will next appear on the computer display screen.

cursor control keys   Set of keyboard keys that move the cursor around the display screen.

customer support   Telephone assistance provided by software manufacturers to address problems arising from specific user situations.

cylinder   Circumferential tracks on disk storage surfaces. For example, track 3 on side 0 of a disk when combined with tracks 3 of sides 1, 2, 3, etc., are collectively called "cylinder 3."

daisy-wheel printer   A type of letter-quality printer using a flat, rotary imprint wheel. Similar to some typewriters.

data   In general, any information being processed by the computer system.

data bus   A common path of printed circuits through which data pass from one part of a computer to another.

data file   One of the two primary types of files DOS works with. Data files are generally created by the user or by computer programs themselves. *Compare* program file.

database   An organized collection of related information (data) stored on the computer's hard disk.

database management system   Applications software that contains tools for defining, organizing, storing, and retrieving data.

database manager   *See* database management system.

database structure   The basic, initial design of the database according to the wishes and needs of the user; what different items of information are included in a database.

daughter board   *See* expansion board.

default   A value assigned or an action taken automatically by a software program unless another is specified. Can be thought of as a "factory setting."

delete   To erase or remove data from a computer's memory or disk storage.

desktop computer   Another term for microcomputer.

desktop publishing   A powerful type of applications software for manipulating text and graphics, allowing a PC user to prepare near-printshop-quality documents.

device   Any piece of computer equipment (often external) thought of as a unit (e.g., monitors, printers, modems).

digital   The representation of information using only arrangements of binary numbers (1 and 0) to represent all characters and values.

directory   A convenient logical division for storing related files.

directory path   The route from one area on a disk to another through the levels of directories and subdirectories.

directory tree   A graphic (or imagined) representation of levels of hierarchical directories. Similar in shape to a family tree.

disk   *See* diskette.

disk controller   The circuitry (often an expansion board) that directs the operation of the disk drives and their respective read/write heads.

diskette   A single, flexible disk of recording material that is a portable but relatively limited form of data storage. Often called a floppy. The most common sizes of diskettes are 3 inches and 5¼ inches. Each size is also available in high density.

disk operating system (DOS)   *See* operating system.

display   A video display device, often called the "monitor" or the "screen."

display adapter   The circuitry (often an expansion board) that converts the computer's commands to "show this" to a visible picture on the display.

document   A general term for most types of work created with a word processor.

documentation   The collection of books and other materials that explains the use and operation of a software program.

DOS   Disk operating system.

DOS prompt   *See* prompt.

dot-matrix printer   A printer whose print head creates printed characters by writing a series of dots.

download   To copy data or files from another computer. *Compare* upload.

EGA   *See* enhanced graphics adapter.

e-mail   Electronic mail sent from one computer to another over a network or by telecommunications.

enhance   In word processing, to make specific text stand out from the rest (e.g., by underlining or using boldface type).

enhanced graphics adapter (EGA)   An advanced color display adapter that allows for sixteen colors (from a palette of 64), high-resolution text, and graphics.

Enter key   Key pressed to begin the execution of a command. Also called the Return key.

erase   *See* delete.

expansion board   Additional circuit boards to enhance the performance or capabilities of the computing system.

expansion card   *See* expansion board.

expansion slot   An opening along the data bus for the addition of expansion boards.

extension   *See* filename extension.

field   In a database, an item of information; similar to a blank on a form.

file   A convenient collection of related data. Files may be retrieved, opened, processed, closed, moved, and placed back into storage.

file server   A central computer that supervises the operation of a network. *Compare* node.

filename   A one- to eight-letter designation assigned to a file.

filename extension   An optional one- to three-letter addition to a DOS filename.

fixed disk   IBM's term for a nonremovable hard disk.

flat file   A simple database management system used to organize a single group of information. *Compare* relational database.

floppy   *See* floppy disk.

floppy disk   An informal term for a diskette.

footer   Repeated text that appears at the bottom, or "foot," of each printed page.

format   In applications software, the basic layout or appearance of a document or spreadsheet, including margins, line spacing, and column width.

formatting   The process of preparing a disk or diskette to receive data; a new disk must be formatted before it can be used. When a disk is formatted, all previous data will be erased and replaced by new sectors and tracks.

function keys   Programmable keys whose purposes depend on the software program being used.

gigabyte (G or GB)   Roughly, a billion bytes.

global   An operation that affects an entire document or spreadsheet.

graph   A visual representation of data, such as a bar graph or pie chart. (Not to be confused with *graphics*.)

graphic interface   The use of pictures, symbols, and icons to provide a menu of operations and applications available to the user. Usually a mouse is used to point to a particular icon to run that program.

graphics   The production of lines, angles, and curves by a computer on a monitor display or printer.

graphics mode   A way of presenting visual data in which the screen is treated as an array of tiny dots. Anything shown on the screen (pictures or alphanumeric characters) is built up from these dots. *Compare* text mode.

hard disk   An internal, usually nonremovable data storage device. Typical capacities range from 20 to over 500 megabytes.

hardware   A general term referring to all of the physical and electronic components of the computer system.

header   Repeated text that appears at the top, or "head," of each printed page.

help   In applications software, a set of instructions or operating reminders that can easily be displayed on-screen.

hierarchical directories   The formal term for the arrangement of directories and subdirectories in a directory tree.

high density   Diskettes that have increased storage capacity.

I/O   Input/output. A general term to describe any input/output device or the data that flow to or from it.

IBM   International Business Machines, Inc.

icon   A small, symbolic picture that represents a command or operation. Touching an icon with a mouse pointer performs the same task as typing a command at a prompt.

ink jet printer   A type of letter-quality printer that "paints" its characters by squirting tiny drops of ink onto the paper.

input   Any data or information that goes into the computer.

integrated circuit   A large number of electrical components and connections densely and microscopically placed on the surface of a semiconductor; often called a chip.

integrated software   A comprehensive applications software package, usually including a word processor, spreadsheet, database manager, and communications programs.

interactive   Requiring input or responses from the user.

interface   The point where two data processing components meet, for example, where a printer cable plugs into a parallel port. The user interface refers to how information is conveyed to the human user, such as the design of the screens and the functions of the keys.

joystick   A manual input device often seen with computer and video games.

justification   In word processing, arranging and spacing words and letters so that margins are aligned. Left justification (that is, along the left margin) is common, right justification less so.

keyboard   Most frequently used input device; resembles a typewriter keyboard.

keypad   On a keyboard, a supplemental set of keys resembling a calculator keypad. Convenient for entering a large amount of numerical data. Cursor control keys are superimposed on the numerical keypad and may be toggled back and forth with the Num Lock key.

kilobyte (K or KB)   Roughly, 1,000 bytes (1,024).

label   In spreadsheets, the contents of a cell beginning with either a letter or one of several text characters. Although they may contain numerals, labels are not affected by arithmetic operations. *Compare* value.

LAN   *See* local area network.

laser printer   A sophisticated letter-quality printer that combines laser and photocopying technology.

letter-quality printer   Any of several printers that produce printed documents comparable in quality to those produced by good typewriters. *See* daisywheel printer; ink jet printer; laser printer.

light pen   An input device that optically scans and "reads" data, often in the form of a bar code.

link   In spreadsheets or databases, two or more separate files may be linked through a common field.

load   To place or copy a program into memory in preparation for running it.

local area network (LAN)   An in-house communications system connecting several microcomputers by cable.

macro   Macro instruction. A work-saving procedure in which a series of frequently used keystrokes and commands are recorded by a software program to be later "played back" by just pressing one or two keys.

mail merge   A word processing feature allowing information from two files (such as text in a form letter and addresses from a mailing list) to be combined quickly and simply so that each form letter looks individually typed.

mainframe computer   A very large computer, usually requiring specialized staff and support.

math co-processor   An optional, supplemental microprocessor that speeds up complex mathematical calculations.

megabyte (M or MB)   Roughly, 1 million bytes; often referred to as "megs."

memory   The high-speed working area of the computer where both the program currently being run and the data being processed are temporarily stored.

menu   In applications software, a list of several options or operations available to the user.

merge   *See* mail merge.

microchannel bus   A special data bus for the IBM PS/2 models 50 and up, which is considered to be technically superior to the older XI/AT bus. It requires different expansion boards from the older bus.

microcomputer   A small, relatively inexpensive, free-standing computer designed for individual use. Also known as a personal computer.

microdiskette   A 3½-inch diskette contained in a hard plastic shell.

microprocessor   The small computer chip in a personal computer that interprets programs and performs instructions.

minicomputer   A medium-sized computer, usually able to run several programs simultaneously.

minidiskette   *See* microdiskette.

modem   Modulator-demodulator. A device that allows computer data to be fed back and forth over telephone lines.

monitor   The video display device.

monochrome   A monitor capable of displaying only one color (usually green or amber) against the background.

mother board   The primary board of the computer; contains the main circuitry, including the microprocessor.

mouse   An input device that controls cursor movement by sliding on a flat surface.

move   The transfer of text, data, or files from one location to another. The original material is then erased. *Compare* copy.

MS-DOS   A proprietary operating system distributed by the Microsoft Corporation.

multitasking   The capability of some computers to perform more than one task or run more than one computer program at a time.

multiuser   The capability of some computers and computer systems to support several interactive terminals at the same time, with the appearance that each terminal is enjoying exclusive use of the system.

network A group of computers connected through cables or telephone lines for the purpose of transferring information from place to place. *See* local area network.

node   Peripheral computers connected to a network. *Compare* file server.

number crunching   Informal term for a spreadsheet's ability to take a large table of related numbers and formulas and perform multiple calculations in a short time.

operating system   A program that supervises and controls the operation of a computer, the operation of other software programs, and the user's communication with the computer.

option board   *See* expansion board.

OS/2   A multitasking operating system designed as an eventual replacement for DOS.

output   Any information or results from the computer for the user.

parallel port   A connection or outlet on the system unit that can transmit 8 bits at a time. Usually connected to printers. *Compare* serial port.

parameter   An addition to a command that governs software, selects options, or establishes limits. *Compare* argument.

parent directory   The directory one level higher than another.

password   In applications software, a specific word required to gain access to protected information.

path   *See* directory path.

PC   Abbreviation for personal computer. *See* microcomputer.

PC-DOS   A proprietary operating system distributed by IBM. Functionally the same as MS-DOS, both of which are usually simply called DOS.

peer-to-peer   A network arrangement whereby each computer has equal status and access to all resources.

peripheral device   Any external piece of equipment attached to the system unit; same as an I/O device.

peripherals   *See* peripheral device.

personal computer (PC)   *See* microcomputer.

pixel   Picture element. A small dot on a display screen that combines with other pixels to make graphics.

plotter   A specialized printer to draw pictures, graphs, schematics, and other pictorial representations.

port   Connections used for transferring information between peripheral devices and the system unit. *See* parallel port; serial port.

POST   Power On Self Test, a self-checking program automatically run every time the computer is switched on.

printer   A peripheral device for producing permanent printed copies of computer output.

program   A complete set of coded instructions that tells a computer how to do something.

program file   One of the two primary types of files DOS works with. Contains the coded instructions of executable programs. *Compare* data file.

programming   The process of writing coded instructions for a program.

prompt   A message or symbol (such as the DOS prompt) displayed by interactive software, requesting information or instructions from the user.

PS/2   A series of computers from IBM, first made available in April 1987.

RAM   *See* random-access memory.

random-access memory (RAM)   "Ordinary" computer memory that can be read
or written to.

read   The ability or process of acquiring data from memory, storage, or a peripheral device. *Compare* write.

read/write slot   The exposed area on a diskette where the disk-drive head can
read and write data.

read-only memory (ROM)   Memory that can be read but not written to except
by special means. It contains instructions for starting the computer, as well
as special routines that perform many functions of the operating system.

reboot   To restart the computer, usually as the result of a problem.

record   One complete entry in a database file.

relational database   A database management system that allows two or more
files to be linked together, forming relations on common data or "tables."
Compare flat file.

resolution   The degree of clarity of characters on a video display or printer.

Return key   *See* Enter key.

ring topology   A type of network whereby each node receives and passes along
all messages in a closed loop until the message reaches its destination. *Compare* bus topology; star topology.

ROM   *See* read-only memory.

root   *See* root directory.

root directory   The highest level directory in the system of hierarchical directories.

row   In a spreadsheet, the horizontal division of a worksheet. On a computer
monitor, the vertical space for one line of text; most monitors can display
twenty-five rows.

save (to disk)   To write data to a disk for storage.

scroll   The action of pushing lines off the top of a video display while writing
new lines at the bottom (or vice versa).

search   To look for a specific character string of information.

search and replace   To look for specific information and replace it with different data.

sector   A subdivision of a track on a disk constituting a unit of disk storage
space.

serial port   A connection or outlet on the system unit that can transmit only 1
bit at a time. Used for a variety of peripheral devices, including modems,
printers, and mice. *Compare* parallel port.

software   The programs or instructions a computer uses. Includes both the operating system and applications software.

sort   To arrange records or data in a particular order.

spreadsheet Applications software that is an electronic version of the traditional financial analysis tools: the columnar pad, the calculator, and the pencil. The spreadsheet is represented on the screen as a grid of columns and rows.

star topology A network arrangement in which all lines converge on a central "host" computer. *Compare* bus topology; ring topology.

string *See* character string.

subdirectory Lower-level directories subordinate to a parent directory.

system board *See* mother board.

system reset *See* reboot.

system unit Hardware unit that houses the majority of the computer's electronic components, including the microprocessor and the disk drives.

telecommunications Data communications via telephone circuits.

teletext Commercial services that provide information and other services to computers via telecommunications.

template In applications software, a predesigned screen automatically set up to receive certain information or to perform specific procedures. Also, a plastic paper cutout to be placed on or near the keyboard to remind users of key operations and procedures.

text mode A way of presenting the entire character set quickly by having all characters built in to the computer's memory. *Compare* graphics mode.

toggle An action typical of certain keys allowing a function to be alternately turned on and off by pressing the same key (similar to a light switch).

token ring Local area network software methodology that works with networks arranged in a ring topology.

topology The design and physical arrangement of a network.

touchscreen A combination input device/monitor that allows information to be conveyed to the computer by touching specific areas on the monitor screen.

track Logical concentric circle on a disk for storing information. *Compare* cylinder.

tutorial Practice sessions that are frequently provided by software manufacturers as an aid to learning their software. Tutorials may be printed in a book or displayed on-screen.

UNIX A multiuser, multitasking operating system, developed by AT&T and originally designed for use of minicomputers. Versions of UNIX are now available for the more powerful versions of microcomputers.

upload To copy data or files to another computer. *Compare* download.

user interface *See* interface.

utility program A general-purpose computer program that performs an activity not specific to any one applications program. Often used for computer "housekeeping" operations, such as managing files.

value In spreadsheets, the contents of a cell beginning with either a numeral or one of several symbols. Values can be manipulated by arithmetic operations. *Compare* label.

VGA   *See* video graphics array.

video graphics array (VGA)   An advanced color display adapter that allows for 16 colors (from a palette of 256), high-resolution text, and graphics. Supplied standard with IBM PS/2 line of computers.

what-if A powerful feature of spreadsheets using formulas and functions to compute the values at cell addresses rather than computing the values themselves. Once the spreadsheet has been constructed, new data can be introduced and the entire spreadsheet recalculated to show the effect of the new data.

windowing   The division of a single display screen into several viewing areas.

word processor   A powerful applications package for creating, revising, and printing text documents.

word wrap   A word processing feature that automatically breaks a line of text at an appropriate point, continuing to the next line.

write   The ability or process of moving information from one place to another and saving it at the destination, such as in memory or on disk. *Compare* read.

write-protect feature   A method of protecting storage media (diskettes) from being accidentally altered or written over; 5¼-inch diskettes have a notch that may be covered by opaque tape, and 3½-inch diskettes have a sliding window that may be opened.

XENIX A version of UNIX.

XT   Advanced model of the IBM PC, which appeared in February 1983. The first IBM computer to include a hard disk drive as standard equipment.

Section Three
Business Documents

A boss discusses a business document with his secretary.

Chapter 17

The Business Letter

Appearance

Despite constantly improving forms of communication, the business letter still exerts enormous influence and deserves your close attention. Why?

Very few customers ever see the home office or a branch office; this is often true even of small businesses. What customers do see is company correspondence. An untidy or ungrammatical letter gives the instant impression that the company's product or service is equally flawed. On the other hand, upon receiving a handsomely spaced, well-constructed, and well-organized letter, a customer unconsciously assumes it has come from an up-to-date, well-organized, and successful business.

Letter writing occupies at least one-third of all office work, and good writing is the secretary's most effective advertisement of his or her capability. Any skills you can acquire or improve in this area do double duty: They help you work more quickly and effectively while advancing your career.

Besides the skills you need for your own writing, you need to learn techniques of letter writing to handle your boss's correspondence. Most successful businesspeople have already mastered the mechanics of language, but many in authoritative positions lack such skills. They rely on their secretaries to see that their letters are satisfactory.

Any letter that comes from your keyboard—whether composed by you or your employer—must have a businesslike appearance that does not distract from the message it has to convey. The letter must be neat and symmetrical and with no typographical, grammatical, or spelling errors. Its language should clearly and simply go to the heart of the matter discussed. Its language and appearance should also be within the conventions of the commercial world. That is the reason each company selects its own style for the presentation to its public.

The way in which a company is known to its customers, its good name, its reputation, and the quality of its products or services all comprise the *corporate image*. Image is very important, and many companies spend fortunes to have the image instantly recognized by the consumer, so no matter what style the company uses, use it consistently. This helps make the company's correspondence characteristically its own. That consistency also translates into dependability in the customer's mind.

Paragraphing

If you are new to the company, it's not likely you'll be invited to decide on which style of letter to use. A certain style may have already been selected long ago after various experiments. In accordance with that style, you'll be instructed to indent paragraphs or to block them and to put a double space between paragraphs that are single spaced. Your boss will no doubt also tell you his or her way of closing a letter, perhaps with the company's name and his or her signature with title below. You should conform to your employer's preference without question.

At the same time you'll be told of "open punctuation" (no marks at the end of each line outside the text of the letter) or "closed punctuation" (marks after the date line, after each line of the addressee's name and address, after the complimentary close, and after the signature). Closed punctuation is usually used with blocked paragraphs.

Beginning the Letter

The Date Line

Some offices show the **standard date line** near the body of the letter, ending at the right margin two spaces above the name of the addressee, which is written flush with the left margin. If the **centered date line** is chosen, it is placed two spaces below the letterhead as though it's part of the letterhead and centered exactly. This is an effective and well-balanced look if the company name and address in the letterhead fall in the center of the page. If the letterhead is spread out across the whole top of the page ending at the right margin, then the standard date line seems more graceful and more balanced.

When paper without a letterhead is used, the date line must be standard and must be a part of the three-line heading. This consists of the address of the writer and the date of the letter:

> 1501 College Station Road
> Bryan, Texas 77802
> May 27, 1995

Never place the name of the writer in the typewritten heading of the letter, for that belongs only at the end of the letter.

In typing the date line, never abbreviate the name of the month or use figures for it. Also, use numerals only for the day of the month; never add *nd, d, rd, st,* or *th.* These sounds are heard but are never written.

WRONG: May 27th, 1995
RIGHT: May 27, 1995
WRONG: June 22d, 1995
RIGHT: June 22, 1995

The Inside Address

The name and address of the addressee should be exactly as typed on the envelope.

If a street address is long enough to require two lines, place the less important of the two above:

Student Union Building
Northwestern State Teachers College
Alva, Oklahoma 76021

If an individual in a company is addressed, show the individual's name (and title) with the company's name below that, single spaced. If there is a long address that must be carried over to a second line, indent the second line three spaces:

Mr. Charles F. Thomas, President
San Francisco National Bank and
    Mortgage Association
1200 Market Street
San Francisco, California 99001

Never abbreviate part of the company name unless the company's registered name uses an abbreviation (Co., Inc., or &) and such abbreviation is shown on the company's official letterhead.

Figures are used for all house numbers except "one" (which is spelled out). If there is a numerical street number, separate the house number and street number by a dash:

3780–87 Street (note: no *th* after 87)

Names of cities are never abbreviated; the names of states are also never abbreviated. There is one exception: Use the official U.S. Postal Service postal state abbreviations on the envelope address. (See Chapter 4, Mailing and Shipping.)

Never use an abbreviation such as a percentage mark for "care of"; always spell the word out. Never use "care of" before a hotel name if the addressee is a guest there and never use it before a company name if the addressee is employed there. However, if the addressee is temporarily receiving mail at the office of the company, "care of" may be used before the company name:

Mr. Joseph Mendelson
Care of The Rockwell Corporation
60 Wall Street
New York, New York 10022

Titles

An individual's name is always preceded by a title—for example, Mr., Ms., Mrs., Miss, Dr., or Col. It's permissible to place honorary initials after the name of an addressee; in that case, always omit the beginning title:

> WRONG: Dr. Philip W. Radford, Ph.D.
> RIGHT: Philip W. Radford, Ph.D.

Reverend and *Honorable* are titles of respect and are preceded by the word *The* (*Mr.* is omitted):

> WRONG: Rev. John Smith
> RIGHT: The Rev. John Smith
> WRONG: Reverend Terrance Anderson
> RIGHT: The Reverend Terrance Anderson

Women and Men

In addressing a woman, it's useful to refer to previous correspondence from the individual to see whether she included a courtesy title when she typed or signed her name. If you have no previous correspondence, use these general guidelines: *Miss* is used for an unmarried woman. *Mrs.* with her husband's full name (if known) is used for a married woman or a widow. If a divorcee retains her married name, use *Mrs.* plus her own name, not her husband's. *Ms.* is used in any of the above cases if the woman prefers it; it's also used if you do not know the woman's marital status or if you're addressing a divorcee who has resumed her maiden name.

Address a professional woman by her title, followed by her given and last name:

Dr. Mary Hungerford

Previous custom was to use *Mr.* as the title when the gender of the addressee was in doubt. Current custom, to avoid giving offense, is more likely to use the addressee's full name without a title, in both the address and the salutation:

Dear Pat Richardson

However, if the letter has some importance, it's worth making a quick call to the other party to get the proper title. Simply say to whomever answers the telephone: "I'm addressing a letter to Pat Richardson. Is that Mr. Richardson or Ms.?" This can save your employer much embarrassment later on.

Business Titles

Business titles are never abbreviated:

WRONG: Mr. John Smith, Sr. Ed.
RIGHT: Mr. John Smith, Senior Editor
WRONG: Ms. Mary Johnson, Asst. Mgr.
RIGHT: Ms. Mary Johnson, Assistant Manager

When you are writing to a person holding more than one office within a company, use the highest title unless you are replying to a specific letter signed by him or her under another title as applying to the subject covered. When you are writing to a department of a company, rather than to a person within the company, place the company name on the first line and the department on the second line:

Foley's Department Store
Electronics Department
120 Irving Mall
Irving, Texas 76022

Attention Line

An "attention line" refers the letter to the person or department in charge of the situation covered. The word *Attention* is followed by the name of the individual or department. Do not abbreviate the word *Attention* or follow it with a colon.

The attention line is placed two spaces below the last line of the name and address of the addressee, either flush with the left margin of the letter or in the center of the page when paragraphs are blocked. When paragraphs are indented, the attention line is placed in the center of the page.

The attention line is never used in a letter to an individual but only in a letter having a plural addressee, in which case the letter is written to the entire company and not to the person named in the attention line. The salutation must always agree (singular or plural) with the name of the addressee, not with the name on the attention line. Example:

Johnson Smith & Company, Inc.
1500 Main Street
Greenville, Texas 75401

Attention Mr. Thomas Hartley

Gentlemen:

Salutation

The salutation is typed two spaces below the addressee's address or the attention line, flush with the left margin. The first word of the salutation begins with a capital, as does the name of the addressee:

> Dear Governor Thompson:
> My Dear Mrs. Thomas:
> Dear Jane,

In business letters the salutation is followed by a colon. In personal letters, the salutation is followed by a comma.

Sometimes you'll be required to write a letter addressed to no particular person or firm (such as a letter of recommendation); then you will use capitals for the salutation:

> TO WHOM IT MAY CONCERN:

Subject Line

The subject line of a letter is an informal way of categorizing or titling a letter. Many letters in business must begin with a subject line after the salutation, a valuable aid in the distribution of mail that also facilitates filing. The subject line can be centered, but when the paragraphs are blocked, it is flush with the left margin.

Do not show "In re" or "Subject" before the subject line. Underline the subject line, but if it occupies more than one line, underline only the bottom line, letting the line extend the length of the longest line in the subject.

Be sure to word the subject line so that it is helpful. If the letter is about an order of silk, a subject line reading simply "Silk" would contribute nothing. If, however, the subject line should read,

> Silk Returned, Our Shipping Order 8939

the clerk opening the letter could promptly route it to the person within the organization best able to reply.

Contents

With the body of the letter, first consider its appearance. You must judge how long the letter will be and how much space it will occupy in order to place it on the page as within a picture frame—never too high, never too low, always with proper side margins. At first, this spacing will be difficult to judge, but quickly you'll learn from experience how to compose the page.

The body of the letter should be brief and straightforward (see Chapter 21, on language usage). The letter should have the same ease as a personal conversation. Although you must write whatever your boss dictates, many times while typing you can ease the language a bit to improve its impression on the reader; it's possible to do this with just a word or two more or less that won't call attention to any change. It's your responsibility to see that the letter going forth is creditable in every way to your employer's interests.

The length of the letter should be in accordance with its importance. If too short, the letter may have a curt tone and may seem to slight the recipient. If the letter is too long, the recipient's attention may wander after the first page, and he or she may not read the letter in its entirety.

Closing the Letter

Complimentary Close

When the salutation has been "Dear Sir" or "My dear Sir," the complimentary closing can be "Yours truly" or "Very truly yours"; no personal connection exists between the writer and the recipient.

"Sincerely" or "Sincerely yours" is appropriate when there is an established personal as well as a business relationship, but it is used only in letters to individuals, never to a company. "Respectfully yours" appears only on letters addressed to a person of acknowledged authority or in letters of great formality.

Avoid the use of such complimentary closes as "Yours for lower prices" or "I remain" and other "hanging phrases." "Cordially yours" is not suitable in a business letter. It is often used but used incorrectly as it is too familiar for business. Avoid it.

The Signature

If in the body of the letter the writer has referred to "we," "us," or "ours," the company, and not an individual in the company, is writing the letter. Consequently, the signature would then consist of the typed name of the company under the complimentary close, the space for the writer's signature, and the typed name of the writer with his or her title. The whole signature is typed in block form beginning under the first letter of the complimentary close. In some blocked-paragraph letters the complimentary close begins at the left margin; then the signature also begins at the left margin.

Very truly yours,
JONES BUILDING COMPANY

Philip W. Jones, President

Never put a line for the writer's signature. This is a superfluous and old-fashioned practice.

When the writer has referred within the letter to "I," "me," "my," or "mine," this means that he or she, not the company, is writing the letter. Therefore the writer's name is typed with his or her title, omitting the company name entirely.

Very truly yours,

Philip W. Jones, President

A woman should include a courtesy title in her typed signature, so as to allow the recipient of the letter to reply appropriately. Parentheses may be used:

(Miss) Louise A. Scott
Ms. Tina Anderson-Tate
Mrs. Jane Roberts

The courtesy title is blocked with the complimentary close, not extended to the left of it. For a married woman, the signature may consist of either the woman's first name and her surname or her husband's name preceded by Mrs. (no parentheses).

Sincerely yours,

Mrs. Elizabeth Bryan

A widow may sign as though her husband were living. A divorced woman no longer uses the given name or initial of her former husband. She may use whatever courtesy title she wishes, whether or not she keeps her married surname.

Other Elements

Reference Initials

It's no longer considered necessary to type reference initials—the initials of the letter writer and the typist. However, if the company requires identification of this kind for the files, show these on the file copy only, not the original. The writer's initials are typed in capitals, the typist's in lowercase. To separate the two, use a colon or a slash. Many companies require only the typist's initials since the writer's initials are obvious from the signature of the letter.

If you're using a typewriter, you can save yourself the trouble of reinserting the file copy in the typewriter by slipping a small memo sheet between the platen and the ribbon as a guard when you type the reference initials. The initials should be flush with the left margin, two spaces lower on the page than the signature.

When using a word processor, write the initials or name of the person dictating the letter on the office file copy.

Enclosures

Mention of enclosures should be placed two lines below the reference initials. It may seem to serve no purpose to add "Enc. 2" if the body of the letter mentions the enclosure of two papers. However, the mailing department may find this notation helpful to sort outgoing mail. In addition, as the recipient of such mail, this helps you keep the contents of letters together as you prepare to distribute them without having to read every line.

Postscript

Sometimes the letter writer will take advantage of the postscript (following the initials, "P.S.," two spaces below the signature or reference initials) to dramatize some bit of information. Never use the postscript to add something that was forgotten during the typing of the letter. Instead, retype the entire letter.

A Last Look

Before you consider the letter finished, decide if it looks like a picture on the page; that is, have you centered the whole thing? Ask yourself: If you received this letter, would you be favorably impressed? Now check your grammar, spelling, and punctuation again.

A business letter should be folded neatly and precisely. The side edges must match, the typing inside the folds must seem to be protected, and only the fewest folds for the perfect fit into the envelope must be used. Upon taking the letter from the envelope, the recipient should be able to begin reading the letter immediately and should find it attractive. Remember that this is the reader's first impression of your organization.

Chapter 18

Other Written Communications

Letters Written by the Secretary

Letters written over your own signature usually include acknowledgments of correspondence received while your boss is away, letters requesting appointments, reservation letters (for hotel rooms, plane tickets, etc.), follow-up letters, and letters requesting information that another secretary can furnish. While these letters are an excellent opportunity to show your capability and initiative, always keep in mind that service to your boss and the company is the main factor in deciding which letters to write without dictation.

Planning the Letter

Good ideas can be clouded by verbosity, while clear forceful words make for quick understanding. Therefore, plan your letters before you write a word. You'll save yourself precious time and effort and add to the company's bottom line because the time element is the greatest cost connected with writing a letter.

To begin, ask yourself: Is this letter supposed to serve the writer, the reader, or both? Will the letter give information or will it request information? Will it ask for action? What other data must it contain? Before you write, be sure that the full file on the subject is on your desk so you can readily refer to previous correspondence or double-check your information. If you're hazy about the subject of the letter, so will the reader be.

In the first sentence, mention your purpose in writing so that the reader immediately knows what the letter is about. Then follow with whatever explanation is necessary, using a positive tone at all times—that is, words chosen to evoke a positive response. Speak directly to the reader from his or her own point of view, not from yours. The reader must see the advantages of replying favorably.

Use concise language, but be as natural as possible, as though you were speaking to the other person. Reserve the last sentence to request a response if there is to be further correspondence on the subject. Always make that last sentence complete, never hanging. A hanging statement is one that leads into the signature, such as "Hoping this meets with your approval, I am . . ." If that's the thought you wish to express, state it as, "I hope this meets with your approval."

In a business letter, there's no place for cute or clever remarks or for slang. Your use of slang may be misinterpreted as your not knowing the correct English equivalent. Also avoid exaggeration, sarcasm, or any remarks derogatory to any person or to any product—even competitors.

For the Employer's Signature

Your boss may prefer that all letters be written over his or her name rather than having some letters written over yours. This may be true even if you compose the letters and have permission to sign the boss's name yourself.

When you're composing such a letter, use the boss's characteristic language and style. If your employer usually dictates in a short, concise manner, word the letter in the same way. If your boss usually goes into detail, do the same. And when you sign your employer's name, try to duplicate his or her handwriting as nearly as possible. In other words, make the reader think that your employer took the time to dictate the letter and sign it. To do less is an insult to the recipient.

Never write "Dictated but not read" or "Signed in Mr. Wilson's absence." It's insulting to the recipient, implying that your employer either didn't have or didn't take the time to reread and sign the letter personally. It also hints that you couldn't be trusted to write what your employer asked you to write.

For the same reasons, don't sign the boss's name and then add your initials beside it. If you find it useful to show the true writer and true signer, make a notation on the file copy, for future reference.

When you write a letter on your employer's behalf but in your own name, sign it, but do not type your name below the signature line. Instead, type:

Sincerely yours,

Secretary to Mr. Wilson

Routine Letters

Encourage your boss to trust you with routine correspondence by emphasizing the enormous time savings it will produce. Then when the boss discovers you can prepare such letters for signature without dictation, he or she may reward you with more challenging correspondence. Following are the types of routine letters you should be able to handle with ease.

Appointments and Acknowledgments

You may request an appointment for your boss or acknowledge letters requesting an appointment. In each letter, always refer to the reason for the appointment and the suggested time; always request a confirmation.

If a certain time has been requested and your employer approves, confirm the appointment accordingly. If your boss will be occupied at the requested time, suggest another and ask for confirmation. Be sure to keep a record of appointments suggested and not yet confirmed. If there is ever an argument that your employer broke an appointment, you will have proof otherwise in writing. For this reason, if the back-and-forth process of setting an appointment moves from the letter to the telephone, always send a letter to confirm it in writing.

Reservations

In writing for hotel reservations, state the type of accommodation desired, the name of the person desiring it, and the date and time of arrival, with the probable date of departure. Then request confirmation.

No doubt the usual reservations for plane or train travel will be made through a travel agent who understands your employer's requirements and makes every effort to satisfy. Travel agents can be invaluable to a business, and their services are free, because their fees are paid by the airline or hotel. When using a travel agency, a telephone call will substitute for a letter to request arrangements; however, do request written confirmation once arrangements have been made.

Follow-up

In some offices, secretaries use a follow-up file—or a tickler file—to check on delayed replies after a certain lapse of time. When you write a follow-up letter, refer to the previous correspondence, identifying the last letter by date as well as content, and perhaps enclosing a copy if it contains a great deal of detail that could be useful should the original not be available to the addressee.

If you have many follow-up letters to write, instead of composing separate reminders, prepare a form request that can be duplicated on the copier machine or in your word processor. When follow-ups are sent outside the company, often the enclosure of a stamped return envelope will speed a reply.

Sample Model Letters

When a letter is typical of ones you send out frequently, make an extra copy, and place it in a special binder or keep a copy in the memory of your computer so that you can refer to it as a model when you have to write that sort of letter again. On a typed letter, note the space plan for margins and center measurements so you'll have the format already arranged. With a computer or word processor, these margins and center measurements are much easier to reset.

Personal Letters

You'll find that many of the letters in this "letter bank" will be from your boss to another businessperson, yet the subject will be personal in nature. These letters are among the most difficult to write, since they must display sincerity in a variety of situations: sending congratulations, declining invitations, offering condolences, and the like.

Figures 18-1 through 18-3 are samples of personal letters to business associates that you may adapt for your own use. Such letters should use the salutation that your boss would normally use for the recipient and should sign the name the employer is called by that recipient.

Personal Service and Hospitality

When a person has done your employer a personal service or has entertained the boss without financial remuneration when he or she is out of town, that person should be thanked in a letter that can be written by you (Figure 18-4).

Introductions

Letters of introduction written by you for the boss's signature may be mailed or prepared for delivery in person. Such letters should contain the name of the

Figure 18-1.   Sample letters of congratulations.

Dear John:

   I have just read in *The Wall Street Journal* of your promotion to General Sales Manager. I don't think that Smith and Company could have chosen a better man for the job. My congratulations to you.

Sincerely yours,

[*signed*] Phil

Dear John:

   I appreciate your generous letter about my promotion to Executive Vice President. Such good wishes and kind words will help me do a better job, I'm sure.

   Thanks for your note and for your valued friendship.

Sincerely yours,

[*signed*] Phil

Figure 18-2.   Sample letters of condolences.

Dear Mrs. Wilson:

It is with great regret that I just read of your son's passing.

I know no words of mine can console you in this sorrowful time, but I do want you to know of my deepest sympathy. You have many friends who are thinking of you.

Sincerely yours,

Philip Brown, President

Dear Mr. Crenshaw:

All of us at Thorne and Sons were saddened to learn of your wife's death. We know there is nothing we can say to help you in this time of grief, but we do want you to know that we extend to you our very deep sympathy.

Sincerely yours,

Philip Brown, President

Dear Mrs. Holmes:

We at Liberty Oil Company were sorry to read of the tornado that struck your Denison factory. We know the loss was very great, but we know also that you will rise and go ahead with rebuilding.

If we can be of service in helping you overcome your present problems, please call on us. We have enjoyed doing business with R. G. Holmes Corporation and look forward to resuming our enjoyable relationship in the near future.

Sincerely yours,

Philip Brown, President

Figure 18-3. Sample letter of thanks.

Dear Henry:

    Your card and beautiful bouquet of roses helped a great deal to make last week bearable to me.

    I am back at the office and feel I shall be good as ever before many days have passed. The accident was a shock, but with good friends like you, I know the days ahead will be brighter.

    You may be sure that I appreciate your friendship all the more at a time like this.

                           Sincerely yours,

                           [*signature only*]

---

introduced person, the reason for the introduction, the personal or business qualifications of the person, and a courtesy statement (Figure 18-5).

Invitations

Letters of invitation should be gracious without undue formality. Always tell when, where, and why (Figure 18-6).

Acceptance of Invitations

Letters of acceptance should be brief, appreciative, and enthusiastic. If the letter of invitation failed to include complete details, the letter of acceptance should ask for specific information (Figure 18-7).

Declinations

Letters declining an invitation should express appreciation and enthusiasm, with an assurance of regret or an explanation (Figure 18-8).

Interoffice Memorandums

If the company you work for is large, much of your correspondence will be with other departments or perhaps with branch offices scattered throughout the com-

Figure 18-4. Sample letter of personal service and hospitality.

Dear Janet:

If it hadn't been for your keen mind and able assistance, our recent sales meeting might have been a complete flop. Because I had never before conducted such a meeting, I certainly was lucky to have your help.

Thank you for your good judgment and wise suggestions.

Sincerely yours,

[*signature only*]

---

pany. The office memorandum, commonly called a memo, is a popular and inexpensive method of communicating with these fellow employees. Some companies provide special forms for memos; preprinted forms are obtainable at most office supply stores.

Memos should be directed only to persons within the organization and should be signed or initialed by the sender. If a memorandum is confidential in nature, enclose it in a sealed envelope. If copies are sent to individuals other than the person or persons addressed, a notation to that effect should be made at the lower left corner of the form.

If you wish to create memo forms "from scratch," use plain white paper. If your office is equipped with a word processor, store the basic form in the computer's memory and retrieve it when needed. Figure 18-9 contains an example.

Postcards

In communicating advertising material to customers or making special offers, double postcards can save time. It's easy for the customer to reply promptly by merely tearing off his or her side of the card and jotting down a brief answer on printed blanks.

Mailing Lists

If you have a mailing list in which the addresses of your regular customers are likely to change frequently, use a card index in a card file box with alphabetical guides. The changes can be made by replacement or removal of cards, and in this way you can keep your mailing list up to date. Otherwise you may find too large a percentage of your outgoing mail is returned marked "Unknown."

(text continues on p. 205)

Figure 18-5. Sample letters of introduction.

To a business associate

Dear Mr. Fielding:

This will introduce a good friend of mine, John August, who is associated with our state's Department of Commerce. He has heard of the fine work you are doing in Ohio and hopes he will have a chance to talk with you for a few minutes when he visits Cincinnati next Tuesday, March 22.

I have asked Mr. August to telephone you upon his arrival in Cincinnati to learn whether you can see him on that day. If you can, I shall appreciate it. I think you will enjoy meeting him.

It was great to see you at the Boston convention, and I look forward to the Buffalo convention in September.

Sincerely yours,

Philip Brown, President

To a personal friend

Dear Tom:

A very good friend of mine, John August, will be passing through Nashville on his way to Boston next Tuesday, and I have asked him to stop by your office. John is a fellow you will enjoy meeting.

I shall appreciate any courtesy you may extend to him while he is in Nashville— his first visit to your great city, by the way.

Sincerely yours,

[*signature only*]

Figure 18-6.   Sample invitations.

To attend a luncheon or dinner

Dear Mr. Bauer:

The American Consolidated Life Insurance Company is holding a dinner next Thursday evening honoring its million-dollar-a-year salespeople. Will you join us as our honored guest?

Since you would be seated at the head table, we are asking you to join us in Room 200 of the Waldorf Hotel at seven-thirty, so that we may arrive at the banquet room in a group.

Sincerely yours,

Miss Nora Drake, President

Dear Roger:

Arthur Whitfield is coming to town next Friday, and Mary Smith and I are entertaining him at a luncheon at the Ritz. We hope you can set aside a couple of hours so as to join us. I am sure Arthur will be happy to see you, as Mary and I shall also.

The luncheon will be held in the Persian Room at twelve fifteen.

Sincerely yours,

[*signature only*]

To give an address

Dear Mr. Lee:

As President of the Chicago Rotary Club, I have been asked to arrange the program for our next Thursday noon meeting. I know that all of our Chicago Rotarians would like to hear the address you gave in Detroit last week (I was privileged to be in attendance there) on the subject of "The International Situation."

Next Thursday's meeting will be held in the Venetian Room of the Drake Hotel. I hope you will be with us to give our members the same treat you afforded the Detroit Rotarians.

                                    Sincerely yours,

                                    Philip Brown, President

Figure 18-7.   Sample acceptances of invitations.

Dear Miss Brett:

It is a pleasure to accept your invitation to attend the dinner next Thursday evening honoring your million-dollar-a-year salespeople.

I shall be in Room 200 of the Waldorf Hotel promptly at seven-thirty, as you suggest.

Thank you very much for your invitation.

                                    Sincerely yours,

                                    Philip Brown
                                    [no typed title]

Dear Mr. Brown:

I shall be delighted to speak to the Chicago Rotary Club next Thursday. Thank you for inviting me.

Your suggestion that I repeat my Detroit address means that I won't have to prepare a new one.

I shall look forward to seeing you in the Venetian Room at noon.

                                    Sincerely yours,

                                    Barrymore Lee

Figure 18-8.   Letters of declination.

Dear Miss Brett:

Only yesterday, I accepted an invitation to speak in Boston on July 4, the date of your dinner meeting honoring your million-dollar-a-year salespeople. This will make it impossible for me to be your guest that evening.

It was kind of you to invite me, and I regret my inability to attend. I hope the occasion will be a very successful one.

Sincerely yours,

Arthur D. Thompson

My dear Mrs. Scott:

In reply to your letter of May 3 inviting me to participate in your association's fund-raising campaign, I appreciate your thoughtfulness in writing to me.

I am familiar with your association's good work, and in the past it has been my pleasure to contribute to it. It is with regret, therefore, that I must tell you that all my available funds for purposes of this nature have been pledged. It is just not possible for me to be a party to your worthy program at this time.

You have my best wishes for a highly successful campaign.

Sincerely yours,

Ms. Virginia Preston

Dear Mr. Bryson:

I dislike writing a letter that will cause someone inconvenience, but this one falls within that category, to my regret.

This morning, I was advised that a close relative had passed away in Denver, and I shall be leaving this afternoon to attend the service tomorrow, the day of your meeting.

I am sorry that I shall not be able to speak to your group and especially that you will have to find a speaker to replace me at this late date. I hope you understand that I am helpless to avoid this trip.

I hope your meeting will be successful in every way.

Sincerely yours,

Miss Nora Drake, President*

*Because this cancellation comes so close to the date of the speech, this letter would immediately be delivered by messenger or would be faxed or telegraphed if the addressee is in another city.

If you use a computer or word processor, you can maintain mailing lists even more easily, updating or removing names from the list as you need.

Meetings

Every corporation holds an annual meeting of stockholders for the election of directors. During the year, it may also hold other meetings when the stockholders' consent is required for some proposed action, such as an increase or decrease in capital stock, an amendment of the corporate charter, or a merger.

As secretary, your duties include preparing notices of the meeting, as well as a proxy form to be used in case a stockholder cannot attend. This proxy gives another person the right to vote for the stockholder. These must be sent to everyone concerned in accordance with the bylaws of the group.

You must arrange for a meeting place and confirm that it will be ready for use at the time specified. You'll also type and distribute the agenda. On the day of the meeting, place all pertinent papers in a folder with the corporate seal on the conference table at the chairperson's seat.

If you act as the recorder of the meeting, sit beside the chairperson in order to hear every word distinctly. If you have difficulty in hearing, signal the chairperson, who will then ask for a repetition of what has been said. Before the meeting, read all resolutions and reports to be presented. Also obtain the list of the persons attending (which you should have from distributing the agenda) and check the absentees ahead of time rather than write down names while the roll is being called. The greater your knowledge is of the meeting's purpose and the attendees, the easier recording will be.

The Minutes

When you transcribe the minutes, you should write them up in formal language according to the following outline:

- ☐ Name of organization
- ☐ Name of body conducting meeting
- ☐ Date, hour, and location of meeting
- ☐ List of those present and those absent
- ☐ Reading of previous minutes and their approval or amendment
- ☐ Unfinished business
- ☐ New business
- ☐ Date of next meeting
- ☐ Time of adjournment
- ☐ Signature of recorder

See Figure 18-10.

Resolutions

Formal resolutions may be made in one of these forms:

> WHEREAS it is necessary to . . . ; and
> WHEREAS conditions are such that . . . ; and
> WHEREAS, moreover, on the 5th day of August, 1995, . . . ;
> Therefore be it
> RESOLVED, That . . . ; and be it
> RESOLVED further, That . . .

Note that the word *whereas* is in caps with no comma following it; the first word after it is not capitalized unless it is a proper name. The word *resolved* is also set in caps but is followed by a comma and a capital letter.

In formal resolutions, the facts are stated simply:

> . . . and the following resolution was unanimously adopted: RESOLVED, That . . . .

Conference Notes

If your employer asks you to report on all that is said in a conference, make place cards for the members of the group expected to meet. As they enter the room, direct them to sit where they have been assigned. Before your own seat, arrange tabs showing the names of the members in the same order as they are seated around the table so that you will know who is speaking at each given moment. This will enable you to take your notes in the form of a dramatic dialogue. Preface one remark with "Hansen" if the man whose name is Hansen has spoken; then preface the next remark with "Rosen" if the next voice has come from the seat you assigned to Mrs. Rosen; and so forth.

When you transcribe your notes, you can show the discussion in this dialogue

Figure 18-9. Sample interoffice memorandum.

TO: Mary Anne Scott, Shipping Department Manager

FROM: Derek Hartley, President

DATE: May 12, 1995

SUBJECT: Meeting to discuss various overseas carriers

A meeting has been scheduled for Tuesday, May 12, in my office to discuss with several carrier representatives suggested methods and costs to deliver our products to international markets. Your attendance is requested.

Distribution:
Tom Alberton
Martha Reeves

---

form, if that's acceptable to your employer; or you can insert a full "stage direction," such as "Mr. Hansen replied:" or "The next speaker was Mrs. Rosen, who said:" In either case, open your transcription with a list of those present, giving the full name or initials and office held, if any, for each.

A recording device is usually used, but you should be ready if it's not available. It may be wise to take notes even when a recording device is used because, unless the meeting is held under strict discipline, there may be a jumble of voices. Your notes will help you decipher the recording.

Office Meetings

Your boss may ask you to record into written form a meeting of various office personnel, perhaps department heads. Elaborate minutes are not required as long as the group is not a governing body within the company, such as the board of directors (Figure 18-11).

Figure 18-10.   Minutes of a typical meeting.

Minutes
of Meeting of
the Historical Society of the University of Texas
Hotel Driscoll, Austin, Texas
May 1, 1995

At the meeting of the Historical Society of the University of Texas at Austin, some 100 charter members being present, the Society was called to order at 1:05 P.M. by Mr. John R. Combs, Chairperson, who requested Mr. Warren T. Scaggs to serve as Temporary Secretary.

Mr. Combs dispensed with the reading of the minutes of the last meeting because a copy had been previously distributed to all members.

A communication from the National Historical Society, read and accepted by the Society, dealt with the planting of redbud trees throughout America.

A communication from Miss Harriet Allen of New York City asked that the Society refrain from its normal pattern of conducting spring tours throughout the State of Texas. Several members, after the reading, expressed disagreement with the views given by Miss Allen.

There was no unfinished business.

New business was the election of officers for the remaining current year. The following nominations were announced by Mr. Warren T. Scaggs, Chairperson of the Nominating Committee:

President	Mrs. Rutherford Tinsdale
Secretary	Mr. Joseph Mapes
Treasurer	Mrs. Theodore R. Tollivar
Members of the Council	Miss Louise Allen
	Mrs. Philip W. Crossman
	Mr. John Stobaugh
	Mrs. John C. McCann

After an unanswered call for nominations from the floor, it was moved by Mrs. William R. Metcalfe that the Secretary cast one ballot for officers nominated. The motion was seconded and carried, and the officers were declared elected.

The next meeting of the Historical Society of the University of Texas at Austin will be held on June 1 at the Hotel Driscoll in Austin, Texas, at 1:00 P.M.

After congratulations to the newly elected officers by the Chairperson, the Society adjourned at 3:25 P.M.

Warren T. Scaggs
Temporary Secretary

Figure 18-11. Sample report of an office meeting.

Meeting of the United Way Committee
January 12, 1995

Attendance

A meeting of the department managers was held in the office of John Smith, Executive Vice President, at 9 A.M. on January 12, 1995. Mr. Smith presided. Present were Martha Johnson, Philip Smith, Martin Allen, Raymond Martinez, Eloise Randolph, Anthony Guerrero, and Patricia Reese. James Augustine was absent.

Items Covered

1. How the company can participate fully in the United Way campaign just begun. Raymond Martinez reviewed last year's company goals and how these goals were reached. Anthony Guerrero suggested our goal for the present year be increased by 10 percent. Recommendations were made by each person present.
2. These suggestions and recommendations will be discussed and voted upon at the February 2 meeting of the committee.

Adjournment

The meeting was adjourned at 10 A.M.

Martha Johnson, Recorder

Chapter 19

Forms of Address

The correct form of address helps to create a favorable impression, no matter whether you are communicating in a letter, by telephone, or in person.

Following is a chart of the correct forms in alphabetical order by the title of the person being addressed.

Chart Code:

EA	Envelope address
S	Salutation of a letter
C	Complimentary closing of a letter
SP	Speaking to
WR	Writing about

Abbot

EA	The Right Reverend Jackson Thomasson, O.S.B., Abbot of _____
S	Dear Father Abbot
C	Respectfully yours
SP	Abbot Thomasson OR Father Abbot
WR	Father Thomasson

Alderman or Selectman

EA	The Honorable Millard Frazier, The Honorable June Frazier
S	Dear Mr./Mrs./Miss/Ms. Frazier
C	Very truly yours OR Sincerely yours
SP	Mr./Mrs./Miss/Ms. Frazier
WR	Mr./Mrs./Miss/Ms. Frazier

Ambassador (United States)

EA	The Honorable Regina A. Strauss, American Ambassador [but in Central or South America: The Ambassador of the United States of America]
S	Sir/Madam OR Dear Mr./Madam Ambassador
C	Sincerely yours OR Very truly yours

SP   Mr./Madam Ambassador
WR   the American Ambassador OR the Ambassador of the United States

Ambassador (foreign)

EA   His Excellency George Brown, Her Excellency Louise Brown
S   Excellency OR Dear Mr./Madam Ambassador
C   Respectfully yours OR Sincerely yours
SP   Mr./Madam Ambassador
WR   the Ambassador of Spain OR the Ambassador

Archbishop (Roman Catholic)

EA   The Most Reverend Archbishop of New York OR The Most Reverend
         John C. Terrell, Archbishop of New York
S   Your Excellency OR Dear Archbishop Terrell
C   Respectfully yours OR Sincerely yours
SP   Your Excellency
WR   the Archbishop of New York OR Archbishop Terrell

Archdeacon

EA   The Venerable Paul A. Morgan
S   Venerable Sir OR My dear Archdeacon
C   Respectfully yours OR Sincerely yours
SP   Archdeacon Morgan
WR   the Archdeacon of Los Angeles

Assembly Representative (see Representative, State)

Attorney General (of the United States)

EA   The Honorable Daniel Jones, Attorney General, Washington, DC
         20503
S   Dear Mr./Madam Attorney General
C   Sincerely yours OR Very truly yours
SP   Mr./Madam Attorney General OR Attorney General Jones
WR   the Attorney General OR Mr./Mrs./Miss/Ms. Jones

Attorney General (of a state)

EA   The Honorable Marsha Smith OR Attorney General of the State of
         Kansas
S   Sir/Madam OR Dear Mr./Madam Attorney General
C   Sincerely yours OR Very truly yours
SP   Attorney General Smith
WR   the Attorney General OR the State Attorney General, OR Mr./Mrs./
         Miss/Ms. Smith

Bishop (Catholic)

EA	The Most Reverend Phillip Johnson, Bishop of _____
S	Your Excellency OR Dear Bishop Johnson
C	Respectfully yours OR Sincerely yours
SP	Bishop Johnson
WR	Bishop Johnson

Bishop (Episcopal)

EA	The Right Reverend Mark Lessing, Bishop of _____
S	Right Reverend Sir OR Dear Bishop Lessing
C	Respectfully yours
SP	Bishop Lessing
WR	the Episcopal Bishop of _____

Bishop (Episcopal, presiding)

EA	The Most Reverend Peter Brown, Presiding Bishop
S	Most Reverend Sir OR Dear Bishop Brown
C	Respectfully yours OR Sincerely yours
SP	Bishop Brown
WR	Bishop Brown

Bishop (Methodist)

EA	The Reverend Andrew Carter
S	Reverend Sir OR Dear Bishop Carter
C	Respectfully yours OR Sincerely yours
SP	Bishop Carter
WR	Bishop Carter

Brother (of a religious order)

EA	Brother Robert, S.J.
S	Dear Brother Robert
C	Respectfully yours OR Sincerely yours
SP	Brother Robert
WR	Brother Robert, S.J.

Brother (superior of a religious order)

EA	Brother Thomas, S.J., Superior
S	Dear Brother Thomas
C	Respectfully yours OR Sincerely yours
SP	Brother Thomas
WR	Brother Thomas

Cabinet Officer of the United States (addressed as "Secretary")

EA	The Honorable Timothy Dutton, Secretary of State, Washington, DC 20044
S	Sir/Madam OR Dear Mr./Madam Secretary
C	Very truly yours OR Sincerely yours
SP	Mr./Madam Secretary
WR	the Secretary of State, Timothy Dutton

Cabinet Officer (former)

EA	The Honorable James Barker
S	Dear Mr./Mrs./Miss/Ms. Barker
C	Very truly yours OR Sincerely yours
SP	Mr./Mrs./Miss/Ms. Barker
WR	Mr./Mrs./Miss/Ms. Barker

Canon

EA	The Reverend Thomas R. Milford
S	Dear Canon Milford
C	Respectfully yours OR Sincerely yours
SP	Canon Milford
WR	Canon Milford

Cardinal (Roman Catholic)

EA	His Eminence John Cardinal Simonton, Archbishop of Chicago, Chicago, Illinois
S	Your Eminence OR My dear Cardinal Simonton OR Dear Cardinal Simonton
C	Respectfully yours OR Sincerely yours
SP	Your Eminence OR Cardinal Simonton
WR	His Eminence Cardinal Simonton OR Cardinal Simonton

Chairperson of a Subcommittee, U.S. Congress

EA	The Honorable John Brown, Chairman, Committee on _____, United States Senate/House
S	Dear Mr. Chairman/Madam Chairwoman
C	Sincerely yours OR Very truly yours
SP	Senator Brown OR Mr. Chairman/Madam Chairwoman
WR	Senator Brown OR Congressman Brown OR the Chairman/Chairwoman of the _____ Senate/House Committee on _____

Chancellor of a university (*see* University Chancellor)

Chaplain (of a college or university)

EA	The Reverend Dean A. Augustine, Chaplain
S	Dear Chaplain Augustine
C	Respectfully yours OR Sincerely yours
SP	Chaplain Augustine
WR	Chaplain Augustine

Chargé d'Affaires ad interim, United States

EA	Gary K. Wilson, Esq., American Chargé d'Affaires ad Interim; OR, if in Central or South America, United States Chargé d'Affaires ad Interim
S	Dear Mr./Mrs./Miss/Ms. Wilson
C	Sincerely yours
SP	Mr./Mrs./Miss/Ms. Wilson
WR	the American Chargé d'Affaires in France OR if in Central or South America, the United States Chargé d'Affaires in France

Clergy, Lutheran

EA	The Reverend Arthur Anderson [*address of church*]
S	Dear Pastor Anderson
C	Respectfully yours
SP	Pastor Anderson
WR	Pastor Anderson

Clergy, Protestant (no degree; excluding Episcopal)

EA	The Reverend Donald Reese [*address of church*]
S	Dear Mr./Mrs./Miss/Ms. Reese
C	Respectfully yours
SP	Mr./Mrs./Miss/Ms. Reese
WR	The Reverend Mr. Reese

Clergy, Protestant (with degree)

EA	The Reverend Dr. William Johnson
S	Dear Dr. Johnson
C	Respectfully yours
SP	Dr. Johnson
WR	The Reverend Dr. Johnson

Clerk of a Court

EA	Elizabeth Pym, Esq., OR Clerk of the Court of _____
S	Dear Mr./Mrs./Miss/Ms. Pym
C	Sincerely yours OR Very truly yours

SP   Mr./Mrs./Miss/Ms. Pym
WR   Mr./Mrs./Miss/Ms. Pym

Congressperson *(see* Representative)

Consul *(United States or other)*

EA   John Robert Henderson, Esquire, American [*or other*] Consul
S   Dear Sir/Madam
C   Very truly yours
SP   Mr./Mrs./Miss/Ms. Henderson
WR   The American Consul in Brazil

Dean *(of a cathedral)*

EA   The Very Reverend John C. Majors OR Dean John C. Majors
S   Dear Dean Majors
C   Sincerely yours OR Respectfully yours
SP   Dean Majors
WR   Dean Majors

Doctor of Dentistry/Divinity/Medicine/Philosophy, etc.

EA   Sara Brown, D.D.S., Sara Brown, Ph.D.
S   Dear Dr. Brown
C   Sincerely yours OR Very truly yours
SP   Dr. Brown
WR   Dr. Brown

Governor *(of a state)*

EA   The Honorable Charles Sullivan, Governor of New York
S   Dear Governor Sullivan
C   Respectfully yours
SP   Governor OR Governor Sullivan
WR   Governor Sullivan

Governor-elect *(of a state)*

EA   The Honorable Diane Jennings, Governor-elect of Ohio
S   Dear Mr./Mrs./Miss/Ms. Jennings
C   Respectfully yours
SP   Mr./Mrs./Miss/Ms. Jennings
WR   Mr./Mrs./Miss/Ms. Jennings

Governor *(former)*

EA   The Honorable Roberta Peyton
S   Dear Mr./Mrs./Miss/Ms. Peyton

C	Sincerely yours
SP	Mr./Mrs./Miss/Ms. Peyton
WR	Mrs. Roberta Peyton, Former Governor of Ohio

Judge

EA	The Honorable George Smithers, Justice [*name of court*]
S	Sir/Madam
C	Sincerely yours OR Very truly yours
SP	Judge Smithers
WR	Judge Smithers

King

EA	His Most Gracious Majesty, King Philip
S	May it please Your Majesty
C	Respectfully
SP	Your Majesty [initially; thereafter, Sir]
WR	His Majesty OR King Philip

Lawyer

EA	James Robert Judd, Esq., OR Mr./Mrs./Miss/Ms. Judd
S	Dear Mr./Mrs./Miss/Ms. Judd
C	Very truly yours OR Sincerely yours
SP	Mr./Mrs./Miss/Ms. Judd
WR	Mr./Mrs./Miss/Ms. Judd

Lieutenant Governor

EA	The Honorable Mary Brown, Lieutenant Governor of Maine
S	Madam/Sir OR Dear Mr./Mrs./Miss/Ms. Brown
C	Respectfully yours OR Sincerely yours
SP	Mr./Mrs./Miss/Ms. Brown
WR	Lieutenant Governor Brown

Mayor

EA	His/Her Honor the Mayor, City Hall [*city, state*]
S	Sir/Madam
C	Very truly yours OR Sincerely yours
SP	Mayor Starnes
WR	Mayor Starnes OR Mayor of Raleigh

Military Enlisted Personnel (United States)

EA	rank, full name, address
S	Sir/Madam OR Dear Sir/Madam
C	Very truly yours

SP	Sergeant Smith, Airman Jones, Private Jackson
WR	Sergeant Smith, Airman Jones, Private Jackson

Military Officer (United States)

EA	rank, full name, address
S	Sir/Madam OR Lieutenant Jones, Admiral Jones
C	Very truly yours
SP	Lieutenant Jones, Admiral Jones
WR	Lieutenant Jones, Admiral Jones

Minister (Protestant, no degree)

EA	The Reverend Robert R. Foley
S	Dear Mr./Mrs./Miss/Ms. Foley, or Reverend Foley
C	Respectfully yours OR Very truly yours
SP	Mr./Mrs./Miss/Ms. Foley OR Reverend Foley
WR	Mr./Mrs./Miss/Ms. Foley OR Reverend Foley

Minister (Protestant, with degree)

EA	The Reverend Robert R. Foley, D.D.
S	Dear Dr. Foley
C	Respectfully yours OR Very truly yours
SP	Dr. Foley
WR	Dr. Foley

Monsignor, Roman Catholic

EA	The Right Reverend Monsignor Johnson
S	Right Reverend Monsignor Johnson
C	Respectfully yours
SP	Monsignor Johnson
WR	Monsignor Johnson

Pope

EA	His Holiness the Pope, Vatican City, Italy
S	Your Holiness OR Most Holy Father
C	Respectfully yours
SP	Your Holiness
WR	His Holiness OR the Pope

Premier

EA	His/Her Excellency [*full name*], Premier of _____
S	Dear Mr./Madam Premier
C	Sincerely yours

SP   Your Excellency
WR   The Premier of _____ or The Premier

President of the United States

EA   The President, The White House, Washington, DC 20500
S   Mr./Madam President or Dear President Jackson
C   Respectfully yours
SP   Mr./Madam President or Sir/Madam
WR   The President or President Jackson

President of the United States (former)

EA   The Honorable Stephen Murray
S   Sir/Madam or Dear Mr./Mrs./Miss/Ms. Murray
C   Respectfully yours
SP   Mr./Mrs./Miss/Ms. Murray
WR   Former President Murray or Mr./Mrs./Miss/Ms. Murray

Priest (Episcopal)

EA   The Reverend Ann Thomason or *if degreed,* The Reverend Dr. Ann
           Thomason
S   Dear Mr./Mrs./Miss/Ms. Thomason or Dr. Thomason or Reverend
           Thomason
C   Respectfully yours
SP   Mr./Mrs./Miss/Ms. Thomason or Dr. Thomason or Father/Mother
           Thomason
WR   Father/Mother Thomason or Dr. Thomason

Priest (Roman Catholic)

EA   The Reverend Leland Smith [*plus initials of his order*]
S   Reverend Father [*formal*] or Dear Father [*less formal*]
C   Respectfully yours
SP   Father Smith
WR   Father Smith

Prime Minister

EA   His/Her Excellency, Prime Minister of _____
S   Excellency or Dear Mr./Madam Prime Minister
C   Respectfully yours
SP   Mr./Madam Prime Minister
WR   The Prime Minister of _____

Prince

EA   His Royal Highness
S   Sir or Your Royal Highness

C   Respectfully
SP   Your Royal Highness
WR His Royal Highness OR Prince George

Princess

EA Her Royal Highness
S   Madam OR Your Royal Highness
C   Respectfully
SP   Your Royal Highness
WR Her Royal Highness OR Princess Mary

Professor

EA Professor [OR *Dr. if Ph.D.*] Gary Keith Wilson, Department of
        Chemistry, Vanderbilt University, Nashville, Tennessee
S   Dear Professor Wilson
C   Very truly yours OR Sincerely yours
SP   Professor OR Dr. Wilson
WR Professor OR Dr. Wilson

Queen

EA Her Most Gracious Majesty, Queen Anne
S   May it please Your Majesty
C   Respectfully
SP   Your Majesty [*initially*], Ma'am [*thereafter*]
WR Her Majesty, Queen Anne

Rabbi

EA Rabbi David L. Fader OR, *if degreed,* Rabbi David L. Fader, D.D.
S   Dear Rabbi Fader OR Dear Dr. Fader
C   Respectfully yours OR Sincerely yours
SP   Rabbi Fader
WR Rabbi Fader

Representative, State (including Assemblyperson, Delegate)

EA The Honorable Nancy Northcutt, The State Assembly OR House of
        Representatives OR The House of Delegates
S   Dear Mr./Mrs./Miss/Ms. Northcutt
C   Sincerely yours OR Very truly yours
SP   Mr./Mrs./Miss/Ms. Northcutt
WR Mr./Mrs./Miss/Ms. Northcutt, the State Representative OR
        Assemblyperson OR Delegate

Representative, Congress

EA	The Honorable Douglas Scrimshaw, United States House of Representatives, Washington, DC 20515
S	Dear Sir/Madam OR Dear Representative Scrimshaw
C	Very truly yours OR Sincerely yours
SP	Mr./Mrs./Miss/Ms. Scrimshaw
WR	Douglas Scrimshaw, U.S. Representative from _____ OR Congressman Douglas Scrimshaw

Representative, Congress (former)

EA	The Honorable Douglas Jones [*local address*]
S	Dear Mr./Mrs./Miss/Ms. Jones
C	Very truly yours OR Sincerely yours
SP	Mr./Mrs./Miss/Ms. Jones
WR	Mr./Mrs./Miss/Ms. Jones

Secretary of State (of a state)

EA	The Honorable James Cobb OR The Secretary of State of _____
S	Dear Mr./Madam Secretary
C	Sincerely yours OR Very truly yours
SP	Mr./Mrs./Miss/Ms. Cobb
WR	Mr./Mrs./Miss/Ms. Cobb

Senator, U.S.

EA	The Honorable Lloyd Merton, United States Senate, Washington, DC 20510
S	Dear Senator Merton
C	Sincerely yours OR Very truly yours
SP	Senator Merton OR Senator
WR	Senator Merton OR The Senator from _____ OR The Senator

Senator (state legislature)

EA	The Honorable Martin Allen, The Senate of _____ [*capital city and state*]
S	Dear Senator Allen
C	Sincerely yours OR Very truly yours
SP	Senator Allen
WR	Senator Allen

Senator-elect

EA	The Honorable Mary Branson, Senator-elect [*local address*]
S	Dear Mr./Mrs./Miss/Ms. Branson
C	Sincerely yours OR Very truly yours

SP   Mr./Mrs./Miss/Ms. Branson
WR   Senator-elect Branson

Sister (member of a religious order)

EA   Sister Mary Martha, S.C.
S   Dear Sister OR Dear Sister Mary Martha
C   Respectfully yours OR Sincerely yours
SP   Sister Mary Martha
WR   Sister Mary Martha

Sister (superior of a religious order)

EA   The Reverend Mother Superior, S.C.
S   Reverend Mother OR Dear Reverend Mother
C   Respectfully yours
SP   Reverend Mother
WR   The Reverend Mother Superior OR The Reverend Mother

Speaker, U.S. House of Representatives

EA   The Speaker of the House of Representatives OR The Honorable
      Allan Carl, Speaker of the House of Representatives
S   Dear Mr./Madam Speaker
C   Sincerely yours OR Very truly yours
SP   Mr./Madam Speaker OR Mr./Mrs./Miss/Ms. Carl
WR   The Speaker OR Mr./Mrs./Miss/Ms. Carl

Supreme Court (United States; associate justice)

EA   Mr. Anthony Barrett, The Supreme Court, Washington, DC 20543
S   Dear Mr./Madam Justice OR Dear Justice Barrett
C   Sincerely yours OR Very truly yours
SP   Mr./Madam Justice Barrett
WR   Mr./Madam Justice Barrett

Supreme Court (United States; chief justice)

EA   The Chief Justice of the United States [NEVER The Chief Justice of
      the Supreme Court]
S   Dear Mr./Madam Chief Justice
C   Respectfully OR Respectfully yours
SP   Mr./Madam Chief Justice
WR   The Chief Justice of the United States OR The Chief Justice

Supreme Court (state; associate justice)

EA   The Honorable Jackson Morrison, Associate Justice of the Supreme
      Court of _____ [*address*]

S	Dear Justice Morrison
C	Sincerely yours OR Very truly yours
SP	Mr./Madam Justice
WR	Mr./Madam Justice Morrison OR Judge Morrison

Supreme Court (state; chief justice)

EA	The Honorable Margaret W. Smoot, Chief Justice of the Supreme Court of _____
S	Dear Mr./Madam Chief Justice
C	Sincerely yours OR Very truly yours
SP	Mr./Madam Chief Justice OR Chief Justice Smoot
WR	Mr./Madam Chief Justice

United Nations delegate (United States)

EA	The Honorable Edwin L. Rutherford, United States Permanent Representative to the United Nations, United Nations, New York, NY 10017
S	Dear Mr./Madam Ambassador
C	Respectfully OR Sincerely yours
SP	Mr./Madam Ambassador
WR	The United States Representative to the United Nations

United Nations Delegate (foreign)

EA	His Excellency Thomas Henson/Her Excellency Rose Henson, Representative of _____ to the United States
S	My dear Mr./Madam Ambassador
C	Respectfully OR Sincerely yours
SP	Mr./Madam Ambassador
WR	The Representative of Canada to the United Nations

United Nations Secretary-General

EA	His Excellency Juan Perez/Her Excellency Juanita Perez, Secretary-General of the United Nations, United Nations, New York, NY 10017
S	Dear Mr./Madam Secretary-General OR Your Excellency
C	Respectfully
SP	Sir/Madam OR Mr./Mrs./Miss/Ms. Perez
WR	The Secretary-General of the United Nations

University Chancellor

EA	Dr. Barbara R. Rodgers, Chancellor [*name and address of university*]
S	Dear Dr. Rodgers
C	Sincerely yours OR Very truly yours

SP	Dr. Rodgers
WR	Dr. Barbara R. Rodgers, Chancellor of _____ University

University or College Dean

EA	Dean Hamilton Smythe OR Dr. Hamilton Smythe, Dean [*name and address of university*]
S	Dear Dr. Smythe OR Dear Dean Smythe
C	Very truly yours OR Sincerely yours
SP	Dean Smythe OR Dr. Smythe
WR	Dr. Smythe, Dean of _____ University

University or College President

EA	Dr. Thomas A. Harmon, President OR President Thomas A. Harmon [*name and address of university*]
S	Dear President Harmon OR Dear Dr. Harmon
C	Sincerely yours OR Very truly yours
SP	Dr. Harmon
WR	Dr. Harmon

Vice President of the United States

EA	The Vice President, United States Senate, Washington, DC 20510
S	Dear Mr./Madam Vice President
C	Respectfully
SP	Mr./Madam Vice President
WR	The Vice President

Warrant Officer

EA	Warrant Officer John C. Calhoun, Jr., OR Chief Warrant Officer John Smith
S	Dear Mr./Mrs./Miss/Ms. Calhoun
C	Very truly yours
SP	Mr./Mrs./Miss/Ms. Calhoun
WR	Warrant Officer Calhoun OR Mr./Mrs./Miss/Ms. Calhoun

Some Additional Guidelines

The Honorable and The Reverend

"The Honorable" is a title of distinction reserved for appointed or elected government officials such as congressional representatives, judges, justices, and cabinet officers. "The Honorable" is never used before a surname alone—for example, The Honorable Thomas Jones, NOT The Honorable Jones. Also, do not combine "The Honorable" with a common courtesy title, such as "Mr." or "Ms."—for example, NOT The Honorable Mr. Thomas Jones. Never abbreviate "The Honorable" in either forms of address or formal writing.

"The Reverend" should be used in official or formal writing. "The Reverend" is often abbreviated to "The Rev." or just "Rev." in informal and unofficial writing. However, when used in conjunction with a full name, "The Reverend" must be used—for example, The Reverend John Reeves or The Reverend Dr. Louise A. McGinnis.

Notice that both titles are used with the full name on the envelope address but not in the salutation of the letter. Also note that "The" always precedes these titles.

Esquire

When the title "Esquire" is used, it is always abbreviated after the full name, and no other title is used before the name—for example, James Rogers, Esq. Although the abbreviation "Esq." is most commonly seen after the surnames of attorneys, it may also be used after the surnames of other professionals—engineers, consuls, architects, court clerks, and justices of the peace. "Esquire" is written in signature lines and addresses, but is never used in salutations. It is commonly used regardless of sex, but there are some who object to using "Esquire" as a title for a woman professional.

Women Clergy

The issue of addressing women clergy reflects the problem of our ever-changing vocabulary. In many instances "Reverend" or "Doctor" will suffice for both men and women, but some denominations address their ordained male members as "Father." The natural tendency then is to address the female counterpart as "Mother," but there may be strong resistance to this title from both the individual and the group. Whenever possible in such a situation, try to discover the preference of the individual.

Retired Military

When military officers retire from active duty, they retain their highest rank, and this rank is always used when they are addressed.

Chapter 20

Legal Documents and Terms

Grammalogues

Business secretaries will probably not be called upon to take legal dictation, but it's helpful to have a brief knowledge of legal grammalogues. (A grammalogue is a shorthand shortcut for full expressions used.) When taking dictation, it's useful to be able to write in one stroke the representation for "time is of the essence," "writ of habeas corpus," "denied certiorari," and other phrases. You can have your notes complete before the person dictating has finished a sentence because you know what the dictator means to say and how to record it quickly.

Document Formats

When you are asked to type a legal document, use plain white legal paper, 8½ inch by 13 or 14 inch, or legal cap paper of the same size having a wide ruled margin at the left and a narrow ruled margin at the right. The typing must be kept within these ruled margins.

Wills are written on heavy noncorrasable paper of legal size without ruled margins.

Always double-space papers and reports, with triple spaces between paragraphs. Retain a 2-inch margin at the top and a 1-inch margin at the bottom of the page. If plain paper is used rather than ruled, leave a 1½-inch margin on the left and a ¾-inch margin on the right.

Indent paragraphs ten spaces; for land descriptions or quotations that are single spaced, indent an additional five spaces.

If carbon copies are used, and when carbon copies are to be signed (called duplicate originals), they are typed on the same kind of paper as the original. Carbon copies not to be signed are made on legal-size onionskin paper.

Number the pages in the center of the bottom of the page (¾ inch from the bottom edge), except for briefs that are numbered in the upper right corner, the first page number not marked.

If an error is made in typing a legal document, retype the entire page because erasures may cause a court contest at a later date. Erasures are never allowed, especially in wills.

Legal documents are bound with a sheet of heavy backing paper (9 inch by 15 inch). The backing sheet should be folded to provide four sections of the sheet 9 inches long. On one of these sections, type an endorsement and label briefly to describe what the document represents. Following is an example of an endorsed mortgage backing:

No. A-31075
RELEASE OF OIL AND GAS LEASE
FROM
WILLIAM P. ALLEN
TO
FIRST CITY BANK OF NEW YORK

Printed legal forms of many kinds, referred to as "law blanks," are obtainable at stationery and office supply stores and at legal stationers. They are easily filled in on the typewriter and are quickly read. They may sometimes serve as a guide in drafting a document.

When writing numbers in legal documents, write them in words, and repeat them immediately in numerals inside parentheses: ten thousand five hundred and seventy-five (10,575) dollars or ten thousand five hundred and seventy-five dollars ($10,575).

Dates may be spelled out, or you may express the day and the year in numerals, with the month always spelled out.

The following words and phrases often used in legal documents are customarily written in full capitals, usually followed by a comma, a colon, or no punctuation:

THIS AGREEMENT, made this second day of. . . .
KNOW ALL MEN BY THESE PRESENT, that . . .
IN WITNESS WHEREOF, I have this day . . .
MEMORANDUM OF AGREEMENT made this twenty-fifth day of . . .

Case Titles

Case titles are always underscored, followed by a comma, the volume and page numbers, and date:

Johnson v. Smith, 201 Okla. 433, 32 Am. Rep. 168 (1901).

Notary Public Forms

In a small office and even in many larger offices, the secretary will probably also be a notary public. Figure 20-1 shows commonly used forms of notary public acknowledgments on legal documents.

Codicils to a Will

Additions to and changes in a will are made by an instrument known as a **codicil,** sometimes written on the last page of the will. It must be dated, formally executed, signed, witnessed, and probated with the will (Figure 20-2).

Agreements and Contracts

Agreements or contracts should state the obligations of each party (Figure 20-3).

Proxy

A proxy is a form of power of attorney given by one person to another, authorizing the second person to vote in lieu of the first person at a meeting of a corporation (Figure 20-4).

Legal Glossary, Including Real Estate Terms

Here is a partial list of common legal terms that you may have occasion to use:

abstract of title   A brief history of the title to a piece of real estate, including data regarding transfer of the property from the time of the first recorded owner to the present owner.

acceleration clause   A clause in a note or deed of trust causing the entire balance to become due and payable should a default in one of the provisions therein be triggered.

accessory after the fact   A person who aids one whom he or she knows to be a felon.

accessory before the fact   A person who instigates or contributes to the commission of a crime but does not actually take part in it.

accrual method   An accounting system that records income when earned and expenses as incurred.

acknowledgment   A certification appearing at the end of a legal paper showing that the paper was duly acknowledged and executed.

ad valorem tax   Tax according to the market value of subject property.

(text continues on p. 229)

Figure 20-1.   Commonly used forms of notary public acknowledgments.

For an individual

State of _____ SS

County of _____

    On the __ day of _____, 199____, before me came _____, known to me to be the individual described in and who executed the foregoing instrument and acknowledged that he (or she) executed the same.

(S) _____

Notary Public

[*Stamp* and Seal*]

For a corporation

State of _____ SS

County of _____

    On the __ day of _____, 199____, before me personally appeared _____, to me known, who, being by me duly sworn, did depose and say that he (or she) resides at _____; that he (or she) is _____ (title) of _____ (Company), the corporation described in and which executed the foregoing instrument; that he knows the seal of said corporation; that the seal affixed to said instrument is such corporate seal; that it was so affixed by order of the _____ (title) of said corporation; and that he (or she) signed his (or her) name thereto by like order.

(S) _____

Notary Public

[*Seal*]

For a partnership

State of _____ SS

---

*The stamp is not required in every state.

County of _____

On the __ day of _____, 199___, before me personally appeared _____, to me known and known to me to be a member of _____ (name of partnership), and the person described in and who executed the foregoing instrument in the firm name of _____, and he (or she) duly acknowledged to me that he (or she) executed the same as and for the act and deed of said firm of _____ (repeat name of partnership).

(S) _____

Notary Public in and for the above named state and county.

[*Seal*]

---

administrator (male), administratrix (female)   A person appointed by a court to administer an estate.

advocate   A person who pleads the cause of another before a tribunal or judicial court.

affidavit   A certification attesting the authenticity of statements made in a legal paper.

alienation clause   A specific clause in a note and/or deed of trust stating that, should the property be sold or transferred in any manner, the entire balance of the note shall be immediately due and payable. To "alienate" is to transfer.

answer   A statement made by the defendant through an attorney stating his or her version of the situation (often called a plea).

appeal   The act of taking a legal case to a higher court.

appurtenances   Improvements that pertain to the land. *See also* tenements; hereditaments.

arraignment   The calling of an accused person into court, reading the indictment to that person, and asking that person whether he or she is guilty or not guilty.

assessment   A levy made on property for improvements.

attachment   A court order authorizing a seizure or a taking into custody of property or monies to satisfy a claim.

attestation   A certification as to the genuineness of a copy.

attorney   One who is legally appointed by another to transact business for him or her.

attorney-in-fact   One who is appointed by another, by means of a letter or a power of attorney, to transact business for him or her out of court.

Figure 20-2. Sample of a codicil to a last will and testament.

I, JOHN PHILIP MOORE, a resident of the City of Chicago, County of Cook, State of Illinois, do hereby make, publish, and declare the following as and for a codicil to the Will and Testament heretofore by me executed, bearing date of the ___th day of ____, 19____.

FIRST: [*state provisions*]

SECOND: [*state provisions*]

In all other respects and except as hereinbefore set forth, I hereby republish, ratify, and confirm my said Will, dated the ___th day of ____, 19____.

WITNESS MY HAND AND SEAL this ___ day of ____, 19____.

(S) _____

[*Seal*]

Sample of attestation

The foregoing Codicil, consisting of one-half page, containing no interlineations or erasures, was on the date thereof signed by the above-named Testator and at the same time published and declared by him (or her) to be a Codicil to his Last Will and Testament. The said Testator signed this instrument in the presence of the undersigned, who acted as attesting witnesses at his (or her) request. Each of the undersigned signed as a witness in the presence of the Testator and in the presence of each other. At the time of the execution of this Codicil the said Testator was of sound mind and memory and under no undue influence of restraint.

NAME:*   ADDRESS:*

(S) _____   _____

(S) _____   _____

---

*The secretary usually types the name and address of each witness beneath these lines.

beneficiary   The person who is benefited by a gift, proceeds of an insurance policy, income from a trust estate, etc.

bequeath   To make a bequest or to give personal property by will.

brief   The written argument of an attorney supporting his or her contention as to the correct interpretation of the law and the proper inference from the evidence in a particular case.

burden of proof   A term meaning that the party making a claim must prove it. Burden of proof rests on the plaintiff.

capital punishment   The death penalty.

certified copy   A copy of an instrument made from the records in a recorder's

Figure 20-3. Sample contract.

THIS AGREEMENT, made this ___ day of ____, 199___, between _____ of _____, First Party (hereinafter called the Seller), and _____, a corporation under the laws of the State of _____, with principal place of business in _____, _____ (city and state), Second Party (hereinafter called the Purchaser),

WITNESSETH:

WHEREAS the Seller has this day agreed to _____; and WHEREAS the Purchaser is willing to _____; and WHEREAS _____; NOW, THEREFORE, it is agreed that _____. WITNESS the signatures of the parties hereto on the date aforesaid.

(S) _____
 Seller

(S) _____
 Purchaser

by _____
 President

[Corporate Seal]

Figure 20-4. Sample proxy.

[Corporate Seal]

I, JOHN WILLIAM SMITH, do hereby constitute and appoint HAROLD JACKSON attorney and agent for me, to vote as my proxy at a meeting of the stockholders of THE JOHN SMITH CORPORATION, according to the number of votes I should be entitled to cast if personally present.

DATE: _____   (S) _____

office and certified to by the recorder as being an exact copy of the paper on file or of record.

certiorari   A writ from a superior court to call up for review the records of an inferior court.

change of venue   A change in the place of trial.

civil action   An action to enforce a civil right or to remedy a private wrong.

complaint   A formal allegation against a party.

conditional binder   A sales agreement that contains certain conditions that must be met before it becomes unconditionally binding on all parties.

conditional sale   A contract covering goods sold and delivered to a buyer on
condition that he or she make periodic payments thereon (or meet other stip-
ulated conditions).

contingency clause   The clause in an agreement that makes the entire agreement
conditional on the happening of a certain event.

corporal punishment   Punishment applied to the body of the offender.

corporation   An entity of joint ownership in which all parties have a share (equal
and unequal) but that acts in the same capacity as an individual owner. Usually governed by a board of directors elected by the shareholders.

criminal action   An action in which it is sought to determine the guilt of a person
who is accused of a crime specifically prohibited by law.

cross-complaint   A complaint seeking affirmative relief against a codefendant.

defalcation   A misappropriation of funds by one who has them in trust.

demographics   The study of population trends and/or buying habits of the public in a certain geographic area.

demurrer   A plea by the defendant asking the court to dismiss the action because
of insufficient cause for complaint.

deposition   A testimony under oath in writing; often taken orally and signed
after it has been recorded.

due-on-sale clause   The clause in the loan papers that gives the lender the right
to call the loan due and payable upon the happening of a certain occurrence,
such as sale of the property.

easement   An acquiring privilege or right of use or enjoyment that one person
may have in the land of another.

eminent domain   That superior dominion of the sovereign power over property
that authorizes the state to appropriate all or any part of it to a necessary
public use, reasonable compensation being awarded.

encumbrance   A claim or lien upon an estate.

environmental impact report   Report required in some states that shows the effects a proposed development will have on the environment of the area. Such
reports study the effects on the wildlife, traffic, schools, terrain, and so forth.

escrow   The procedure of placing all papers and money concerning a transaction
in the hands of a disinterested third party with instructions on how such
items are to be treated in the event all conditions are or are not met.

exclusionary zoning   Zoning sometimes used to exclude multiple-family dwell-
ings from predominantly single-family neighborhoods.

exclusive agency listing (real estate)   A listing that contains a termination date
in which an owner and broker enter into a written contract for the broker to
sell a property. The broker, as agent for the seller, will receive a commission
if the property is sold during the term of the listing by that broker or by any
other, but not if the owner sells the property independent of the broker's
efforts.

exclusive right-to-sell listing (real estate)   Similar to an exclusive agency listing, except that even if the owner sells the property before the termination date, the owner must still pay a commission to the broker.

executed agreement   An agreement that has been signed by all parties to it.

factor times gross income   An investment analysis formula for judging the worth of a piece of income property by multiplying the annual gross income by a factor derived from the ratio of gross income to the selling price of similar properties.

Farm Home Administration (FMHA)   A branch of the U.S. Department of Agriculture concerned with making home loans in rural areas that lack the usual financing sources.

Federal Housing Administration loans   Loans made by conventional lenders but with a portion insured by the Federal Housing Administration.

felony   Any of various crimes graver in their penal consequences than those called misdemeanors.

FHA   Federal Housing Administration.

fiduciary   The person named in a trust or agency agreement to act for another on his or her behalf and in the same manner as if acting for himself or herself.

first deed of trust   A mortgage security instrument that has first priority over any other voluntary financing liens on a property.

FMHA   Farm Home Administration.

foreclosure   The process in which property used as security for a mortgage is sold to satisfy the debt when a borrower defaults in payment of the mortgage note or on other terms in the mortgage document.

foreclosure suit   A suit brought to foreclose a mortgage.

foreclosure under court action   Foreclosure procedure that is handled in a court of law and allows the lender to obtain a deficiency judgment against the borrower. It also allows the borrower a year's right to redeem the property by paying all back monies and costs incurred to and from the date of foreclosure.

foreclosure under right of sale (deed of trust)   An automatic procedure that allows the lender to foreclose on the property through the power-of-sale provision in the contract. It usually takes about four months. The original borrower is released from responsibility for the debt in exchange for the sale of the property. However, in some cases, the borrower may be held liable for any difference between the loan amount and the sale amount.

franchise   Right to operate a business under the name and operating procedures of a large, often nationwide parent company.

garnishment   Legal notice to one to appear in court, usually regarding the attachment of property to secure a debt.

general agent   One who performs continuing services for the principal.

general partnership   An entity of ownership in which all partners in it hold voting rights as to decisions being made and in which all partners share in the profits and liabilities as their interests appear.

grand jury   An appointed group of citizens to examine accusations against persons charged with crime and to issue bills of indictment if the evidence warrants.

habeas corpus   A common law writ to bring a party before a court or judge, usually when the party is confined to jail.

hereditaments   Rights and property inherited or inheritable. *See also* appurtenances; tenements.

holographic will   A will entirely written, dated, and signed in the handwriting of the maker.

impeachment   Arraignment of a public officer for misconduct while in office.

indictment   The formal written statement charging one or more persons with an offense, as framed by the prosecuting authority of the state and issued by the grand jury.

inflation   Abnormal increase in the volume of money and credit that results in a substantial, continuing rise in the general price level.

injunction   A court writ requiring a party to perform or to forbear certain acts.

interlocutory   Intermediate; not final or definite.

intestate   A person who dies without having a will.

judgment   The decree or sentence of a court.

jurisdiction   The legal power, right, or authority to hear and determine a cause or causes.

larceny   The unlawful taking of objects with intent to deprive the rightful owner.

law of agency   The section of statutes pertaining to the relationship that is created when one entity is authorized to act on legal matters for the benefit of another.

legatee   One to whom a legacy is bequeathed.

letters of administration   The instrument by which an administrator or administratrix is authorized to administer the estate of a deceased person.

letters patent   An instrument covering rights and title to an invention or public lands.

letters testamentary   An instrument authorizing an executor of a will to act.

leverage   The process whereby an investment can be burdened with a loan or loans and still provide a higher yield than if an investor had paid all cash for it.

libel   Written public defamation.

limited partnership   Syndication in which many parties can participate, except that the limited partners have no voice in the operation of the venture and do not suffer any recourse from potential liabilities beyond their initial investment.

line of credit   A prearranged commitment from a lending institution to advance up to a specific amount of money to a customer of that bank.

liquidity   The facility with which an asset can be converted to cash.

malfeasance   The performing of an act that a person ought not to perform.

mandamus   A writ issued by a superior court directing some inferior court or person in authority to perform some specific duty.

misdemeanor   A crime less than a felony.

misfeasance   A trespass or injurious act.

money supply   A figure issued weekly by the Federal Reserve Bank indicating the amount of money in circulation in the United States during the past week.

mortgage   A written conveyance of property intended to be a security for the payment of money. There are two parties to a mortgage: the mortgagor (the borrower) and the mortgagee (the lender).

motion   An application made to a court to obtain an order, ruling, or direction.

net operating income (NOI)   A figure arrived at in completing an investment analysis form that indicates the amount of income to be derived from the property after the vacancy factor and all other operating expenses have been deducted from the gross income but before any loan payments are applied.

NOI   *See* net operating income.

notary public   A public officer who attests to or certifies deeds, affidavits, and depositions.

notice of default   A notice recorded by the trustee under a deed of trust that indicates that the trustor (borrower) is in default on the note and is in danger of foreclosure.

one-time capital gain credit   A provision in the Internal Revenue Code that allows a taxpayer who is over fifty-five years of age to sell his or her home once without having to pay income tax on up to $125,000 of the profits.

PACs   *See* political action committees.

perjury   False swearing; voluntary violation of an oath.

petit jury   A body of twelve persons selected impartially to hear cases and render decisions under the direction of a judge.

plea   An allegation of fact, as distinguished from a demurrer; in common law practice, a defendant's answer to the plaintiff's declaration or, in criminal practice, the accused person's answer to the charge against him or her.

political action committees (PACs)   Committees allowed by the federal government to collect contributions that are used for the political advancement of candidates or causes favorable to the aims of the organization forming the committee.

prepaid interest   Interest charged by a lender before it is actually due or earned.

prepayment privilege   The privilege spelled out in a loan agreement that allows the borrower to pay off a loan ahead of maturity.

probate   Official proof, especially of an instrument offered as the last will and testament of a person deceased.

promissory note   The note evidencing a debt and outlining the terms under which the debt is to be repaid.

proxy   Written power to act for another in a specific instance.

quasi-franchise   An organization to which a company can belong that does not pose the requirements of a regular franchise.

quiet title suit   Proceedings brought to perfect the title to property.

rent control   A practice that rigidly controls the amount of rents that a landlord can charge on his or her units.

restraining order   A court order temporarily restraining a party from committing a certain act until the court can decide whether an injunction should be issued.

right of redemption   The right to redeem a property foreclosed on through court action, usually because of default on a mortgage but sometimes on a deed of trust.

S corporation   A special kind of corporation allowed by law that provides all of the protective benefits of a regular corporation but also allows income and deductions to pass through to the shareholders, much the same as in a partnership.

second deed of trust   A deed of trust second in priority to the first deed of trust.

security device   A device such as a mortgage or deed of trust that is used to secure real property for the repayment of the terms on a note.

slander   A false report maliciously uttered and tending to injure the reputation of another.

square footage   The area of a given property (either the land plot or the building alone). Land sales are often computed on a price per square foot, and commercial and industrial buildings are leased by this method.

statute of limitations   A statute assigning a certain time after which rights cannot be enforced by legal action.

stay of execution   Court order to withhold execution of a judgment.

subpoena   A writ commanding the addressee to attend court.

subpoena duces tecum   A subpoena that orders a witness to bring certain documents into court.

summons   A warning or citation to appear in court.

tax-deferred exchange   An arrangement under Section 1031 of the Internal Revenue Code that allows an owner to accept another property of like kind in exchange for his or her present holding, thereby eliminating payment of tax on the profit from the one he or she is disposing of.

tax shelter   An accounting term describing an investment that throws off tax deductions from interest and depreciation allowances.

tenements   Rights and interests that pertain to the land. *See also* appurtenances; hereditaments.

testator (male), testatrix (female)   A person who leaves a will in force at death.

title company   A company that specializes in searching the abstract of titles to a property and then insuring that title for a new buyer for a fee. Some title companies in some areas of the country can also handle escrow for real estate transactions.

transfer tax   The tax charged by many cities, counties, and states for the privilege of transferring title to property.

trust   An equitable right or interest in property distinct from the legal ownership.

trustee under deed of trust   The entity under a deed of trust that holds a form of title to the property to ensure the repayment of a debt (usually a corporation formed by the lender).

Truth-in-Lending laws   A group of laws enforced by the Federal Trade Commission to ensure that consumers are made fully aware of the cost of credit and are protected against false credit claims in advertising.

two-party exchange   An Internal Revenue Code Section 1031 tax-deferred exchange in which only two parties are involved as distinct from a three-party or multiparty exchange.

usury   Interest in excess of the legal rate charged to a borrower for the use of money.

verdict   The decision of a jury on the matter submitted in trial.

vested rights   Rights that are permanent and undisputed.

waiver   Act of intentionally abandoning some known right, claim, or privilege; also the instrument evidencing such an act.

without prejudice   Without effect on any rights that existed previously.

writ   An order issued by a court commanding the performance or nonperformance of some act.

zoning   Laws in most cities, counties, and states that stipulate the uses to which any property may be put.

Section Four

Language Usage

A secretary questions the language used in a letter that she is preparing for the boss.

Chapter 21

Correct English Usage

Language: Key to Your Success

Give careful attention to your use of the English language. The ability to write and speak correctly is so important to a business career that you'll find the following to be almost always true: As you improve your speech, you will also naturally improve your business success.

Words, phrases, and sentences that are outworn should not be used in a business letter. Stock phrases, like slang, give the impression that the writer has not thought the idea through and has not chosen the best language for expressing those ideas. It's necessary first to understand thoroughly what you want to say and then to say it forcefully with words as natural to you as those of a conversation. This will help you accomplish the purpose of communication.

To help yourself write naturally, consider how you would respond to a luncheon invitation from an acquaintance. Would you say, "In accordance with your request that I have lunch with you, I beg to advise that I shall be happy to do so"? No. You would be more likely to say, "Thanks. I'll be glad to have lunch with you."

Verbose Expressions

You should be alert to everything you write. Beware of words that do not mean exactly what you want to say. Also beware of phrases that are careless, vague, or wordy.

The following partial list gives examples of such pitfalls. After studying this list, protect yourself from similar mistakes. As a famous company once said in its ads, "The audience is listening!"

Verbose Expressions	*What You Really Mean*
I beg to be advised	Please tell me
Thank you kindly	Thank you
I feel that you are able to appreciate	You can appreciate
Which you will remember is in connection with	Regarding

I am not at present in a posi-tion to	I am unable to
I would, therefore, ask that you kindly write	Please write
We would appreciate it if you would investigate the matter and inform us and report	Please check the matter
You have my permission to	You may
I am in receipt of a complaint from John Smith	John Smith complains
You have not, I believe, fa-vored us with a reply	You have not replied
I acknowledge receipt of your letter	I received your letter

Correct Usage

In addition to being verbose, many letter writers frequently misuse parts of speech. The following examples are given to alert you to these other such mistakes. Some of the examples are grammatically correct for colloquial use but not for formal speech and writing—which is the only kind you should use in business.

affect, effect—*Affect* is most commonly used as a verb, meaning "to influence." It is used as a noun only as a psychological term, meaning "feeling or emotion." *Effect* is a verb meaning "to bring about." It is also used as a noun, meaning "a result or consequence, or a mental impression."

> WRONG: The light effects my vision.
> RIGHT: The light affects my vision.
> WRONG: Can you affect a change in the operation?
> RIGHT: Can you effect a change in the operation?

already, all ready—*Already* denotes time; *all ready* denotes preparation.

> RIGHT: She had already arrived.
> RIGHT: We are all ready to leave.

all right—Always spell *all right* as two words, never one.

> WRONG: It will be alright if you wish to go.
> RIGHT: It will be all right if you wish to go.

altogether, all together—*Altogether* means "quite" or "in all." *All together* means "in one place."

> RIGHT: She is altogether pleasant.
> RIGHT: His bills came to fifty-seven dollars altogether.
> RIGHT: The books were all together on one shelf.

any, either—*Any* refers to one of several. *Either* refers to one of two.

RIGHT: You may have any of the six books.
RIGHT: Either of those two cars will be acceptable.

awful, awfully—Never use as a synonym for *very.*

WRONG: She performed an awful hard task.
RIGHT: She performed a very difficult task.
WRONG: Bill is awfully smart.
RIGHT: Bill is unusually smart.

a while, awhile—*Awhile* is an adverb and should never be used as the object of a preposition (which can only be a noun or pronoun).

WRONG: Please come to my home for awhile before you start your journey.
RIGHT: Please come to my home for a while before you start your journey.
RIGHT: Relax awhile before you begin the task.

badly—*Badly* is an adverb, but it is often mistakenly used as an adjective.

WRONG: He wanted badly to go with them.
RIGHT: He wanted very much to go with them.
WRONG: She felt badly after her operation.
RIGHT: She did not feel well after her operation.

because—*Because* is not to be used in place of *that.*

WRONG: The reason he did not attend the party is because he was in Chicago.
RIGHT: The reason he did not attend the party is that he was in Chicago.
RIGHT: He did not attend the party because he was in Chicago.

between, among—*Between* is used to differentiate two, and only two, objects. *Among* is used to differentiate more than two.

RIGHT: The dog was sitting between John and me.
RIGHT: There were three good books among the many he gave me.

both alike—It's illogical to use the combination *both alike* since two items can't be alike if one is not.

WRONG: The cars are both alike.
RIGHT: The two cars are alike. They are both of the latest model.

both, each—*Both* is used to describe a condition that applies to two entities. *Each* is used to describe a single entity.

WRONG: There is a picture on both sides of the mantel.
RIGHT: There is a picture on each side of the mantel.

bring, take—*Bring* is used to denote movement toward someone or something, while *take* is used to denote movement from someone or something.

RIGHT: Bring me the book.
RIGHT: Take the book to him.

bushel—Add on *s* when referring to more than one bushel.

WRONG: Eight bushel of oats
RIGHT: Eight bushels of oats

business—Don't use *business* when you really mean *right*.

WRONG: What business is it of theirs to question my action?
RIGHT: What right have they to question my action?

came by—*Came by* is a colloquial phrase.

WRONG: He came by to see me.
RIGHT: He came to see me.

can't seem—*Seem* is a verb that means look or appear. Using *can't* with seem is awkward.

WRONG: I can't seem to make the journey in an hour.
RIGHT: It seems impossible for me to make the journey in one hour.

combination—Don't confuse *combine,* normally a verb unless referring to farm equipment, with *combination,* which is a noun referring to a group of entities.

WRONG: That combine will be a large one.
RIGHT: That combination will be a large one.

cooperate—*Cooperate* is a verb that means to work together. Therefore, *cooperate together* is redundant.

WRONG: If they cooperate together, their purpose will be accomplished.
RIGHT: If they cooperate, their purpose will be accomplished.

council, counsel, consul—A *council* is a group of persons convened for advisory purposes. *Counsel* is advice; the word sometimes means "attorney." A *consul* is an official appointed by a government to report on matters that the official observes while residing in a foreign land.

credible, credulous—*Credible* means "believable" or "worthy of being believed." *Credulous* means "inclined to believe too readily."

RIGHT: He related the incident in a credible manner.
RIGHT: She is too credulous for her own good.

data—*Data* is always plural. *Datum* is the singular form.

WRONG: This data proves that our business is growing.
RIGHT: These data prove that our business is growing.

deal—*Deal* should not be used informally to refer to a business agreement.

WRONG: She made a deal to buy the house.
RIGHT: She made an agreement to buy the house.

different from, different than—*Different from* takes an object; *different than* is used to introduce a clause.

WRONG: That coat is different than mine.
RIGHT: That coat is different from mine.
RIGHT: He was different than I remembered.

don't—*Don't* means *do not; doesn't* means *does not.*

WRONG: He don't care to go with us.
RIGHT: He doesn't care to go with us.

each, their—Pronouns must agree in number and person with the words to which they refer.

WRONG: *Each* drives *their* own car.
RIGHT: *Each* drives *his* own car.
RIGHT: Each of the women listed her needs. [The singular pronoun *each* is the subject.]

either, neither—*Either* and *neither* refer to two.

WRONG: Neither of the four books suited him.
RIGHT: None of the four books suited him.
WRONG: Either of the three books is the one I want.
RIGHT: Either of the two books will do.
RIGHT: Any of the three books will suit me.

enthuse, enthusiastic—*Enthuse* is used only as a colloquialism. For the formal language needed for business writing, use *to be enthusiastic.*

WRONG: He was enthused over winning the award.
RIGHT: He was enthusiastic about winning the award.

except, unless—*Except* is a preposition used to introduce a prepositional phrase. *Unless* is an adverbial conjunction used to introduce a subordinate clause. They are not interchangeable. *Except* may be used as a conjunction only when it's followed by the word *that;* however, that construction, although correct, is often awkward, and *unless* is preferable.

WRONG: The horse cannot be entered in the race except the judges permit.
RIGHT: The horse cannot be entered in the race except that the judges permit.
RIGHT: The horse cannot be entered in the race unless the judges permit.

expect—Don't use *expect* to mean *think* or *suppose.*

WRONG: I expect she was well received.
RIGHT: I suppose she was well received.

farther, further—*Farther* shows a specific, quantifiable distance. *Further* shows degree or extent.

RIGHT: I walked farther than he did.
RIGHT: He will go further with your help than without it.

fix—*Fix* means to repair. Don't use it to mean a bad situation.

WRONG: She is in a desperate fix.
RIGHT: She is desperate because of her present situation.

foot, feet—*Foot* is singular, *feet* is plural.

WRONG: The room is twelve foot long.
RIGHT: The room is twelve feet long.

got—Don't use *got*, when you could use *have*, *has*, or *must*.

WRONG: I have got a new car.
RIGHT: I have a new car.
RIGHT: He got a new job.
WRONG: I've got to stop at his house. [*colloquial*]
RIGHT: I must stop at his house OR I have to stop at his house.

gotten—This is an obsolete term. Do not use; replace with *got*.

guess—Don't use *guess* when you really mean *think*.

WRONG: I guess you are right.
RIGHT: I think you are right.
RIGHT: In the word game, Marcus was the first to guess correctly.

inaugurate—Don't use *inaugurate* in place of *started* or *began*.

WRONG: The program was inaugurated on August 1.
RIGHT: The President of the United States was inaugurated on January 4.
RIGHT: The program was begun on August 1.

inside of, within—Don't use *inside of* where you could use *within*.

WRONG: He will visit us inside of a week.
RIGHT: He will visit us within a week.

invite—Don't confuse *invite* (a verb) with *invitation* (a noun).

WRONG: I have an invite to the party.
RIGHT: I have an invitation to the party.

its, it's—*Its* (without an apostrophe) is a possessive pronoun. *It's* (with an apostrophe) is a contraction meaning "it is."

RIGHT: It's getting dark [meaning "It is getting dark"].
RIGHT: The ship was flying its flag at half-mast.

kind—*Kind* is singular; *kinds* is plural.

WRONG: She asked for those kind of flowers.
RIGHT: She asked for those kinds of flowers.
RIGHT: She asked for that kind of flowers.

kind of, sort of—*kind of* and *sort of* are unclear. Be definite when speaking or writing.

WRONG: He appeared to be kind of ill.
RIGHT: He appeared to be rather ill.
WRONG: She was sort of ill at ease.
RIGHT: She was somewhat ill at ease.

learn, teach—Before you can *learn*, someone must first *teach* you.

WRONG: He learned me how to type.
RIGHT: She taught me how to type.
RIGHT: If I teach him correctly, he will learn quickly.

less, fewer—*Less* refers to a smaller amount, degree, or value. *Fewer* refers to a quantifiable number.

> **RIGHT:** This mine contains less gold than the Jackass Mine.
> **RIGHT:** This city has fewer people today than it had a year ago.

let, leave—*Let* means "to permit." *Leave* means "to depart," "to bequeath," or "to allow to remain."

> **WRONG:** Leave her go with us.
> **RIGHT:** Let her go with us.

liable, likely—*Liable* should be used when referring to legal responsibility.

> **RIGHT:** The landlord is liable for damages.
> **RIGHT:** That horse is likely to win the race.

lie, lay—Many people confuse the two because the word *lay* is both the present tense of *lay* (*lay, lay, laid*) and the past tense of *lie* (*lie, lay, lain*). *Lie* means "to remain in position" or "to rest." It is intransitive, meaning no object ever accompanies it. *Lay* means "to place something somewhere." It is transitive, meaning an object always accompanies it.

> **WRONG:** He lays down after lunch every day.
> **RIGHT:** He lies down after lunch every day.
> **RIGHT:** Yesterday he lay on the couch for two hours.
> **RIGHT:** Will you please lay the book on the table?
> **RIGHT:** The pen lay on the desk all day.

like, as—*Like* is a preposition always followed by a noun or pronoun in the objective case. *As* is an adverbial conjunction used to introduce a subordinate clause.

> **WRONG:** It appears like he isn't coming.
> **RIGHT:** It appears as if he isn't coming.
> **RIGHT:** Though he was such a little boy, he marched like a major.

line—*Line* should not be used in place of *business.*

> **WRONG:** He is in the jewelry line.
> **RIGHT:** He is in the jewelry business.

loan—A loan should be used as a noun to refer to an agreement to borrow. To allow someone to borrow is *to lend.*

> **WRONG:** Loan me your pen.
> **RIGHT:** Lend me your pen.
> **RIGHT:** He went to the bank to receive a loan.

lost—Don't use extra words—like *out*—that are not necessary for meaning.

> **WRONG:** He lost out.
> **RIGHT:** He lost.

lots—Don't use *lots* when referring to an amount of something.

> **WRONG:** She receives lots of fan mail.
> **RIGHT:** She receives a great deal of fan mail.

mad, angry—Use *angry* rather than *mad*. Remember, dogs go mad, people get angry.

WRONG: Mary was mad at Jane.
RIGHT: Mary was angry with Jane.

may, can—*May* refers to permission. *Can* refers to ability.

RIGHT: May I go with you?
RIGHT: Can he drive a car?

might of, would of, could of—This construction is the result of poor pronunciation. The correct phrases are *might have, would have,* and *could have.*

WRONG: If you could of arranged it, I would of gone.
RIGHT: If you could have arranged it, I would have gone.

most, almost—*Most of all* is a colloquial expression. Use *most of* or *almost* instead.

WRONG: We walked most all the way.
RIGHT: We walked most of the way.
RIGHT: We walked almost all the way.

never—*Never* means never; it does not refer to a limited period of time.

WRONG: We never saw your dog since yesterday.
RIGHT: We have not seen your dog since yesterday.
RIGHT: We never saw your dog. What breed was he?

off—*Off* is always used alone and not with *of.*

WRONG: The ribbon was taken off of the package.
RIGHT: The ribbon was taken off the package.

only—Be careful of where you place this adverb; position determines which word you modify.

WRONG: I could only get him to play one piece.
RIGHT: I could get him to play only one piece.

open—*Open* should be used without *up.*

WRONG: We open up the doors promptly at noon.
RIGHT: We open the doors promptly at noon.

party—*Party* can be used to refer to a person in legal documents, but it is too formal for common use. A party can also be a celebration.

WRONG: The party I called was disturbed.
RIGHT: The person I called was disturbed.
RIGHT: (in legal documents): The party of the second part hereby agrees . . .
RIGHT: He celebrated his birthday with a party.

people—*People* refers to a large group of individuals. When referring to people of a particular organization or place, it's better to use *people* before the name.

WRONG: The General Motors people
RIGHT: The people of General Motors; the people of Massachusetts

percent—This is one word following an amount, never *per cent.*

RIGHT: Six percent interest was charged.

percentage—Use when no amount is given.

RIGHT: What percentage of interest was charged?

posted, informed—Don't use *posted* in place of *informed.*

WRONG: You are well posted on the subject.
RIGHT: You are well informed about Australia.

raise, rise—*Raise* is a transitive verb and must always take an object. *Rise* is a transitive verb and never takes an object.

RIGHT: They raise the question at every meeting.
RIGHT: I rise to make a motion.

real—Don't use *real* when you really mean *very.*

WRONG: He is real handsome.
RIGHT: He is very handsome.

run—When referring to a business or organization, don't use *run* in place of *manage.*

WRONG: He runs the bakery.
RIGHT: He manages the bakery.

same—Don't use *same* to refer to the subject of a sentence.

WRONG: Your letter arrived and I acknowledge same with thanks.
RIGHT: Your letter arrived and I acknowledge it with thanks.

shape (meaning tangible form)—Don't use *shape* to refer to the status of something.

WRONG: The transaction was completed in good shape.
RIGHT: The transaction was completed to everyone's satisfaction.

shall, will—Use *shall* to express a simple expected action with the first person. Use *will* with second and third persons. However, to express determination or command, reverse the order; use *will* for the first person and *shall* for the second and third.

RIGHT: I shall go tomorrow.
RIGHT: He will go, too.
RIGHT: You will be at school by the time we arrive.
RIGHT: I will go tomorrow, and no one can stop me.
RIGHT: He shall go with me even if I must force him.
RIGHT: You shall never do that again.

should, would—Use *should* with the first person and *would* with the second and third persons to express expected action. However, using *should* and *would* instead of *shall* and *will* implies a doubt that the action will take place. *Should* and *would* may also be used with all persons, but in these instances, the meaning of the verbs is different. *Should* may be used with all persons to show obligation. *Would* may be used with all persons to show habit or determination.

RIGHT: A child should love his parents.
RIGHT: If I had enough money, I would buy a car.

sit, set—

RIGHT: She sits near her husband at every meeting.
RIGHT: She sets the plates on the table in an orderly manner.
RIGHT: She sets the hen over the eggs and hopes they will be hatched.

so—Avoid overuse of this adverbial conjunction. *Consequently, therefore,* and *inasmuch as* are good substitutes when you want to vary the style.

AVOID: It had snowed over a foot that day; so we drove the Jeep into town.
RIGHT: It had snowed over a foot that day, consequently we drove the Jeep into town.

sometime, some time—*Sometime* means occasional. *Some time* means an amount of time.

WRONG: I will go sometime this morning.
RIGHT: If I have some time this morning, I shall do the job for you.

to, at—Do not use either with *where*.

WRONG: Where are you at?
RIGHT: Where are you?
RIGHT: Where did he go to?
RIGHT: Where did he go?

try and, come and, be sure and—Don't use a word if it is not necessary to convey your meaning.

WRONG: Try and be here at noon.
RIGHT: Try to be here at noon.
WRONG: Come and see me tomorrow.
RIGHT: Come to see me tomorrow.
WRONG: Be sure and watch out as you cross the street.
RIGHT: Be sure to watch out as you cross the street.

wait on—When *wait* refers to time, *on* is not needed. When it refers to the actions of a waiter or waitress, *wait on* is acceptable.

WRONG: Please do not wait on me if I am not at the station when you arrive.
RIGHT: Please do not wait for me if I am not there when you arrive.
RIGHT: The headwaiter assigned the red-haired woman to wait on me.

where—Whether used as an adverb or a conjunction, *where* denotes position or place. It should never be used as a substitute for *that* introducing a clause.

WRONG: Did you read in the paper where our mayor was honored at a banquet?
RIGHT: Did you read in the paper that our mayor was honored at a banquet?

which—When used to introduce a clause, *which* must refer to a specific noun or pronoun and not to a whole situation.

WRONG: He did not arrive in time for the meeting, which caused the president embarrassment.
RIGHT: His failure to arrive in time for the meeting caused the president embarrassment.
RIGHT: His failure to arrive, which caused the president embarrassment, was the reason for his dismissal.

who, which, that—*Who* is used to refer to people. *Which* and *that* refer to objects.

RIGHT: She is the woman who smiled at him.
RIGHT: She is the kind of person whom everyone likes.
RIGHT: I read the book on Eisenhower, which I found fascinating.

Additional Examples

Pronouns

Pronouns in the nominative case—*I, we, he, she, they*—serve as subjects of verbs but never objects of verbs or prepositions. You can often tell that the wrong case is being used because the sentence sounds odd. However, when compound subjects or compound objects are used, it may be difficult to hear the correct case. To test such an instance, drop the other subject or object and repeat the sentence with only the pronoun in question.

I—nominative case, never an object

WRONG: Just between you and I . . .
RIGHT: Just between you and me . . .
WRONG: He asked that the money be given to you and I.
TEST: He asked that the money be given to I.
RIGHT: He asked that the money be given to you and me.
TEST: He asked that the money be given to me.

she, he—nominative case, never an object

WRONG: If you stay there, the ball will hit you and she.
TEST: If you stay there, the ball will hit she.
RIGHT: If you stay there, the ball will hit you and him.
TEST: If you stay there, the ball will hit him.

they—nominative case, never an object

WRONG: I will give the money to you and they.
TEST: I will give the money to they.
RIGHT: I will give the money to you and them.

TEST: I will give the money to them.
WRONG: You and them are welcome to come.
TEST: Them are welcome to come.
RIGHT: You and they are welcome to come.
TEST: They are welcome to come.

we—nominative case, never an object

WRONG: Us boys are ready to play the game.
TEST: Us are ready to play the game.
RIGHT: We boys are ready to play the game.
TEST: We are ready to play the game.

Similarly, pronouns in the subjective case—*me, us, her, him, them*—are always used as objects, of either verbs or prepositions, and never as subjects. With a compound subject, use the same way of testing as above, changing the number of the verb as needed.

me, us—objective case, never a subject

WRONG: Mark and me went to the movies.
TEST: Me went to the movies.
RIGHT: Mark and I went to the movies.
TEST: I went to the movies.
WRONG: Janet and us sat on the top bleacher.
TEST: Us sat on the top bleacher.
RIGHT: Janet and we sat on the top bleacher.
TEST: We sat on the top bleacher.

her, him, them—*Her, his,* and *their* are used to convey possession. *She, he,* and *they* are the subjective case.

WRONG: Tommy and her [him, them] argued every day.
TEST: Her [him, them] argued every day.
RIGHT: Tommy and she [he, they] argued every day.

Dangling Participles

A dangling participle modifies the noun or pronoun to which it refers. Since position determines the referent, how you construct the sentence determines the meaning.

WRONG: Walking down Main Street, the art museum is visible. (This implies the art museum is walking down Main Street.)
RIGHT: Walking down Main Street, you can see the art museum.

Chapter 22

Spelling

Dictionary Uses

The constant study of spelling and the exact meaning of words are an important aspect of every secretary's career. Always keep a dictionary close at hand. Besides providing spelling and definitions, this invaluable aid also sets out such information as the following:

- Syllabication (useful when you want to split a word at the end of a type-written line)
- Variant spellings, with the preferred spelling listed first
- Pronunciations, with the preferred form shown first
- Capitalization
- Hyphenation
- Italicization
- Part of speech
- Plural of nouns
- Cases of pronouns
- Verb tenses
- Comparative and superlative forms of irregular adverbs and adjectives
- Derivations of the word
- Synonyms and antonyms
- Status label (if a word is colloquial, obsolete, etc.)

Some words whose spelling frequently puzzles many of us are discussed in this chapter in order to sharpen your awareness of spelling in general.

Plurals

1. The general rule is to form the plural of a noun by adding *s:*

book	books
clock	clocks
pen	pens

2. A noun ending in *o* preceded by a vowel takes an *s* for the plural:

curio	curios
folio	folios
radio	radios
ratio	ratios
studio	studios

Some nouns ending in *o,* preceded by a consonant, take *es* to form the plural, while others take *s:*

banjo	banjos
buffalo	buffaloes
cargo	cargoes
Eskimo	Eskimos
hero	heroes
mosquito	mosquitoes
motto	mottoes
piano	pianos
potato	potatoes
soprano	sopranos
tomato	tomatoes

3. A singular noun ending in *ch, sh, s, x,* or *z* takes *es* for the plural:

bush	bushes
chintz	chintzes
dress	dresses
inch	inches
wax	waxes

4. A noun ending in *y* preceded by a consonant changes the *y* to *i* and adds *es* for the plural:

ability	abilities
auxiliary	auxiliaries
discrepancy	discrepancies
facility	facilities
industry	industries
lady	ladies
society	societies

5. A noun ending in *y* preceded by a vowel takes only an *s* for the plural:

attorney	attorneys
galley	galleys
kidney	kidneys
monkey	monkeys
turkey	turkeys

6. Some plurals end in *en:*

child	children
man	men
ox	oxen

7. Some nouns ending in *f* or *fe* change the *f* or *fe* to *v* and add *es* for the plural:

calf	calves
knife	knives
leaf	leaves
life	lives
loaf	loaves
shelf	shelves

But there are some exceptions:

bailiff	baliffs
belief	beliefs
chief	chiefs
gulf	gulfs
roof	roofs

8. Some nouns require a vowel change for the plural:

foot	feet
goose	geese
mouse	mice
tooth	teeth

9. The plural of numerals, signs, and letters is shown by adding an *s* (or an apostrophe and an *s* to avoid confusion):

COD	CODs
one B	four B's

10. To proper names ending in *s* or in an *s* sound, add *es* for the plural:

Brooks	the Brookses
Burns	the Burnses
Jones	the Joneses

11. A compound noun, when hyphenated or when consisting of two separate words, shows the plural form in the most important element:

attorney-in-fact	attorneys-in-fact
brigadier general	brigadier generals
brother-in-law	brothers-in-law
notary public	notaries public
passer-by	passers-by

12. The plural of solid compounds (a compound noun written as one word) is formed at the end of the solid compound:

bookshelf	bookshelves
cupful	cupfuls
lumberman	lumbermen
stepchild	stepchildren
stepdaughter	stepdaughters

13. Some nouns have the same form for singular and plural:
Chinese
corps
deer
salmon
sheep

vermin
wheat

14. Some nouns are always treated as singular:
    civics
    mathematics
    measles
    milk
    molasses
    music
    news
    statistics

15. Some nouns are always treated as plural:
    pants
    proceeds
    remains
    riches
    scissors
    thanks
    trousers
    tweezers

The Suffix

1. Words whose roots end with *ge* or *ce* generally retain the *e* when a suffix is added:

change	changeable
damage	damageable
disadvantage	disadvantageous
outrage	outrageous

2. A final silent *e* is usually dropped before a suffix that begins with a vowel:

argue	arguing
change	changing
conceive	conceivable

3. A final silent *e* is usually retained before a suffix that begins with a consonant:

achieve	achievement
definite	definitely

4. In words ending in *c*, add *k* before a suffix beginning with *e, i,* or *y,* so that the hard sound of the original *c* is retained:

frolic	frolicked	frolicking
mimic	mimicked	mimicking
picnic	picnicked	picnicking

5. A word ending in *ie* changes the *ie* to *y* when adding a suffix:

die	dying
lie	lying

tie	tying
vie	vying

6. Words that end in *y* preceded by a vowel retain the *y* when adding the suffix:

survey	surveying	surveyor

7. Words that end with *y* preceded by a consonant change *y* to *i* when adding a suffix, except when the suffix is *ing:*

embody	embodying
rely	relying
satisfy	satisfying

8. A final consonant is usually doubled when it is preceded by a single vowel and takes a suffix:

mop	mopping

9. A final consonant is doubled when it is followed by a suffix, and the last syllable is accented when the suffix is added:

acquit	acquitted

10. The final consonant is not doubled when the accent is shifted to a preceding syllable when the suffix is added:

refer	referring	BUT reference

or when the final consonant is preceded by two vowels:

fooled	fooling

Irregular Spelling

1. Irregular spellings to watch closely:
   acknowledgment
   awful
   judgment
   ninth
   truly
   wholly

2. While they may sound the same, there are three ways to spell words ending in *ceed, cede,* and *sede:*
   exceed
   intercede
   precede
   proceed
   recede
   secede
   succeed
   supersede

MEMORIZE: The only English word that ends in *sede* is *supersede.* The only English words that end in *ceed* are *exceed, proceed,* and *succeed.*

Capitalization

Proper nouns that denote the names of specific persons or places are capitalized, though names that are common to a group are not. Following are examples of words that are capitalized:

Acts of Congress

Civil Rights Act
Taft-Hartley Act
BUT labor relations law [*a description*]
the recent amendment to the
Constitution
the Child Labor Amendment
the Eighteenth Amendment

Associations

Society of Professional Engineers
American Business Association
Young Women's Christian Association
American Heart Association

Book Titles and Their Subdivisions

The American Way, Chapter VI
Remembrance of Things Past, Volume II

Bulletins and Periodical Titles

New York Retail Bulletin
Wall Street Journal

Cars of Railroads and Automobile Models

Car 54, Train 93
Plymouth
Cadillac

Churches and Church Dignitaries

Fifth Avenue Presbyterian Church
the Archbishop of New York
Bishop John Barnes

Cities

Jefferson City, Missouri
Los Angeles
BUT the city of Los Angeles

Clubs

Possum Kingdom Club
The Do-Gooders
The Union League Club
BUT many Republican clubs in the West

Codes

the Code of Building Maintenance
BUT the building code
Code VI

Compass Points Designating a Specific Region

the Northeast [*section of the country*]
the Pacific Northwest
BUT Just drive north
the West
BUT west of town

Constitutions

the Constitution of Texas
the Constitution of the United States
BUT the constitution of any nation

Corporations

American Brake Corporation
Container Corporation of America
BUT The corporation was dissolved.

Courts

the Criminal Court of Appeals
BUT a court of appeals
the Supreme Court
the Magistrate's Court
BUT a county court

Decorations

Purple Heart
Good Conduct Medal

Croix de Guerre
BUT Soldiers are given decorations to signal their acts of heroism.

Degrees (academic)

B.A.
D.D.
M.D.
Ph.D.

Districts

First Congressional District
BUT a congressional district
Educational Courses
English II
Spanish Grammar
Mathematics Made Easy
BUT He is studying physics and chemistry.

Epithets

First Lady of the State
Alexander the Great

Fleets

the Third Fleet
BUT The ship was part of the fleet.

Foundations

Carnegie Foundation
Ford Foundation
BUT He established a foundation.

Geographic Divisions

Lone Star State
Sooner State
BUT There are fifty states in our country.
Northern Hemisphere
South Pole
Old World
Near East
Government Divisions
Federal Reserve Board
the Boston Fire Department
BUT The department was headed by Mr. Charles Bleeker.

Historical Terms

Dark Ages
Renaissance
Christian Era
World War II
Battle of the Bulge
Declaration of Independence
Magna Carta

Holidays

Thanksgiving Day
Passover
Easter Sunday
New Year's Eve

Libraries

Carnegie Library
Albany Public Library
BUT The library is a source of information.

Localities

Western Europe
East Africa
Wheat Belt
West Side
Mississippi Delta

Military Services

United States Navy
Signal Corps
Second Battalion
Company B
Squadron 28

Nobility and Royalty

Queen of Belgium
BUT Many queens were honored here.
Duke of Windsor
BUT She was proud to have met a duke.

Oceans and Continents

Pacific Ocean
BUT He was glad to be crossing the ocean.

Parks

Greenleaf Park
Texoma State Park
Yellowstone National Park
BUT The park was in a southern state.

Personification

He was recognized by the Chair and
spoke briefly.
He sang about Summer in all its glory.
BUT In summer the days are longer.

Planets and Other Heavenly Bodies

Mars
Venus
Big Dipper
EXCEPTIONS: moon, sun, stars

Peoples and Tribes

Jews
Christians
Malay
Chickasaw

Rivers

Mississippi River
Wabash River
BUT The Mississippi and Wabash
rivers were flooding after the torrential
rains.

Sports Stadiums and Teams

Dallas Cowboys
Madison Square Garden
Super Bowl
Dodgers

Chapter 23

Pronunciation

Perfecting Your Speech

How you pronounce the words you choose to say can dramatically support—or undercut—the substance of what you're saying. Incorrect pronunciation or slurred enunciation reflects poorly on one's intelligence and ability. While this judgment may be unfair, it's reality: First impressions count. To make a favorable impression, try to perfect your speech.

Begin by carefully listening to the speech of others and comparing it with your own. What are the differences, especially between yourself and the people you most admire? Consult the dictionary when you hear differences to see whether you or the other person has made a mistake. This moment of truth will quickly improve your pronunciation and help you enlarge your vocabulary. It is one of the finest steps toward cultivation of improved speech patterns.

Following is a partial list of words often mispronounced; perhaps a vowel or a consonant sound is mispronounced, or a syllable is commonly dropped, added, or slurred. Sometimes letters that should be silent are sounded, or vice versa. Study the correct pronunciation carefully. You may be accustomed to pronouncing several of these words differently, but remember: Colloquial pronunciation is not preferable for business standards. Words followed by a double asterisk (**) denote that word is among the most mispronounced in the English language.

Word List

abject (ab' jekt)
absolutely (ab' so lute lee)
abstemious (ab stee' mee us)
absurd (ab serd')
accede (ak seed')
accept (ak sept')
accession (ak sesh' un)
accessories (ak sess' o reez)
accidentally (ak si den' tal e)
acclimate (a kly' mut)**
address (a dress' — both noun
    and verb)**

admirable (ad' ma ra bl)**
adult (a dult' — NOT add' ult)**
aerial (air' ree al)
ally (al ly' — verb; al' ly — noun)
applicable (ap' pli ka bl)**
architect (ar' ki tekt)
arctic (ark' tik)
area (air' ee a)
attacked (a takt')
attitude (at' i tyud)
attorney (a ter' nee)**
autopsy (aw' top see)**

avenue (av' a nyu)
aviation (ay vi ay' shun)

battery (bat' er e, NOT bat' tree)
being (pronounce the g)
beneficent (be neff' i sent)
bicycle (by' sik l)
biography (by og' ra fee)
breadth (bredth; pronounce the d)

casualty (cazh' ul tee)
champion (cham' pee un)
chastisement (chass tyze' ment)
chauffeur (show' ferr)**
chestnut (chess' nut)
chocolate (chock' o lut)
clique (kleek)**
comment (com' ment)
compromise (com' pro myze)
concave (con cayv')
concentrate (con' sen trayt)
concierge (con se arzh')**
condolence (con doe' lens)
conversant (con ver' sunt)**
convex (con vex')
corps (kor)
creek (kreek, NOT krik)
cruel (kroo' el)

data (day' tah)
deaf (def)
decade (deck' ayd)
decisive (dee sy' siv)
defect (de fekt)
deficit (def' i sit)
demonstrable (de mon' stra bl)
depot (dee' po)
depths (pronounce the th)
dessert (de zert')
detour (dee' toor)
diamond (dy' a mund)
distribute (dis trib' yute)
divide (di vyd')
doing (doo' ing pronounce the g)
drowned (drownd; one syllable,
   NOT drownded)

duly (dyu' lee)
duty (dyu' tee)

edition (eh dish' un)
educate (edd' yu kate)
elm (as written; NOT ellum)
envelop (verb—en vell' up)
envelope (noun—en' va lowp)
epitome (ee pitt' o mee)
equitable (ek' wi ta bl)**
era (ihr' a)
err (urr; rhymes with fur)
etiquette (ett' i kett)
every (ev' a ree)
exigency (eks' i jen see)
exponent (eks po' nent)
exquisite (eks' kwi zit)
extant (eks' tent)
extraordinary (eks tror' di ner ee)**

facts (pronounce the t)
family (fam' a lee)
fasten (fass' en)
favorite (fay' vo ritt)
figure (fig' yur)
film (as written; NOT fillum)
finance (verb: fi nans')**
finance (noun: fi' nans)
financial (fin nan' shul)
financier (fin nan seer')
forehead (for' id)
forte (for' tay)
formidable (for' mi da bl)**
fragmentary (frag' men ter ee)
friendship (frend' ship; pronounce the d)

genuine (jenn' yu inn)
gingham (ghing' um)
glisten (gliss' en)
gondola (gonn' do la)
government (guv' ern ment;
   pronounce both n's)
grievous (gree' vuss)
guardian (gar' dee un)

hasten (hayss' en)
height (hyt; does NOT end in *th*)
heinous (hay' nuss)**
herculean (herk yu lee' un)
heroism (her' o izm)
homeopathy (ho mee opp' a thee)
horizon (ho ryz' un)
hostile (hoss' til)**
hundred (as written; NOT hunnerd)

idea (eye dee' a)
ignoramus (ig no ray' muss)
immediate (im mee' dee ut)
impious (im' pee uss)
incognito (in cog nee' toe)
incomparable (in com' pa ra bl)
indictment (in dyt' ment)
industry (in' dus tree)**
inexorable (in eks' o ra bl)
inexplicable (in eks' pli ka bl)
infamous (in' fa muss)
inquiry (in kwy' ree)**
Iowa (I' o wah)
irrevocable (ir rev' o ka bl)**
Italian (Itt al' yun)
italics (ih tal' iks)

judiciary (joo dish' a ree)
just (as written; NOT jest)

knew (nyu)

lapel (la pel')
large (larj—NO *d* sound)
latent (lay' tent)
length (pronounce the *g*; NOT *lenth*)
library (as written; NOT ly' bay ree)
lieu (lyu)
lightning (lyt' ning; NOT lyt' en ning)
long-lived (long' lyvd')
longevity (lon jev' i tee)
luxury (luk' shu ree; NOT lug'
   shu ree)**
lyceum (ly see' um)

manufacture (man yu fakt' yur)
maturity (ma tyu' rit tee)

memorable (mem' uh ra bl)
mischievous (miss' cha vuss)**
municipal (myu niss' i pul)
museum (myu zee' um)

new (nyu)

oblique (o bleek')
office (off' fiss; NOT aw' fuss)
often (off' en)
on (as written; NOT awn)
ordeal (or deel')
osteopath (oss' tee o path)
osteopathy (oss tee opp' a thee)
overalls (as written; NOT over halls)

parade (pa rayd'; NOT prayd)
partner (as written; NOT pard' ner)
patron (pay' trun)
pecan (pe kon')
pecuniary (pee kyu' nee er ee)**
peremptory (per emp' te ree)
piano (pee an' o)
picture (pik' tyur)
pique (peek)
plumber (plum' er)
positively (poz' it tiv lee)
possess (po zess')
precedence (pre see' dens)**
preface (pref' iss)
preferable (pref' er a bl)
prescription (pre scrip' shun)
presentation (prez en tay' shun)

radiator (ray' dee ay tor)
radio (ray' dee o)
rambling (as written; NOT ram'
   bol ing)
realm (as written; NOT rellum)
recognize (rek' og nyz)
recourse (ree' cors)
refutable (re fyut' a bl)
reputable (rep' yut a bl)
research (re serch')
resources (ree sors' ez)
respite (res' pit)**

revocable (rev' o ka bl)**
robust (ro bust')**
romance (ro mans')
Roosevelt (Ro' za velt; NEVER
    Roose' a velt)**
route (root)

sagacious (sa gay' shuss)
schism (siz' em)
simultaneous (sy mul tay' nee uss)
short-lived (short' lyvde')**
slippery (as written; NOT slip' ree)
solace (sol' uss)**
solder (sod' er)
sphere (sfeer)**
status (stay' tuss)**
strictly (as written; NOT strick' li)
subpoena (sup pee' na)
subtle (sut' tl)
suit (sute)
superfluous (soo per' floo uss)
surprise (ser pryz')

telegrapher (tell egg' ra fer)
temperament (as written; NOT
    tem' per ment)**
tenet (ten' ett)
theater (thee' a ter)**

tract (as written; NOT track)**
trembling (as written; NOT
    trem' bol ing)
tremendous (tre men' dus)
tribune (trib' yun)
tube (tyub)
Tuesday (tyuz' day)**
tumult (tyu' mult)

umbrella (as written; NOT
    um ba rel' lah)**
usurp (yu serp')
Utica (yu' tik a)

vagary (va gair' ee)**
vehement (vee' a ment)**
vehicle (vee' ih kel)**
verbose (ver bowss')

was (wahz)
water (waw' ter)**
what (hwot; NOT wot)**
wheel (hweel; NOT weel)**
whether (hweth' er)**
white (hwyt)**
worsted (woos' ted)**
wrestle (res' l)

Chapter 24
Punctuation

Purpose of Punctuation

The sole purpose of punctuation is to make the text clear. If a mark of punctuation does not clarify the text, it should be omitted. Of course, you'll follow your boss's preference if he or she instructs you, for example, to insert more commas or semi-colons than today's magazines and newspapers typically use. When public changes occur, not every person immediately approves. But if a matter is left to your discretion, remember that the old tried-and-true comma rule also applies for many other marks of punctuation: "When in doubt, leave it out."

Nevertheless, there are still standards and formalities in punctuation that you must fully grasp, not only to satisfy your boss but also to help promote your own career. Once it leaves the office, your work speaks for itself. You want it to be a source of pride for both your employer and you.

Following is a list of punctuation marks with usage rules and examples for each.

The Period

A period is used at the end of a declarative sentence to denote a full pause:

I am going to town. You may go with me if you wish.

Use a period, not a question mark, when the sentence contains an indirect question:

He could not understand why she was leaving.

Also use a period for a request phrased as a question:

Will you please return the diskette when you are finished.

The period is used in decimals to separate a whole number from a decimal fraction:

5.6 percent
$19.50

It is also used in abbreviations:

Mrs.
Ph.D.
etc.

The Comma

The presence of a comma, or its absence, can cause different interpretations of a written sentence. It is thus of vast importance, particularly in legal documents.

Series

Commas are used to separate nouns in a series or adjectives in a series of the same rank modifying the same noun:

The workers picked cherries, peaches, and plums.
We swam in cool, clear, fresh water.

Some bosses may prefer to omit the comma before the *and* in such sentences unless it's needed for clarity.
Sometimes a term consisting of years, months, and days is considered not a series but a single unit of time. No commas are used:

Interest will be computed for 6 years 3 months and 2 days.

Compound and Complex Sentences

A comma is used between the clauses of a compound sentence:

John went to the theater, but he left before the play ended.

But do not confuse this with a compound predicate, which takes no comma:

John went to the theater but left before the play ended.

An adverbial clause usually follows the independent clause, and no comma is used. But for emphasis, the order of the clauses is sometimes transposed. Then a comma is used.

USUAL ORDER: John was met by a large delegation when he came home.
TRANSPOSED ORDER: When John came home, he was met by a large delegation.

Introductory Expressions

Introductory expressions, such as transitional words and phrases, mild exclamations, and other independent expressions, are set off by a comma when they occur alone at the beginning of a sentence:

> Yes, I will go.
> Well, perhaps she is right.
> Nevertheless, I wish he had waited for me.
> To tell the truth, I think you should go.
> As a rule, he arrives very early.

A few introductory expressions are more emphatic without punctuation, however, and need not be followed by a comma:

> Doubtless she just couldn't be here.
> At least you tried.
> Undoubtedly the plane's engines both failed.
> Indeed you may bring your friends with you.

To distinguish between the two, ask whether you naturally pause after the word or words in question. A comma is used to signal the natural pause.

Other Transitional Words

A comma is used to set off the transitional words *however, therefore,* and *moreover* when used within the sentence or as the first or last word of the sentence:

> Jean may not arrive until noon, however.
> Her problem, therefore, must be solved at once.
> I will be there, moreover, as soon as I can.

Sometimes *though* is used to mean *however* and should be set off with commas:

> I will be there, though, if at all possible.

Prepositional Phrases

No comma is used for prepositional phrases within a sentence unless the phrase comes between the subject and the predicate of the clause:

> I am sure that because of your generosity we will be able to build the new dormitory.
> The bag, in addition to a hatbox, will be sent to you today.

Contrasting Phrases

Contrasting expressions within a sentence are set off by commas:

> The lion, not the tiger, growled.
> We walk slowly, never quickly, to the garage.
> This letter was meant for you, not for me.
> BUT This letter was meant for you but not for me.

Nonrestrictive Modifiers

Nonrestrictive modifiers are phrases or clauses that could be omitted without affecting the meaning of the main clause. These should be set off from the rest of the sentence by a comma or by parenthetical commas:

> John, my favorite friend, is visiting me.
> That car is, I believe, a new model.
> Mary Brown, who lives next door, is in the third grade.
> BUT That is the girl who lives next door.

Infinitive Phrases

An infinitive phrase used independently is set off by commas:

> The color is too dark, to list one fault.

If the phrase is used as a modifier, it is not punctuated:

> The piano is too large to fit in the room.

Dialogue

A comma is used to separate a dialogue quotation from the main sentence:

> "Please go with me," the boy said.
> "What do you think," Mr. Bleeker asked, "the Mayor will do next?"

Commas also separate the name of the person addressed in dialogue from the remainder of the sentence:

> "Will you come with me, John?"
> "But, Jane, how do you know that the plane is late?"

A confirming question within a sentence is set off by commas:

> "He left, did he not, on the noon plane?"

Repeated Words

A comma is used for clarity and to avoid confusion when the same word is repeated:

Whoever goes, goes without my consent.

Omission

When words are omitted in one part of a sentence because they were used in a previous part, a comma is used to show where the words were omitted:

Sam's first car was a Cadillac, and mine, a Ford.

Transposed Adjective Order

An adjective normally precedes the noun it modifies. When an adjective follows a noun, the adjective is set off by commas; when an adjective precedes a noun but also precedes the article before the noun, a comma follows the adjective:

The physician, dignified and competent, told them the bad news.
Dignified and competent, the physician told them the bad news.

Numbers

A comma is used in writing large numbers, separating the thousands digits from the hundreds, the millions digits from the thousands, and so forth:

249,586
1,345,000

A comma is used to separate two or more unrelated numbers:

On August 1, 1992, 437 people visited the museum.
Out of eighty, twenty were discarded.

Do not forget the second comma when the date occurs in the middle of the sentence:

She left for England on June 22, 1993, and returned a month later.

However, it is acceptable if your boss prefers no commas at all:

She left for England on June 22 1993 and returned a month later.

Addresses

Elements of an address are set off by commas:

> He lives at 410 Hawthorne Street, Chicago, Illinois, near the University of Chicago campus.

> On an envelope address, there is no comma between the state and the zip code.

Titles

A comma is used to separate a name and a title:

> The letter was from Mrs. Masterson, our President, and contained a list of instructions.

Set off *Jr.* and *Sr.* from a proper name by a comma. A Roman numeral is not set off by a comma:

> Philip W. Thompson, Sr.
> Philip W. Thompson III

Degrees are also set off by a comma:

> Jennifer Galt, M.D.

But descriptive titles are not:

> Attila the Hun

Company Names

Company names consisting of a series of names omit the last comma in the series:

> Pate, Tate and Waite

When "and Company" completes a series of names, the last comma is also omitted:

> Pate, Tate, Waite and Company

Set off *Incorporated* from the name of a company by a comma:

> Johnson Brothers, Incorporated

The Question Mark

A question mark closes a question:

What time is it?

A question mark is used to express a doubt:

He is older (?) than she.

If the question is indirect, no question mark is used:

I wonder whether he will be here.

When a question is asked in the middle of a sentence, the question is enclosed by commas and the sentence ends with a question mark:

They are arriving, aren't they, on the noon train?

When the question is enclosed in parentheses, the question mark is inside the parentheses, not at the end of the sentence:

The magazine (did you see it?) describes the city in great detail.

If the question mark is part of a quotation, it is placed inside the closing quotation mark; if it is not a part of the quotation, it is placed outside the closing quotation mark:

The statement ended, "And is that all?"
What did she mean by "jobless years"?

If the last word in a question is an abbreviation and thus contains a period, the question mark is also used:

Do you think he will arrive by 4 P.M.?

When it is desired to make a question of a statement, the question mark is used:

He is arriving today?
Really?

The Exclamation Point

An exclamation point is used when making extravagant claims or to express deep feeling:

> Here is the finest car on the market!
> The announcement was unbelievable!

An exclamation point is used after a word or phrase charged with emotion:

> Quick! We don't want to be late.

It is also used for double emphasis:

> Did you catch that innuendo!

CAUTION: Some people get into the habit of using exclamation points far too often to express strong emotion, and they end up blunting the very purpose of the punctuation. For effective writing, show emotion through the choice of words instead, and reserve exclamation points for only the strongest of feelings.

The Semicolon

A semicolon is used when the conjunction is omitted between parts of a compound sentence:

> I went with them; I should have stayed at home.

A semicolon precedes words such as *however, moreover,* or *otherwise* when they introduce the second of two connected full sentences:

> She is arriving at noon; however, she will not stay long.

If parts of a series contain inner punctuation such as a comma, the parts are separated by a semicolon:

> He came to see his mother, who was ill; his sister, who lived in the next town; and his old schoolmate.

The Colon

Introducing a List or Quotation

The colon generally follows a sentence introducing a tabulation or a long quotation.

The following quotation is from the *Detroit Free Press:* "Regardless of what may be accomplished, the company will still be involved."

During your first year, you will study such subjects as these: algebra, physics, chemistry, and psychology.

EXCEPTION: When the tabulated list is the object of a verb or a preposition, a colon is never used:

During your first year, you will study algebra, physics, chemistry, and psychology.

Emphasis or Anticipation

The colon is also used to stress a word, phrase, or clause that follows it or when a sentence creates anticipation for what immediately follows:

The newspaper published a startling statement: the city had been completely destroyed by fire.

Time

The colon is used to separate hours and minutes in expressions of time:

4:15 A.M. CST

Titles

The colon is used to separate a title from a subtitle:

Gone With the Wind: A Story of the Old South

Quotation Marks

Quoted Materials

Double quotation marks are used to set off any material quoted within a sentence or paragraph. If the quoted material consists of several paragraphs, the opening quotation mark is used at the beginning of the quotation and at the beginning of each paragraph within the quotation; a closing quotation mark, however, is used only at the conclusion of the quotation. It is not used at the end of each paragraph within the quotation, as many people mistakenly think. For the sake of brevity, each paragraph in the following example is only one sentence long, which would not normally occur in well-constructed writing:

The passage he read aloud was from the first chapter:
"The discovery of this energy brings us to the problem of how to allow it to be used.

"The use of atomic power throws us back to the Greek legend of Prometheus and the age-old question of whether force should be exerted against law.

"The man of today must decide whether he will use this power for destruction or for peaceful purposes."

When he had finished the reading, there was loud applause.

Quotations Within Quotations

Single quotation marks indicate a quotation within the quotation:

He said, "Did you hear John make the statement, 'I will not go with her,' or were you not present at the time he spoke?"

Titles

In printed text, the titles of essays, articles, poems, stories, or chapters are set off within quotation marks; titles of plays, books, and periodical publications are italicized:

The name of the article was "I Believe."
The title of the book was *Journey Into Night*.
It was first published in *Harper's Magazine*.

Quotation Marks and Punctuation

Place quotation marks outside the comma and the period:

"Don't stop now," he said, "when you have so little left to finish."

Place quotation marks inside the colon and the semicolon:

He called her a "little witch"; that was right after she broke his model plane.

Place quotation marks outside an exclamation point or a question mark when the quoted material alone is an exclamation or a question:

"I passed my test!"

Place quotation marks inside an exclamation point or a question mark when the quoted material alone is not an exclamation or a question:

Didn't he claim to be "too tired"?

The Apostrophe

Contractions

As a mark of omission, the apostrophe may denote that a word has been contracted intentionally:

> It's time to go.
> Haven't you finished the task?

Possession

To show possession, use an apostrophe followed by an *s* after a singular noun:

> the city's founder

Use it alone after plural nouns ending in *s:*

> the books' titles

Plural nouns not ending in *s* form the possessive by adding an apostrophe and an *s:*

> men's clubs
> sheep's clothing

The plural of compound nouns and joint possessive nouns is formed by adding an apostrophe followed by an *s* to the second word only:

> the Secretary-Treasurer's decision
> Mary and John's cassette player

But if the items are separately owned, the compound nouns each add an apostrophe followed by an *s:*

> Mary's and John's coats

No apostrophe is used with possessive pronouns:

> his
> hers
> its
> yours
> ours
> theirs

The apostrophe is used to express duration of time:

a day's traveling time
twelve months' duration

For a proper name ending in *s,* use an apostrophe followed by an *s:*

Lewis's hat
Miss Bliss's book

Two proper names are traditionally observed as exceptions:

Moses' robe
Jesus' parable

For plural proper names ending in *s,* use an apostrophe only:

The Joneses' boots were left in the hall.

The Dash

The dash (in typing, indicated by two hyphens) is used to introduce an added thought:

I shall go with you—you don't mind, do you?

The dash also breaks the continuity of a thought:

"The Scherzo Sonata" by Tolstoi is a sad story—but the writing is magnificent.

It is sometimes used before and after a parenthetical expression in place of commas:

Henry Higgins—bareheaded and without a coat—left the house and ran down the road.

Ellipses

To show omission of words in quoted material, three spaced dots (ellipses) are used if material is deleted within the sentence. When the last part of a quoted sentence is omitted, it is followed by its punctuation plus three spaced dots. At the end of the quotation, only the punctuation is used:

"Five hundred firemen . . . attended the ball. . . .
Mr. Brown went on to say: "The shoe department functions smoothly. . . . Many salespeople have won prizes for efficiency."

Ellipsis dots may also be used to mark a thought expressed hesitantly:

He said, "If . . . if I do go with you, will you return early?"

Parentheses

Parentheses are used to enclose matter that is introduced by way of explanation:

If the lessor (the person owning the property) agrees, the lessee (the person renting the property) may have a dog on the premises.

Parentheses are used to enclose figures that enumerate items:

The book contained chapters on (1) capitalization, (2) spelling rules, (3) troublesome verbs, and (4) punctuation.

They are also used to enclosed citations of authority:

The definition of action is "the process or state of being active (*American College Dictionary*)."

And they are used to enclose figures repeated for clarity, as in legal documents:

He was willed five thousand dollars ($5,000) by his uncle.
You will be paid twenty (20) percent interest.

Italics

Italics are sometimes used for emphasis:

Notice where you *are,* not where you *have been.*

But the best writing avoids italics for this purpose, depending on choice of language to bring out the emphasis.

As mentioned earlier, italics are used for the names of books, pamphlets, and periodicals:

Saturday Evening Post
Black Beauty
Washington Daily News

The names of ships are italicized but not abbreviations in front of them.

Sea Witch
USS *Heinz*

NOTE: When using a typewriter and not a word processor or computer, indicate italics by underlining.

Sea Witch
USS Heinz
Washington Daily News

Chapter 25

Numerals

Words or Figures?

Your main concern with numbers is whether to spell them out in words or to express them in figures. As so often happens with matters of English usage, there are many times when both forms are correct, and you will regularly come across variations not covered in a book of rules, so use your discretion. Clarity is always your strongest guideline.

Printed Text

Prose Text

Generally, in prose text, numbers under 101 are spelled out, and numbers over 101 are shown in figures. The more formal the text is, the greater is the tendency to express the number in words.

In printed text, a number used for comparison with other numbers in the same section should be in numerical form:

An excavation of 500 feet can be finished as rapidly as 200 feet if the right equipment is used.

At the Beginning of a Sentence

A number appearing at the beginning of a sentence, if it can be expressed in one or two words, should be spelled out:

Sixteen new cars were delivered.
Thirty or forty bushels were needed.
NOT 2,746,892 copies were purchased.

The last example should be rewritten so that the figure appears later in the sentence:

The company purchased 2,746,892 copies.

Legal Documents

In legal documents, numbers are written in both words and figures to prevent misunderstanding, and the same is true in papers that transfer land title:

> The west thirty (30) feet of Lot Nine (9) in Block Four (4) . . .

Round Numbers

Approximate round numbers are spelled out:

> The station is about fifty blocks away.
> He found nearly two thousand dollars.

Sets of Numbers

To differentiate two sets of numbers occurring in the same sentence, use words for one and figures for the other:

> Three of the men drove 2,000 miles each; four drove 3,000 miles each; and only one drove the complete 5,000 miles.

If the sentence cannot be rewritten, use a comma or dash to separate the numbers:

> During the year 1992, 20 million people visited the park.
> We received 1,213, 113 of which . . .

Large Numbers

As a general rule, write out numbers up to and including one hundred, and use figures for numbers over one hundred. But for large numbers, if a number can be written as one or two words, do so:

> four hundred
> five million
> two billion

Use the short form for writing numbers over a thousand not pertaining to money:

> fourteen hundred
> NOT one thousand four hundred

Large, even amounts may combine figures and words:

production of 37 million paper clips
a budget of $146 billion

If a figure or the word several precedes *hundred, thousand, million, billion,* and so on, the singular form is used. After *many,* the plural form is used:

six hundred pages
several million years
many hundreds of pages

Separating Digits

All numbers above 999 are written with commas to separate every group of three digits, counting from the units place:

1,001
123,000
1,436,936

EXCEPTIONS: Commas are omitted in long decimal fractions, page numbers, addresses, telephone numbers, room numbers, and form numbers:

.10356
Page 3487
1467 Wilshire Boulevard
(201) 555-9088
Room 2630
Form 2317-A

Commas are also omitted in four-digit year numbers, but they are added for years with five or more digits:

The company began in 1992.
The pottery shards were dated at about 14,000 B.C.
This science fiction novel takes place in the year 27,345 A.D.

Patent numbers are written with commas:

Patent No. 3,436,987

But serial numbers are written without commas:

Motor Number 245889954
Policy Number 894566

Dollars and Cents

Figures

Use figures for money:

> 1 cent
> 5 cents
> 20,000 dollars OR $20,000

However, as with other numbers, amounts of money are always written out when beginning a sentence:

> One cent was contributed by each child.
> NOT 1 ¢ was contributed by each child.

A series of prices is written in figures only:

> These were shoes priced at $50, $60, and $85.

Dollar and Cent Signs

Use the dollar sign before the number, not the word *dollar* or *dollars* after the number:

> The duplex rents for $700 per month.

If a large number combines figures and words, use the dollar sign before the figure:

> The budget called for $850 billion.
> NOT The budget calls for 850 million dollars.

Repeat the dollar sign with successive numbers:

> The bonds could be purchased in denominations of $10,000, $12,000, $15,000, and $20,000.

EXCEPTION: Omit all but the first dollar sign when numbers are in tabulated form:

> The bonds could be purchased in denominations of the following amounts:
> $10,000
>   12,000
>   15,000
>   20,000

The dollar sign is not used when the figure given is in cents alone. Use the cent sign (¢) after amounts less than one dollar, but never use the cent sign with a decimal point:

25¢
NOT .25¢, for that would mean one-fourth of a cent

EXCEPTION: The only time the dollar sign is used when the figure is in cents alone is in statistical work when the part of the dollar is carried out to more than two decimal places:

$0.3564

Decimal Points

Decimal points are another way of writing fractions, especially large fractions. When a decimal occurs with no unit before it, use a cipher for quick interpretation:

a 0.75-yard measurement
rainfall of 0.356 inch

Sometimes the fraction is part of a dollar. When the amount of dollars given is not followed by cents, omit the decimal point and the ciphers:

$3
$1,200
BUT $17.75

The decimal point and ciphers are not used with even amounts of money unless in tabulated form. If tabulated, and some amounts contain cents and some do not, the even amounts should contain ciphers:

$19.36
  5.00
  2.14
 37.00
  1.23
   .19
   .02

Time

When a figure and a word come together as an adjective to express time, connect the two with a hyphen:

a 24-hour day
BUT a day of 24 hours
two 2-year 12-percent notes
BUT two notes for two years at 12 percent

Hours, minutes, and seconds are separated by a colon:

10:05:02 A.M.

Never use "this A.M." instead of "this morning." With A.M. or P.M. the word *o'clock* should not be used:

I will meet you at 4 P.M.
I will meet you at four o'clock this afternoon.

Ciphers after the number of the hour are unnecessary. For exact noon and midnight, it is correct to use the words:

I will meet you at noon.
The horn blew at midnight.

Dates

The day is written in numerals, without *th, st,* or *d,* unless the day is written before the name of the month:

May 1, 1995
NOT May 1st, 1995
BUT On the 2d of June 1994
In the August 21 and September 3 editions (NOT 21st or 3d)

In legal documents, dates are spelled out:

the twelfth day of May, A.D. Nineteen Hundred and Ninety-Five

The Hyphen

Written-out numbers below one hundred are hyphenated:

thirty-three
ninety-nine
twenty-seven

Hundreds and thousands are not hyphenated:

six hundred thousand
three hundred million

When modifying a noun, numbers are hyphenated, as are any compound adjectives:

a five-thousand-foot mountain
a three-foot rule

Fractions of less than one are hyphenated:

one-third
three-quarters
BUT one twenty-third

Mixed numbers are not hyphenated between the whole number and the fraction, both when written as words and figures:

one and one-half
12¾

Do not write one part of the fraction as a numeral and the other as a word:

one-fourth-inch bolt
NOT 1 fourth-inch bolt

When a mixed number is the subject of a sentence, the noun is plural. However, the verb is singular because the quantity is considered as a single unit:

1⅝ inches is needed
2¾ miles is the length of the track

Age

Use the general rule in giving the age of a person or a period of time (write out up to and including one hundred; use figures over one hundred):

She is twelve years old.
He has held the same position for twenty-six years.
She is now 105 years of age.
The company has been in this city for 102 years.

In compound adjectives denoting age, the words designating time may be used before *old*, but in that event the words *year* and *day* must appear in the singular:

a 12-week-old baby elephant
a 6-month-old pony

a 200-year-old building
a 3-day-old kitten

Dimensions

The signs reserved for technical writing are ' for *feet*, " for *inches*, and × for *by:*

9' × 12' (9 feet by 12 feet)
8" × 10" (8 inches by 10 inches)

In regular prose text, write out the word *by* for ×.
    Ciphers can be used to indicate exact measurement if they improve clarity:

9'0" × 12'0" × 20'6"

Weights and Measures

Abbreviations are used without capitalization:

6 lb. 3 oz.
OR 6 pounds 3 ounces
192 bbl.
OR 192 barrels

In a compound adjective showing a weight or a measure, the numeral is hyphenated to a singular noun:

600-mile-an-hour speed
BUT speed of 600 miles an hour
a 40-hour workweek
BUT a workweek of 40 hours

Percentages

The numeral is retained whether or not a percentage sign is used:

a 5% price reduction
a loss of 10 percent
almost 30 percent of the population

For percentages in succession, use the sign after each numeral:

30% to 50%
6%, 8%, and 10%

Page Numbering

For all page numbering, use figures to show the numbers. Commas are not used in page numbers greater than 999.

Page Number Formats

On legal documents, a page number is centered at the bottom of each page; on other papers, it is usually shown at the top. Manuscripts and briefs are numbered in the upper right corner; papers that are to be bound at the left are numbered in the lower right corner. In each case, all numbers should appear at exactly the same place on all pages.

Title pages are not numbered. A first page of a work or of a chapter is not marked with a number, although the numbering of the following pages takes into consideration the number of the first page.

It is acceptable to use a short dash before and after the page number, -3-, without a period. Never use quotation marks and never type the word *page* before the number. Frequently, the number stands alone—2—without a period.

The Abbreviation for *Number*

The abbreviation for *number, no.,* or the number sign— # —is usually omitted:

Building 38
NOT Building No. 38
Invoice 3457
NOT Invoice #3457
Page 92
NOT page no. 92

In text, however, it may be convenient to use the abbreviation:

When he came to No. 16, he halted.
The only houses to be painted this year are No. 16, 17, and 18.

Plurals of Numbers

Form the plural of a numeral or other character by adding *s* or *es* to the word. If the number is a figure, use the *s* or *'s* as your boss prefers:

5s and 6s OR 5's and 6's
fives and sixes
the 1990s OR the 1990's
DC-8Bs OR DC-8B's

Roman Numerals

Roman numerals are often used in outlines and some dates. Here are the most commonly used Roman numerals:

Arabic	*Roman*	*Arabic*	*Roman*
1	I	40	XL
2	II	50	L
3	III	60	LX
4	IV	70	LXX
5	V	80	LXXX
6	VI	90	XC
7	VII	100	C
8	VIII	150	CL
9	IX	200	CC
10	X	300	CCC
11	XI	400	CD
12	XII	500	D
13	XIII	600	DC
14	XIV	700	DCC
15	XV	800	DCCC
16	XVI	900	CM
17	XVII	1,000	M
18	XVIII	1,500	MD
19	XIX	2,000	MM
20	XX	3,000	MMM
30	XXX		

A dash over a Roman numeral multiples it by 1,000:

4,000	MMMM or M$\overline{\text{V}}$	100,000	$\overline{\text{C}}$
5,000	$\overline{\text{V}}$	1,000,000	$\overline{\text{M}}$
6,000	$\overline{\text{VI}}$		

Use these forms for dates:

1900	MCM	1960	MCMLX
1910	MCMX	1970	MCMLXX
1920	MCMXX	1980	MCMLXXX
1930	MCMXXX	1990	MCMXC
1940	MCMXL	2000	MM
1950	MCML		

Section Five
Financial
Activities

Financial activities such as bookkeeping and banking are common responsibilities for many secretaries.

Chapter 26

Bookkeeping and Accounting

Financial Record Keeping

Bookkeeping and accounting are fields requiring special training. Smaller companies may assign these duties to the secretary, especially with today's new computerized accounting programs. Larger companies typically have an in-house accounting department or contract for the services of an accountant to prepare tax statements and other important records. Even so, it's useful to familiarize yourself with the simple mechanics of bookkeeping and accounting no matter what size company you work for. The more informed you are, the more valuable you are to the company.

Property Rights

Assets

Property owned by a business organization and used in its operation is known as **assets.** The proprietor or owner of the business may be one person, two persons (in a partnership), half a dozen persons, or numerous persons operating a corporation. The interest of the owner or proprietor in the assets of the business is called **proprietorship, net worth,** or **capital.** If the business is free of claims against these assets, except for those of the proprietor, then assets equals proprietorship. For example, if John King purchased a stationery store for $10,000, his financial condition would be expressed in this way: Assets $10,000 equal proprietorship $10,000.

Liabilities

A business owner may obtain additional property by borrowing money to purchase the property needed or by purchasing the property with a promise to pay for that property at some future date. Those from whom business owners borrow are known as **creditors.** The creditor has a claim on the property until the proprietor pays in accordance with an agreement. This claim is known as the **liabilities** of the business.

For example, Mary Brown borrows $5,000 from a bank to enlarge the building used for her dry cleaning establishment. The bank thus becomes her creditor. This $5,000 increase in Brown's assets is accompanied by the bank's corresponding claim on her assets until the borrowed $5,000 is repaid. To fill the newly enlarged building, Brown purchases additional equipment and merchandise from the American Dry Cleaning Equipment Company amounting to $5,000; the American Dry Cleaning Company thus becomes another creditor. If Brown fails to pay this $5,000, the company can enforce its claim by legal action; this potential claim of the company on Brown's assets is another liability.

Assets of a business are, therefore, subject to two kinds of claims: (1) those arising from the rights of creditors and (2) those arising from the rights of the proprietor. The sum of these rights is equal to the value of the assets. Thus, assets equal liabilities plus proprietorship.

Effect of Business Transactions

The proprietor must know the effect of all business transactions on his or her assets, liabilities, and proprietorship in order to make decisions regarding future operations. Accounts furnish the proprietor with a record for this purpose, which is why it's critical that accounts be concrete, precise, and accurate.

For example, if the proprietor is considering hiring additional sales associates, he or she should know the results of the existing sales force to be able to estimate the probable results of hiring additional personnel. If the proprietor is considering purchasing additional merchandise, equipment, or space, attention should be given to the results from existing facilities.

The efficient proprietor is always seeking information concerning the effect of past operations in order to plan future operations. Such plans are known as **budgets.** Therefore, the primary purpose of accounting records is to give the proprietor information concerning the nature of his or her liabilities and proprietorship, as well as to furnish a concrete record of the effect of the business operation on these.

The purposes of accounting are to (1) record, (2) analyze and classify, and (3) summarize the activities of the business and their effects on each enterprise. Accounting simply reduces to writing the activities of a business.

Accounting Statements

Accounting statements (1) list a description of and amounts of property, together with ownership rights, and (2) report the effects of the operations on the owner's equity.

The first statement is known as the **balance sheet** (Figure 26-1). The balance sheet shows the assets, together with the rights of the creditors and the rights of

Figure 26-1. Balance sheet.

BALANCE SHEET

November 30, 19X3

Current assets

Cash on hand and in bank	$ 4,000	
Merchandise inventory	90,000	
Accounts receivable	6,000	
Total current assets		$100,000

Fixed assets

Real estate—land		18,000
Real estate—building		
Original cost	$64,000	
Less depreciation	3,000	61,000
Furniture, fixtures, and equipment		
Original cost	$12,000	
Less depreciation	600	
		11,400

Total assets		$190,400

Current liabilities

Accounts payable	$32,000	
Notes payable	16,000	
Total current liabilities		$ 48,000

Long-term debt		22,000
Capital		120,400
Total liabilities and capital		$190,400

the proprietor. The second statement is known as the **income statement** or **profit-and-loss statement** (Figure 26-2). It shows income and costs of operation, with the resulting increase or decrease in proprietorship. The balance sheet shows the financial condition of the business at a given time; the income statement covers the periods between any two balance sheets.

These summaries are interesting to persons other than the proprietor. When the owner of the business wishes to borrow money from a bank, the bank officers, in order to judge the owner's ability to repay the loan, ask for information con-

Figure 26-2. Profit-and-loss statement.

PROFIT-AND-LOSS STATEMENT

November 30, 19X3

Sales		$200,000
Cost of sales		140,000
Gross income		60,000
Operating expenses		
Selling expenses	$25,000	
General expenses	10,000	
Operating expenses		35,000
Operating income		25,000
Other expense		
Interest expense		1,200
Net income before taxes		23,800
Income taxes		6,600
Net income		$17,200

cerning the assets and liabilities and the profits earned in previous periods. Creditors request the same information before selling merchandise on account. The Internal Revenue Service (IRS) also requires a similar statement to be assured that the income tax for the coming year is being estimated properly.

Assets

A large business has hundreds and even thousands of assets to list; these are classified as current assets, fixed assets, and deferred charges to expenses.

Current assets appear in the form of cash or items that may reasonably be expected to be converted into cash in the near future by the regular operation of the business. This includes stocks, bonds, mutual funds, and other negotiable financial instruments. When listed on the balance sheet, these assets are arranged in the order in which they will be converted. Columns are also provided to show the quantity, description, price, and extensions. When all these sheets are extended and totaled, their sum is entered on the balance sheet as merchandise inventory.

Fixed assets are those of a permanent (or fixed) nature that will not be converted into cash as long as they serve the needs of the business. They are not intended for resale but are expected to wear out in the course of the business. They include store equipment, office equipment, delivery equipment, building, and land.

Deferred charges to expenses are assets purchased for use in the business that will be consumed in the near future—for example, store supplies, office supplies, and prepaid insurance.

Liabilities

The classification commonly used for liabilities is similar to that for assets: current liabilities, fixed liabilities, and deferred credits to income.

Current liabilities are those that will be due within a short time. For example, if John King purchases equipment on account with the agreement that he will pay for it within thirty days, this transaction results in a current liability. A liability is considered to be a current one if it comes due within one year after the balance sheet date. Under this heading are notes payable, accounts payable, and accrued liabilities.

Notes payable are promises given by the proprietor to someone to whom he or she owes money. The proprietor may give these to a creditor from whom he or she has purchased equipment or merchandise, or to a bank when borrowing money.

Accounts payable are the financial obligations of a business, usually arising from a purchase on account, when the buyer has given his or her promise to pay at some future time for the goods received.

Accrued liabilities are amounts owed to the government on taxes, to employees on wages, or to creditors on interest. If one of these is unusually high, it may be set up singly under some designation such as "taxes payable," "wages payable," and so forth.

Fixed liabilities are those that will not be due for a comparatively long time after they are contracted. They usually arise in the purchase of fixed assets and include liabilities that will not be liquidated within one year from the date of the balance sheet—for example, mortgages payable or bonds payable.

A **mortgage payable** represents a debt owed by a business for which the creditor possesses a mortgage on a particular asset.

Bonds payable are long-term obligations of corporations commonly evidenced by bonds, a debt to be paid more than one year hence.

Deferred credits to income are the unearned portion of a payment when a business is paid in advance for a service. For example, an insurance company receives in one fiscal period a payment for insurance that extends over a future fiscal period. The unearned portion of the premium is a deferred credit to income and would usually be listed as unearned premium income.

The Balance Sheet

Usually the purpose of any business is to increase its proprietorship—that is, to make money. The amount of profit or loss incurred during a given period is the most important single fact.

A balance sheet (see Figure 26-1) shows the proprietor the amount of his or her proprietorship to help determine whether the proprietorship is increasing or decreasing; it does not, however, show the cause of the increase or decrease.

The Income Statement

At various intervals, the proprietor has to plan to increase profit and eliminate future losses. For this, a report is needed to show the amount of sales, the cost of procuring and selling the goods that are sold, and the difference between the two, which is the **profit** or **loss.** The income statement (see Figure 26-2) gives such information, as well as the gross profit on sales, operating expenses, and depreciation. The period it covers is known as the **fiscal period.**

Income Statement Terms

There are a variety of important terms included on an income statement that need some explanation.

- **Sales.** The gross return from operations. Different businesses use different terms for their sales, depending on whether the business sells commodities or services. For example, sales in a mercantile business are the total amount of money customers have paid or agreed to pay for merchandise sold to them. Airlines have passenger revenue or freight revenue, whereas professional men and women have fees. Investment trusts have interest income and dividend income.

- **Cost of goods sold.** The purchase price paid by a business for the goods it has sold, as distinguished from the sales price. Cost of goods sold is made up of (1) the price charged by the seller as shown on the invoice of sale and (2) the shipping and handling charged for the delivery of the goods.

- **Gross profit on sales.** Derived by subtracting the cost of merchandise sold from the total sales, representing the profit that would be made if no expenses were incurred in conducting the business. Because expenses are always incurred, they must be considered in determining profit. The expenses of operating the business must be deducted to obtain the net profit.

- **Operating expenses.** Include all commodities and services expended in the operation of a business: services of personnel, paper and twine, electricity, fuel, postage, and so forth.

- **Depreciation.** The cost arising from the decrease in value of the fixed assets. Not only are supplies and services used to operate a business, but fixed assets, such as office equipment and store equipment, are gradually worn out through use.

The income statement shows the result of the operations of a specific business during a particular period of time. It lists the income from sales and subtracts from this the expenses of the business in making such sales. The last figure is the net profit from operations.

The Account

Each time a business performs a transaction, a change is made in one or more elements of the equation "assets equal liabilities plus proprietorship." Regardless of the number of transactions, the results of all changes must be ascertained in order to prepare an accurate balance sheet and an accurate income statement at the end of the fiscal period. To accomplish this, each transaction must be recorded as it occurs. The account is the method used to record these individual transactions, and it is from this word that the subject of accounting receives its name.

The Account Record

The **account** is the record of each item entered on the balance sheet and on the income statement—that is, the increases and decreases that occur. In its simplest form, the account provides (1) the name of the customer, (2) transactions decreasing the amount of proprietorship, and (3) transactions increasing the amount of the same item.

The Ledger

The **ledger** is a book containing a group of accounts. It contains a page for each account, or several pages if the account is large. A separate account is maintained for each entry on the balance sheet and the income statement. Accounts are arranged in the ledger in the same order in which they are listed on the accounting statements. Current asset accounts precede fixed asset accounts, and all asset accounts come before liability accounts. Proprietorship accounts are listed last. Loose leaf ledgers should be used, so that new accounts may be inserted alphabetically.

Trial Balance

If the bookkeeper has correctly recorded each transaction, the total of all the debits in all the accounts will equal the total of the credits in all the accounts. A test is made at intervals, usually at the end of the month, to check whether the debits do equal the credits; this test, known as a **trial balance,** summarizes the ledger information. If the sum of the debits does not equal the sum of the credits, an error has been made, and then the bookkeeper has the job of reconciling.

Mixed Accounts

If all transactions recorded in the accounts coincide with the accounting period as shown on the balance sheet and the income statement, the trial balance is a satisfactory check. But it is impossible to arrange transactions so that there will be no carry-overs between accounting periods. A means must therefore be provided to meet this condition; this is called a **mixed account:** an account with a balance that is partly a balance sheet amount and partly an income statement amount.

For example, the trial balance amount for the account called Office Supplies summarizes all office supplies purchased plus those on hand at the beginning of the period covered. To find out how many office supplies have been used during the accounting period, an inventory of office supplies is taken. The office supplies on hand are a balance sheet entry; the office supplies used are an income statement entry. Therefore the account Office Supplies is a mixed account.

The adjustment of mixed accounts must determine the correct balance sheet amount and the correct income statement amount for any trial balance entry that is mixed. For example, a typewriter is recorded as an asset at the time of purchase and appears in the trial balance. The depreciation of the typewriter is not recorded each day and must, instead, be recorded by an adjustment at the end of the accounting period.

Other types of business operations continually affect accounts, for example, as insurance expires and wages and salaries accrue. It's necessary to record all such mixed accounts. A purchase of office supplies is debited to the asset account Office Supplies, or it can be debited to the expense account Office Supplies Used. By means of an account for Office Supplies Used or Expired Insurance, the adjustment can be made. This is an asset adjustment. A liability adjustment is made similarly.

Adjusted Trial Balance

The trial balance summarizes only transactions during the accounting period. Insurance has expired, supplies have been used in operating the business, office and other salaries are incomplete, and equipment has depreciated. The adjustments must be combined with trial balance amounts by means of an **adjusted trial balance.**

Payroll

A good bookkeeping system must provide accurate information concerning the payroll. Because of Social Security laws, income-tax-withholding laws, and other state and federal regulations, any and all of this information must be instantly available. Therefore, an individual payroll record book should be maintained (Figure 26-3).

The following information is needed for accurate and complete payroll accounting:

- ☐ Name of employee, with address and personal data
- ☐ Social Security number
- ☐ Company number (if any)
- ☐ Department number (if any)

☐ Date employment began and ended (and reason for separation)

☐ Dates worked, rate of pay, hours per day worked, regular and overtime status

☐ Regular salaries paid if not on hourly basis

☐ Deductions (federal withholding tax, Social Security taxes, state and local taxes, medical insurance premiums, union dues, retirement plan contributions, etc.)

☐ Totals by month, quarter, and year

Travel-and-Entertainment and Auto-Expense Records

If your boss travels as part of the job, he or she may ask your help in maintaining a record of travel and entertainment expenses. If the boss uses his or her personal vehicle for business travel, you'll need to maintain a vehicle expense record as well. The IRS requires detailed records with documentary evidence for each, especially for expenses over the "standard amounts" it specifies. Such records should be accurate.

Travel and Entertainment Expenses

Records for all travel and entertainment expenses should show:

☐ Expenditure amount

☐ Date of departure and date of return for every trip

☐ Number of days spent on business versus days spent on pleasure

☐ Business purpose of the expenditure

☐ Place of travel or place of entertainment (if clients were entertained)

☐ Relationship to the business of the person or persons being entertained by the taxpayer

Evidence for these expenses is required, such as credit card charge copies and receipts of all bills paid for lodging and meals while traveling. In addition, travel expense report forms are useful to keep track of out-of-pocket expenses, such as tolls and telephone calls. These forms are obtainable from any office supply store (see Figures 26-4 and 26-5).

Automobile Expenses

Anyone who uses a personal automobile for business purposes (other than commuting) is entitled by the IRS to deduct such expenses on his or her income tax return. If the personal vehicle is used entirely for business, all expenses can be deducted; if the vehicle has both business and personal use, its expenses may be deducted in part.

(text continues on p. 304)

Figure 26-3. Sample payroll book entries.

WEEK ENDING

#	NAME	MARRIED/SINGLE	EXEMPTIONS	SUN	MON	TUE	WED	THU	FRI	SAT	TOTAL HOURS	RATE	REGULAR	OVERTIME	OTHER
1	Cynthia Yost	S	1		7	7	7	7	7	3	reg. 38 / o.t.	6.00	228.00		
2	Deborah A. Orr	S	2		8	8	8	8	8	4	reg. 40 / o.t. 4	6.00 / 9.00	240.00	36.00	
3	Irena L. Winson	S	2		8	8	8	8	8		reg. 40 / o.t.	6.00	240.00		
4	Nancy D. Sabol	M	2		7	7	8	8	7	4	reg. 40 / o.t. 3	7.00 / 10.50	280.00	31.50	
5	Glenn L. Baldwin	S	1		6	6	6	6	6		reg. 30 / o.t.	7.00	210.00		
6	Joseph L. LeClerc	M	3		6	7	7	7	8		reg. 35 / o.t.	6.50	227.50		
7	Nicholas Vassor	S	1		8	8	8	8	8	2	reg. 40 / o.t. 2	7.00 / 10.50	280.00	21.00	
8											reg. / o.t.				
9											reg. / o.t.				
10											reg. / o.t.				
11											reg. / o.t.				
12											reg. / o.t.				
13											reg. / o.t.				
14											reg. / o.t.				
15											reg. / o.t.				
	TOTALS												1705.50	88.50	

Specimen

		DEDUCTIONS						NET PAY	TOTAL WAGES	CUMULATIVE TOTALS				
	TOTAL WAGES	SOC. SEC.	MEDICARE	U.S. WITH. TAX	STATE WITH. TAX					SOC. SEC.	MEDICARE	U.S. WITH. TAX	STATE WITH. TAX	
1	225.00	14.14	3.31	24.00	6.00			180.55	962.00	56.56	13.24	96.00	24.00	1
2	276.00	17.11	4.00	25.00	6.25			223.64	1104.00	68.44	16.00	100.00	25.00	2
3	240.00	14.88	3.48	21.00	5.25			195.39	960.00	59.52	13.92	84.00	21.00	3
4	311.50	19.31	4.52	25.00	6.25			256.42	1246.00	77.24	18.08	100.00	25.00	4
5	210.00	13.02	3.05	22.00	5.50			166.43	846.00	52.08	12.20	88.00	22.00	5
6	227.50	14.11	3.30	5.00	1.25			203.84	910.00	56.44	13.20	20.00	5.00	6
7	301.00	18.66	4.36	36.00	9.00			232.98	1204.00	74.64	17.44	144.00	36.00	7
8														8
9														9
10														10
11														11
12														12
13														13
14														14
15														15
	1794.00	111.23	26.02	158.00	39.50			1459.25	7196.00	444.92	104.08	632.00	156.00	

Figure 26-4. Sample expense report form.

EXPENSE REPORT

Expense Report

NAME	DEPT. OR SALES OFFICE	REPORT DATE	DATE OF TRIP	FROM /	TO /

BUSINESS PURPOSE

ACCOUNT NO.

DATE	TRANSPORTATION		AUTOMOBILE EXPENSES ★★★	LOCAL TAXI, CARFARE, TOLLS, ETC.	LODGING	MEALS (ITEMIZE BUSINESS ★★★)			ENTERTAINMENT ★★★	MISCELLANEOUS ★★★	TOTAL
	AIR, RAIL, BUS, ETC.	LIMOUSINE, CAR RENTAL, ETC.				BREAKFAST	LUNCH	DINNER			
SUN											
MON											
TUE											
WED											
THU											
FRI											
SAT											
TOTAL											

AUTOMOBILE EXPENSES ★★★

DATE	MILEAGE	GAS, PARKING, REPAIRS, SERVICE	AMOUNT

MISCELLANEOUS EXPENSES ★★★

DATE	DETAIL	AMOUNT

ENTERTAINMENT AND BUSINESS MEALS ONLY ★★★

DATE	ENTERTAINED (NAME, COMPANY, TITLE)	PLACE	BUSINESS PURPOSE	AMOUNT

EXPENSE SUMMARY

	AMOUNT
TOTAL EXPENSES REPORTED	
LESS CASH ADVANCE	
TOTAL DUE EMPLOYEE/EMPLOYER	

INSTRUCTIONS

☐ DEDUCT FROM MY ADVANCE
☐ MAIL TO:

Expense Report

SIGNATURE _____
9032

APPROVED BY _____ DATE _____

Figure 26-5. Sample travel expense record book.

SUMMARY OF EXPENSES

WEEK ENDING _____

ACCT. NO.	ACCOUNT	TOTAL THIS WEEK		TOTAL LAST WEEK		TOTAL TO DATE	
1	BREAKFAST						
2	LUNCH						
3	DINNER						
4	HOTEL OR MOTEL						
5	TRANSPORTATION: PLANE						
6	RAILROAD						
7	TAXI OR BUS						
8	AUTO RENTAL, ETC.						
9	BAGGAGE CHARGES						
10	ENTERTAINMENT						
11	GIFTS						
12	TIPS						
13	TELEPHONE						
14	TOLLS						
15	POSTAGE						
16	AUTO EXPENSES: GAS, OIL, LUBRICATION, ETC.						
17	REPAIRS						
18	TIRES, SUPPLIES, ETC.						
19	PARKING						
20	WASHING						
21	INSURANCE						
22	................MILES @ c						
23	OFFICE EXPENSE						
24	TRADE SHOWS						
25	MISCELLANEOUS						
26							
27							
28							
29							
30							
	TOTALS						
	LESS CREDIT CARD (EMPLOYER)						
	BALANCE						

A printed form, Record of Automobile Expenses, is obtainable in most office supply stores (Figure 26-6). So is a pocket-size booklet that can be handily kept in a briefcase or automobile glove compartment.

If the boss does not want to keep detailed records of automobile expenses, an optional deduction method is allowed. Instead of deducting a vehicle's actual fixed and operating expenses with a separate deduction for depreciation (for an individual), the boss could deduct a standard mileage rate for annual business miles traveled. State and local taxes (not including gasoline tax) and interest payments on loans to purchase business vehicles are deductible as well.

These laws change frequently, and it would be wise for you or your employer to secure up-to-date IRS booklets for rules on required record maintenance and reporting to make sure you're keeping adequate records. But even with these booklets, your employer should also utilize the services of a competent accountant.

For information on other taxes, see Chapter 29.

Figure 26-6. Sample automobile expense record.

AUTOMOBILE EXPENSES   MONTH OF_____ 19____

DAY	MILES TRAVELED	GASOLINE GALS.	AMOUNT	OIL & LUBE	PARKING and TOLLS	REPAIRS	TIRES	WASH.	ACCESS.	MISC.	DAY
1											1
2											2
3											3
4											4
5											5
6											6
7											7
8											8
9											9
10											10
11											11
12											12
13											13
14											14
15											15
16											16
17											17
18											18
19											19
20											20
21											21
22											22
23											23
24											24
25											25
26											26
27											27
28											28
29											29
30											30
31											31
TOTAL											

Figure 26-7. Sample cash budget.

| | *JUNE* | |
	Budget	*Actual*

Expected Cash Receipts

(1) Cash sales
(2) Accounts receivable collections
(3) Other cash income
(4) Total cash receipts

Expected Cash Payment

(5) Inventory
(6) Payroll (including owner)
(7) Other expenses (including maintenance)
(8) Selling expenses
(9) New equipment
(10) Advertising expenses
(11) Other expected payments (including taxes,
     interest, loan)
(12) Total cash payments
(13) Expected cash balance at beginning of month
(14) Cash increase or decrease (item 4 less item 12)
(15) Expected cash balance at end of month (item 13
     plus item 14—may be negative)
(16) Working cash balance needed
(17) Short-term loan needed (item 15, if item 16 is
     larger)
(18) Cash available for capital expenditures and short-
     term investments (item 15 less item 16, if 15 is
     larger)

Capital Cash

(19) Cash available (item 18)
(20) Desired capital cash (for item 9)
(21) Long-term loan needed (item 20 less item 19, if 20
     is larger)

Figure 26-8. An estimate of start-up costs for a retail shop.

Inventory	$50,000
Fixtures and equipment	7,000
Decoration	9,000
Legal and professional fees	2,000
Utility deposits	100
Preopening promotions	1,800
Cash contingency fund	2,000
Insurance	500
Supplies and equipment	1,500
Security rent	2,000
Miscellaneous	500
Total	$76,400

Figure 26-9. Estimate of monthly expenses for a retail shop.

Salaries	$2,000
Rental	800
Utilities and telephone	200
Inventory replenishment	4,000
Advertising	100
Supplies and postage	200
Insurance	125
Maintenance	70
Professional fees	100
Delivery expense	250
Interest on loan	80
Subscriptions and dues	40
Miscellaneous	250
Monthly total	$8,215

Annualized expenses: $98,580

Cash Budgets

A **cash budget**—an estimate of expected cash receipts and expenditures—is necessary for any business, especially a small business where every dime counts. Cash budgets should be prepared six months ahead or, if possible, twelve months ahead with revision as needed.

When you help your boss develop a cash budget, it must be a realistic estimate. What the boss hopes will happen is not to be considered. A cash budget is completely useless unless it is based on realistic, sober judgment springing entirely from experience.

Figure 26-7 shows a cash budget form for one month. It can be extended for as many months or even years as you find useful.

Records for Lenders

Start-Up Costs Estimate

If your employer is just starting a business, a lender is likely to request a specific list and total estimate of the business's start-up costs. Figure 26-8 shows a sample. You might help your employer gather the necessary information.

Monthly Expenses Estimate

As with a start-up estimate, a lender is likely also to request an estimate of probable monthly expenses, which when multiplied by twelve will be an estimate of first-year expenses. Figure 26-9 shows a suggested form to use.

Chapter 27

Business and Personal Taxes

The Secretary's Role

Although your secretarial duties may not include filling out tax forms, it can be important to know what taxes are payable when and what forms are required. If you work for a small business, the greater your chance is of being asked to help in this area. But if in no way else, you can help by keeping a list of tax forms and due dates and by reminding your employer a few weeks in advance of each deadline.

Business Taxes

Corporate Taxes

Federal Taxes

If the business that employs you is a corporation, a corporate tax form is due each year. This is Form 1120, and it's due March 15 of each calendar year, one month prior to the due date for personal returns. Throughout the year, estimated tax payments are also due; these are payable January 15, April 15, June 15, and September 15. To pay estimated taxes, a tax coupon book must be obtained from the Internal Revenue Service (IRS). This coupon book is used to make payments for a variety of different taxes. When filled out correctly, the coupon shows the type of tax (in this case 1120), along with the particular quarter of the year the payment is being made for. Rather than send these payments directly to the IRS, you may pay them at the bank where the company maintains its checking account.

State Taxes

If your state charges an income tax (and most do), the corporation must also pay estimated state taxes. You must obtain a state coupon book and make quarterly payments. However, in most cases these payments are made directly to the state by sending them in the mail.

Franchise Tax

The franchise tax is an annual tax on corporations payable to the secretary of state's office in order to keep the corporation's status current. Usually the state sends the company a bill.

Sales Tax

If your employer is involved in the sale of goods or provides certain services, he or she may be liable to collect and pay sales tax. Sales tax amounts vary across the country, and forms sent by the state and county will explain how much to collect. Periodically, usually once each month, sales tax reports are sent out to each business. These must be filled out and returned with a check for the sales tax collected.

Employment Taxes

A variety of employment taxes must be filed and paid. For example, the federal and state taxes, Social Security tax, and Medicare fees that are withheld from employee paychecks must be paid periodically to the IRS and the state taxing authority. Federal and state guides for employers are available to explain how much to withhold from an employee's check and when payments are due. These withholding tax payments must be made promptly. In some cases the deadline is as fast as three days following the pay date. Form 941 must be filled out each quarter for federal tax reporting. Payments are made by using the tax coupon books at your local bank.

Another withholding tax is the unemployment tax, levied against businesses by your local state government throughout the year. If the company files with the state department of labor and the U.S. Department of Labor, it will receive reporting forms a few weeks before the filing deadlines. State taxes and report forms are sent to the state through the mail along with payment. On the federal level, this tax requires filling out Form 940 once each year and using the coupon book to make the payment at the company's local bank.

Self-Employment Tax

If your boss does business as a partnership or a sole proprietor, he or she receives profits directly from the company. No Social Security tax is withheld from these profits. Therefore, when it comes time to file annual tax returns, your employer must pay a self-employment tax and file Schedule SE. At the same time, any nonincorporated business owner must also file a Schedule C to report his or her business income.

Just as employees on a payroll must pay their taxes throughout the year through withholding, so anyone owing self-employment tax must make estimated tax payments throughout the year. This can be done using 1040ES forms available from the IRS and sending payments into the IRS office for the particular IRS estimated tax region.

Employee or Independent Contractor?

What about you? Are you self-employed? If you are a part-time secretary and do not have "employee" status, your employer may consider you an **independent contractor**. This means that the employer will not withhold taxes from your check, and, like a business owner, you are then liable for paying your own taxes. Depending on how much you earn, you may be required to make estimated tax payments throughout the year.

Determining Your Status

Whether you are an employee or a contractor is a difficult question to answer. The Department of Labor and IRS usually state that if you work at the company's place of business, use its tools, and work specific hours set by the company, then you are an employee. If you work at home, use your own computer, and come and go when you please, then you might be considered a contractor.

Effects of Status

The difference in your status can determine whether your employer is liable to pay half of your Social Security taxes (rather than you being solely responsible for self-employment taxes). In addition, an employer may pay unemployment tax and workers compensation.

Workers compensation, sometimes called "workers comp," is a state-funded insurance policy for employees who become injured or disabled while on the job. If you are injured, the insurance policy will pay for some of your medical bills, as well as a portion of your wages while you are off the job. Workers compensation is required in many states but varies depending on the business size.

Property and Net Worth Taxes

In most states, businesses pay local county and state governments a tax on inventory and on real property such as land or buildings. This tax is filed once each year. Land property tax bills are usually mailed each year, just like those that are sent to you if you own a home.

Net worth taxes are usually reported and paid at the same time the annual tax return is filled out. It requires that taxes be paid on business assets as well as cash and investments.

Business Licenses

All partnerships and sole proprietors along with some corporations are required to obtain a business license from the city and sometimes from the county where they are located and do business. To obtain a business license, the business owner must fill out paperwork and pay an annual fee. Business licenses can be renewed each year by paying an annual fee.

Tax Assistance

Many tax planning aids are available for your boss from the IRS and your state department of revenue. Check your telephone book for the correct numbers, and call to ask for employers' guides and needed forms. Keep these on hand so your boss will always have them available in order to meet a deadline.

Chapter 28
Banking

The Company's Bank

One important relationship every business must establish is with a bank. Many of the resulting financial details—whether from a checking account, business loan, or credit card—will be handled by the company's secretary. The smaller the company is, the greater will be your involvement with your company's banking.

What if the bank gave away money, and you did not get in line? That's essentially what can happen if you don't understand a bank's full spectrum of financial products and services and use the correct ones when available. To save your company the most in fees while helping it nail down the most in interest, you need to know exactly what a bank can do for you.

Checking Accounts

The most basic account that every business needs is a checking account. There are several different types available, ranging from the basic checking account with a monthly fee, to the NOW account, the Super NOW account, and the money market account. Knowing which account the business qualifies for can help you reduce its monthly fees and even earn interest on its deposit. This is important information to pass on to your employer.

Basic Checking Account

A basic checking account is a convenient way to spend money without making frequent trips to the bank. It also allows you to pay bills through the mail without sending cash, something that should never be done. In addition, a basic checking account provides you with a monthly record of the company's transactions, which helps you track income and expenses more easily. Most financial institutions do not pay interest on the money a business keeps in a basic checking account; instead, the banks charge a monthly fee. However, there is usually no minimum balance required to maintain this account.

NOW Account

A variation of the basic checking account is the NOW account, as it is known in the banking industry. This checking account has all the features of the basic checking account and pays interest on money in the account. NOW accounts require a minimum balance to be maintained. If the company's balance falls below that minimum, the account will be charged a monthly fee just like a basic checking account.

Super NOW Account

Like the NOW account, the Super NOW is a checking account that bears interest. However, it pays a higher rate of interest than a NOW, which can fluctuate from month to month. The minimum balance required to maintain this account is usually $2,500.

Money Market Account

A money market account is similar to a Super NOW since it pays interest at the market rate, but the number of monthly transactions is limited by law. Like the Super NOW, a minimum balance is required to earn market interest rates, but only six transfers of funds such as checks, withdrawals, or wire transfers may be made each month. A money market account may substitute for a regular savings account for businesses that wish to invest on a short-term basis and still have quick access to their money.

Petty Cash

Most businesses keep a small amount of cash on hand to pay for cash items and to make change for customers. This cash must be accounted for with receipts for each expenditure. You can obtain petty cash by writing a check payable to "cash" or to a particular employee. In either case, whoever cashes the check will be responsible for making sure that accurate records are kept of expenditures.

Savings Accounts

If your employer's business has excess cash available, a variety of accounts can help save those funds for the future: a regular savings account, certificates of deposit (CDs), jumbo CDs, individual retirement accounts, savings bonds, automatic savings plans, and other retirement accounts.

A savings account is an ideal place to deposit cash or checks, providing a safe way to save for any purpose. In addition, excess funds earn interest while in the account. Unlimited withdrawals are permitted, but no checks may be written against the account. Interest rates may vary from one period to the next; the compounding of interest also varies among financial institutions.

Investment Accounts

Certificates of Deposit

Certificates of deposit (CDs) provide an investment option that pays a higher rate of interest than a savings account. A CD's interest rate and minimum deposit may vary depending on the term, such as six months or one year; however, once a CD is purchased, the interest rate is fixed. There are substantial penalties if the company needs to withdraw its funds before the term of the CD expires.

Another type of CD is the jumbo CD, so-called because it requires a minimum of $100,000 to open. The rate of interest is higher than that of a regular CD and varies depending on the term. Usually the longer the term is, the higher is the interest rate. Like a regular CD, there is a substantial penalty for early withdrawal.

Savings Bonds

The purchase of government-backed U.S. savings bonds is another safe way to invest and save money. Series double E government bonds are available in denominations from $50 to $10,000 and carry a competitive interest rate. Earned interest is not subject to state or local taxes, and federal tax may be deferred until the bonds are redeemed and the interest is received.

Trust Services

One benefit offered by many large corporations is a retirement plan. Even small businesses may have retirement plans for some or all employees. Some retirement plans are offered by banks, and others can be set up through a mutual fund. The basic choices are a profit-sharing pension plan, a money-purchase pension plan, a 401k plan, a Keogh, and an individual retirement account.

Simplified Pension Plan

A simplified employee pension plan can be adopted by small corporations. It usually consists of either a profit-sharing pension plan or a money-purchase pension plan or both. These plans can be set up by using fill-in-the-blank forms to determine the specifics for your business. With a simplified employee pension plan (SEP), the business contributes a percentage of the employee's annual salary into a pension account. This account is tax deferred and cannot be withdrawn by the employee until retirement age. With a profit-sharing plan, a certain percentage is determined each year; the percentage can vary from year to year. It is not necessarily based on profits, and the business may have to contribute to the retirement fund even if there is a loss. With a money-purchase plan, the business must make a predetermined percentage contribution each year regardless of the business performance.

401k Plan

With a 401k plan, funds are deducted from the employee's salary and are deposited into the retirement account. The funds are tax deferred, and the interest earned on the account is also tax deferred. Sometimes the business may match the contribution of the employee up to a predetermined percentage and dollar amount limit determined by law.

Keogh Plan

If your boss is a self-employed individual in a small business, he or she may be interested in a special retirement plan called a Keogh, which provides a basic qualifying self-employment retirement plan for unincorporated business owners and their employees. Keogh participants may contribute up to 25 percent of their salaries and earned income into the retirement account, up to a dollar limit. Both the yearly contribution and interest earned on the account are tax deferred.

Individual Retirement Account

If the company does not offer its employees a retirement plan and your individual income falls within certain limits, you may qualify for an individual retirement account (IRA). The money that you deposit into an IRA can be deducted from your income before paying taxes. The interest earned by the account is tax deferred until you reach retirement age.

Other Services

Your boss and the company may be able to profit from some of the other many miscellaneous convenience services offered by financial institutions.

ATM Cards

ATM stands for "automated teller machine," a convenient way to get cash twenty-four hours a day. Besides providing you with petty cash for the office, the card allows you to check account balances, make deposits, and perform many other routine banking activities at your convenience. To use an ATM, the customer must be issued an ATM card, which is sometimes called a debit card. By using a secret password the customer is protected, and every transaction is conducted in private.

Safe Deposit Boxes

Many financial institutions have spaces within their vaults that are available for rental. These safe deposit boxes are a safe and fireproof way to store valuable documents and other small items of value. Only the owner of the box can access it using a special two-key system. Usually safe deposit boxes are available in several different sizes for a nominal annual rental fee.

Bill Paying by Telephone

Many banks allow you to pay routine bills such as utilities with just a telephone call, a boon for overworked secretaries. The organizations that your company must pay have prearranged code numbers. Use a touch-tone telephone to arrange payment from your company's account, and the financial institution makes sure your bill is paid immediately. A monthly statement of each transaction may be available to record expenditures.

Banking by Mail

If you do not want to or cannot visit a financial institution in person, you can use a bank-by-mail service. Primarily this service is for making deposits. Users are provided with preaddressed envelopes and deposit tickets to mail checks for deposit into their accounts.

Wire Transfers

If you need to send money quickly from one account to another, a wire transfer is the fastest way. It moves funds by telephone and electronic bookkeeping into another bank account in any part of the country or world.

It's important that you have some type of written authorization between the two parties involved, since once the funds have been transferred, they cannot be returned. To complete the transaction you need to know the names of the two account holders, the financial institutions involved, the American Banking Association numbers (a reference number that designates a particular bank), and the account numbers. You should get a receipt when the transaction is completed. A small transaction fee is required for the transfer, but the method is a safe and convenient way to transfer funds in a flash.

Foreign Currency Exchange

Foreign currency exchange can be a big help to a business in the import/export trade. The user of this service can convert money from one country to that of another at the current exchange rate. For businesspeople going abroad, changing currency in advance is much more convenient than waiting until they arrive at their destination. Later, after the business trip, you can exchange the boss's left-over foreign currency back into U.S. funds. Since the financial institution can adjust the exchange rate, there is usually a built-in fee for this service.

Bank Checks

When a business check or cash is not appropriate—such as transactions involving large dollar amounts—there is a variety of bank checks available, widely accepted as a safe, guaranteed substitute for cash. **Cashier's checks** are issued by the bank and guarantee that funds are available. **Money orders** serve the same purpose but are usually issued in smaller amounts. **Traveler's checks** are sold in denominations such as $10, $20, $50, or $100, and can be refunded if lost or stolen.

Notary Service

Another useful business service offered by many banks is a notary service. Notaries verify the identity of individuals who need to sign certain official and legal documents. A notary can witness the signature and seal the signatures with a special stamp. Sometimes there is a small fee for this service, but many banks provide it free to customers who have an active account.

Checks

One of the most fundamental activities of any small business is the exchange of products and services for something else of value, normally money. This is called a **transaction**. Selling a product to a customer who pays cash is a typical transaction. But what about customers who pay by check? There are many transactions that do not involve cash, such as writing a check, accepting a check, making deposits or withdrawals at the bank, or transferring funds. It's important to understand the details of these transactions to protect your boss and the company from fraud and theft.

The most common transaction you will be involved in concerns checks, either personal or business. There are many different types and styles of checks, from the plain to the colorful. Yet all checks have some common basic elements such as numbers and names, and there is a specific set of requirements necessary before a check can be negotiable or cashable.

The first step in learning to negotiate a check is knowing the significance of each of its parts. There are two general areas to focus on: the preprinted information and the information filled in by the check writer. (See Figure 28-1.)

Looking at the preprinted information first, you will find the following:

- In the upper left corner is the *name of the maker*—the person or persons who own the account. The maker is also sometimes called the *drawer*.
- The *name and location of the financial institution* should also be printed on the check, usually just below the name of the maker. Often the bank includes its logo here.
- The *sequential number of the check* is printed in the upper right corner.

Figure 28-1. Sample of a business check.

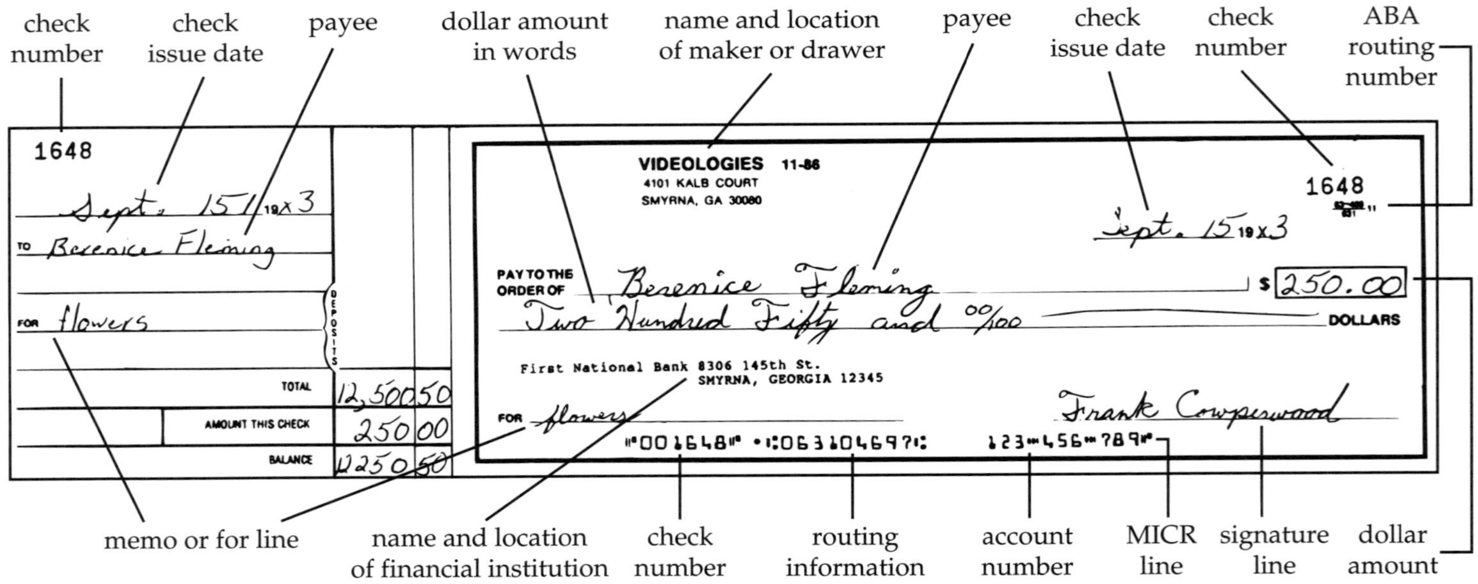

- Below the check number to the right of the date line is a fraction. This is called the American Banker's Association routing number and is referred to as the *ABA routing number*. When decoded, this number tells where the bank is located, the city, the specific bank branch, and the Federal Reserve bank serving this financial institution.
- The *MICR line*, printed along the bottom of the check, contains the account number and the check number. (MICR means magnetic ink character recognition; it is a number that can be read by a computer.)

The parts of a check that most concern you are those filled in by the maker.

- The *date line* provides space for the date the check was written.
- The *pay-to-the-order-of* line indicates whom the maker intends to pay. This person or business is called the *payee*.
- A line for the *dollar amount* to be written in figures is next to the payee line.
- Underneath the payee line is a line for the maker to write the *dollar amount in words*.
- A *"for"* or *"memo"* line is provided on the bottom left corner for the maker to note what the check is for.
- The maker's signature goes on the *signature line* along the bottom right edge of the check.

Just as a bank examines a check you want to cash, you too should learn what to look for to make sure the checks you accept are legally negotiable:

☐ There must be a date written on the date line of the check.

☐ The pay-to-the-order-of line must be filled in. Checks written to the company cannot be cashed; they can only be deposited.

☐ The dollar amount must be filled in, both in numbers and in words, and the two amounts must match.

☐ The check must be signed by the maker, that is, the person listed on the printed part of the check. Look to see if two or more people must sign the check to make it legal. You'll know because there will be two signature lines on it and often the printed words "two signatures required" as well.

☐ The name and location of the financial institution must be printed on the check.

☐ Examine the check for alterations. Scratch-throughs, white-outs, or any other indication that the check has been altered may make it unacceptable by the bank.

Deposits

One of the goals of most financial institutions is to receive and retain deposits. Money taken into customer accounts through deposits provides the primary source of funds for the institution to loan and invest. If the company you work for is successful, you may make many routine deposits. There are two different types you can make: demand deposits and time deposits.

Demand deposits are made into checking and regular savings accounts where the money is readily available. The company can make a withdrawal at any time. On the other hand, with a **time deposit** such as a certificate of deposit, the company's money may be tied up for a period of time.

Making Deposits

You cannot walk into any bank on the street and deposit a check someone has given you or the company. Checks received by a business and made payable to the business name can be deposited only at a bank where the business has an established account. You cannot, for instance, go to the bank of the person who wrote the check and try to cash it there.

Another area of making deposits that confuses many people is something the banks classify as "on us" and "not-on-us" checks. An **on-us** check is one that is written and then deposited or cashed at the same bank. A **not-on-us** check is just what the name says: a check deposited at a bank that does not hold the account from which funds will be drawn. In most cases, there will be a longer delay in getting funds transferred when a transaction involves a not-on-us check. The delay can be longer if the transaction involves an out-of-state or a foreign bank. When there is a delay, most often a hold will be placed on the deposit for a specified period of days. This means that the funds are not available as actual cash until the hold has expired and the funds have been transferred into the company's bank account.

When you make a deposit, you are giving the bank access to company funds. The deposit slip gives the bank permission to put money into the company's account or to collect funds from checks the company has received. It's your responsibility to make sure you have followed the correct procedures making the deposit and that you get a receipt to ensure the company receives proper credit for the transaction. Therefore it is important that you understand what is involved in making a deposit.

The Deposit Transaction

Generally a deposit transaction requires a deposit slip, items to be deposited, processing of the deposit by the bank teller, and issuing a receipt and/or cash back from the deposit. The transaction begins with the deposit slip. This key instrument of negotiation tells who is making the deposit, into what account the deposit is being made, and what amount is being deposited from what items.

Deposit Slip

A deposit slip (Figure 28-2) must have the name and address of the account owner, either preprinted on the slip or written by hand. There must also be a

Figure 28-2. Sample of a business deposit slip.

date. In addition, there must be an MICR encoded account number to ensure proper crediting to your account. Most important, there should be a list of the items being deposited. These items must be listed in the form of currency, coins, and checks. Each check must be listed separately by amount. Additional space is usually provided on the back of the slip when depositing numerous checks. The subtotal of any checks deposited must be listed on the back and must also be filled in on the front part of the slip. Then all of the amounts for currency, coins, and checks should be totaled.

All checks deposited must be endorsed on the back. You must include the name of the company, its account number, and the words "for deposit only."

Processing by the Bank Teller

Bank tellers are trained to check and doublecheck every transaction. Therefore you should expect the teller to add up your deposit and to doublecheck your totals on the deposit slip. The teller should also verify the company's account number and make sure that all checks have been endorsed.

One important area to note concerns depositing cash items. Cash items are not just cash but any items that are accepted for deposit and credited to the company's account. They include all currency, coins, and many types of checks. Noncash or collection items are accepted for handling but are not immediately credited to the account. These include checks that are not MICR encoded, foreign checks, promissory notes, and other items with documents or special instructions attached.

The important thing to remember is that depending on whether you deposit cash or noncash items, the company may not have instant access to the funds in its account for a specified period of time. If these banking details are your responsibility, it's up to you to find out when funds will be available. In this way the boss will not accidentally write a check with insufficient funds.

Withdrawals

Along with writing checks and making deposits, there may be times when you will be asked to make a withdrawal of cash from the company's checking or savings account. Withdrawing money from a checking account requires that you write a check on the company's account payable to yourself or to "cash." Some savings accounts also have checks that may be written to make a withdrawal. However, in some cases when you do not have checks available you can use a withdrawal slip (Figure 28-3).

A withdrawal slip must include the following information: the date, the amount of the withdrawal, the account number, and the signature of someone who has been approved to make withdrawals. If anything is missing or incorrect, the bank teller will ask you to correct your mistake or submit a new withdrawal slip.

If the withdrawal slip is correct, the teller will verify the signature with the one on file with the account. You should also be asked for proper identification. The teller must then check to make sure the company has funds available to cover the withdrawal. If it does, you will be given the cash and a receipt.

When withdrawing money from a business account, it's important to keep a few accounting and tax procedures in mind. All transactions must be accounted for. When you take cash from a business account, you must note the purpose. Usually the purpose will be to fund a petty cash account so you can pay for business supplies, stamps, or other incidentals. You must account for all cash you spend by getting receipts for your purchases. And before taking additional cash out of the business account, you should account for any previous withdrawals.

Figure 28-3. Sample withdrawal slip.

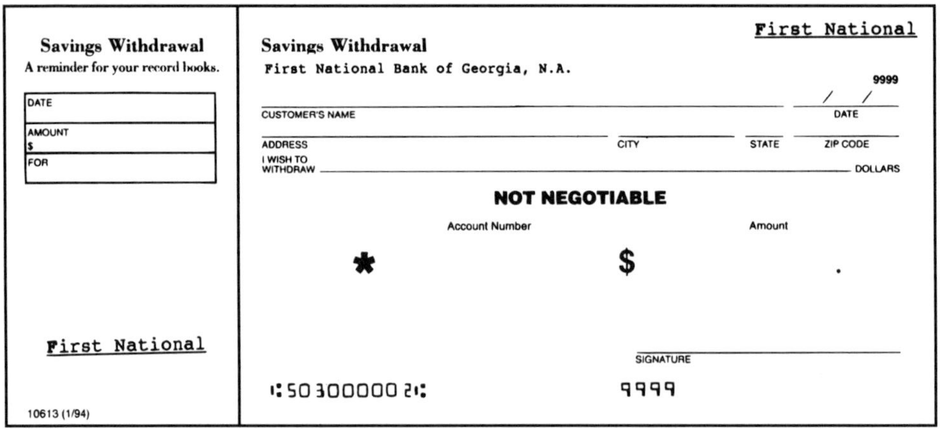
Savings Withdrawal
A reminder for your record books.
DATE
AMOUNT
$
FOR
First National
10613 (1/94)

First National
Savings Withdrawal
First National Bank of Georgia, N.A.
9999
/ /
CUSTOMER'S NAME
DATE
ADDRESS
CITY
STATE
ZIP CODE
I WISH TO WITHDRAW
DOLLARS
NOT NEGOTIABLE
Account Number
Amount
* $.
SIGNATURE
⑆50300000 21⑆ 9999

Special Situations

In addition to understanding normal business banking transactions, it's important that you understand what to do in some special circumstances. For instance, what if the boss accidentally writes or receives in payment an insufficient or "hot" check? Or what if you're asked to withdraw $10,000 or more in cash from the business account?

Returned Checks

A check may be returned to the company for any number of reasons such as a missing signature, closed account, or insufficient funds. If you receive a returned check, your best bet is to contact the person who gave the company the check and try to collect cash instead. If the person is not cooperative, you or the boss should contact local law enforcement authorities since theft of goods or services by check is against the law.

If the company inadvertently should give someone a check that is returned, be prepared to pay cash and possibly to pay a special fee. You should make every effort to settle this matter amicably and at once. The company can be held legally responsible for the returned check; at the least it could suffer a damaging blow to its reputation.

Large Transactions

Transactions involving $10,000 or more in cash require special attention. The U.S. Treasury Department requires all financial institutions to provide the Internal Revenue Service (IRS) with information on large currency transactions. This information helps the IRS's criminal tax and regulatory investigations by discouraging the use of cash in illegal transactions. Some customers, such as retail businesses, may be exempted by this reporting. However, unless the company has been previously exempted, you must fill out the large currency transaction form. This can usually be done with the help of a teller or customer service representative.

If you are involved with withdrawals exceeding $10,000 and since carrying large amounts of cash is unsafe, what can you do instead? Let's say the boss is purchasing a car for the business. Many car dealers will not accept a check from the company account and allow the boss to drive away in the new car. Instead, he or she must provide the seller with something that is as good as cash.

Cashier's or Certified Check

A cashier's check or a certified check could be used to pay for the car since they verify that funds are available. A cashier's check is issued by a financial institution and is paid for at the time it is issued. A certified check is from the company account, and it has been officially certified by the bank that funds are available and have been set aside to pay this particular check. Both checks are as good as cash and allow the boss to complete the purchase.

Money Order

Money orders are often used by people who don't have checking accounts. They are sold for specific amounts by financial institutions and retail stores. They are made payable to the order of a particular business or individual when they are purchased. Therefore they are as good as cash if you receive one from someone else. They also provide a receipt that can be used to prove payment or to get a refund in the case of theft or loss.

Traveler's Checks

Traveler's checks are also commonly used in many business transactions instead of cash. These special checks are issued by a financial institution in common denominations just like currency. When you purchase a traveler's check, you must endorse the check once before you leave the bank. When you get ready to pay for a transaction with a traveler's check, you then endorse the check a second time. If you accept a traveler's check as payment for goods or services, you should make sure both signatures are the same. This double-signature feature protects the purchaser of the checks in case they are lost or stolen. Receipts are also provided for this same purpose. Usually some form of identification is required when using traveler's checks.

Credit Cards

Depending on what type of business you work for, you may also be involved in transactions involving credit cards. Credit cards are often used as payment in transactions and are widely accepted all over the world for purchases of goods and services.

Credit cards are issued by a financial institution just like a loan. Each card has a unique account number, which can be verified electronically or by checking the list of accounts published by the card company. A credit card purchase slip is required to complete a transaction. It must include a stamp of the card, the account number, the name of the card holder, and the expiration date. The purchase slip must also include the amount of the purchase and be signed by the card holder. In some cases, such as mail order purchases, this information can be obtained over the telephone and filled in by hand.

Reconciling Bank Statements

Each month the bank will provide a statement for the previous month that lists company checks that have cleared and deposits made. The statement will also list any special fees or charges for items such as printing new checks, covering re-turned checks, renting safe deposit boxes, and so forth. Along with the statement the bank will provide copies of the canceled checks written against the account.

As soon as bank statements come in, they should be doublechecked against the company's checkbook records for mistakes and possible fraud. This process is called **reconciling** or **balancing the checkbook**. If the duty falls to you, follow these guidelines:

☐ Put the checks returned with the statement into numerical order.

☐ Make sure each check is for the same amount that is listed in the company checkbook, and note in the checkbook that it has cleared.

☐ Look at the bank statement to make sure each check is listed correctly there.

☐ Follow the same procedures to verify deposits. Make sure the bank has credited the account for the same amount that you have listed in the company checkbook.

Usually checks that were written or deposits made at the end of a reporting period will not appear on the statement, and sometimes recipients of checks fail to deposit them promptly; all of these checks will be missing from the bank state-ment. Because of this, there will usually be a difference between the bank balance shown on the statement and the balance shown in the checkbook. Follow the simple guidelines for reconciling usually printed on the back of the statement. These guidelines will take into account missing checks and deposits made after the cut-off date, items that won't show up until next month's statement.

Although you're busy with many other duties, it's usually a good idea to reconcile the company's bank records as soon as they come in each month. Allowing them to pile up may result in account balance errors and eventual bank charges for returned checks. Also, there are time limits for correcting a mistake if you believe the bank is at fault. To protect your company's rights, its financial security, and its reputation, reconcile the statements as quickly as possible.

Once you've reconciled the statements, keep them in a safe place, where they are available only to people authorized by the business owners. These statements are often needed in the event of tax audits and when applying for business loans. Duplicates of missing statements may be obtained by writing or calling the com-pany's bank.

Chapter 29

Special Business and Financial Information for the Small Business Secretary

Frequently Asked Questions

Many secretaries work in what are considered to be "small businesses" (though under certain definitions, companies with as many 1,500 employees are considered to be small!). If you're such a secretary, you may perform different roles from those of a secretary in a larger office. In a small business there's often no payroll department, no accounting department, no purchasing department, no human resources: there's only you. Because of this, you may find yourself with enormous responsibility, privy to the boss's most private concerns about the business.

As the boss's right hand, you'll be the first person he or she turns to with questions. Here, in a brief format, are answers to some of the most frequently asked questions your boss may have about the company.

- *How does the boss go about registering the company's name?* Contact the county clerk in the county where the business is or will be located.

- *How can the boss incorporate the business?* In most states, this can be done either with or without an attorney. Write to your state's secretary of state in the state's capital city for information.

- *How can the boss obtain a copyright?* Write for information from:

Copyright Information
Library of Congress
Washington, DC 20559
(202) 479–0700

- *How can the boss obtain a patent or a trademark?* Write for information from:

Commissioner of Patents and Trademarks
Washington, DC 20231
(703) 557–3158 or (703) 557–3881

- *How can the boss receive patent, trademark, search, and technology assistance?* Technical Applications Centers or Technology and Transfer Centers are located throughout the nation. Write to the Commissioner of Patents at the address above for the location nearest the company.
- *Where can the boss receive business tax information?* To obtain a State Resale Tax Permit for the boss, write to the Comptroller of Public Accounts, State Capitol Building, in your state's capital city. To obtain a Federal Employee Tax Number for the boss, write the Internal Revenue Service (IRS) at a district office near you or at Washington, D.C. Or the boss can attend a workshop conducted by the IRS in your area, usually once or twice weekly. Call the nearest office of the IRS for details and dates.
- *Where can the boss receive import and export information?* For importing information, contact your nearest U.S. Customs Department District Office. For information about exporting the company's products, contact an International Assistance Center; these are located throughout the nation and can supply you with an abundance of information concerning exports. A local Small Business Association Office can give you the location of a center near you.

Trading With Other Countries

Most small businesses strive to become large businesses and in doing so may seek world markets for their products and services. If your employer is among that group, he or she should ask the International Trade Administration (ITA) of the U.S. Department of Commerce for assistance. The ITA functions to help citizens benefit from foreign trade. The agency explains how to begin exporting the company's products and how to locate buyers and distributors for those products and services.

The ITA publishes *A Basic Guide to Exporting*. For information on ordering a copy, write to:

Superintendent of Documents
U.S. Government Printing Office
Washington, DC 20402

This excellent publication is invaluable to business owners who wish to enter international markets.

Also of assistance is the U.S. Department of State. Using Country Desk Officers, the Department of State advises representatives of American companies about the economic climate and political situation of the country each officer represents. For further information, write directly to:

Office of Commercial Affairs
EBIOCA
U.S. Department of State
Washington, DC 20520

Because of language barriers, it might be wise for the small business owner just beginning to enter foreign markets to start with countries where English is the spoken language. Chapter 5 contains a list of the languages spoken in nations around the world. You will note that there are many countries where English is the spoken language. But regardless of language, before committing to any one country, the boss might consider such questions as these:

- What is the standard of living in each country?
- What is the level of education prevailing in each country?
- What is the anticipated market for the company's product or service?
- What information can be discovered about competitive products or services now offered to that country?
- What is the price structure prevailing for similar products or services?

Another important agency is the Export-Import Bank of the United States. This independent organization of the U.S. government helps finance America's exports by offering loans to foreign purchasers of American goods and services. The agency works with commercial banks in this country and overseas to provide financial arrangements, which helps U.S. exporters offer credit assistance to their foreign buyers. For details and assistance, write to:

Export-Import Bank of the United States
811 Vermont Avenue, NW
Washington, DC 20571

Sources of Financing

Some of the following sources provide money for all kinds of businesses, small and large. As you will notice by their titles, certain sources concern themselves with groups singled out by Congress for special financial aid. Others supply money to get certain kinds of things done by business:

- Small-business investment companies
- State and local development companies
- Environmental Protection Administration

- Veterans Administration
- Area Development Administration
- Bureau of Commercial Fisheries
- Commodity Credit Corporation
- Bureau of Indian Affairs
- Treasury Department
- Federal Housing Authority
- Federal Reserve System

Small Business Administration

What is the U.S. Small Business Administration? How can that agency be of assistance to your boss if he or she is a small business owner? The answer to this question is so lengthy the rest of the chapter has been devoted to it.

The Small Business Administration (SBA) helps build America's future by being at the forefront of developing this vital sector of the economy. Following is some general information about the SBA. This fundamental knowledge will be useful if the boss asks you to find out what the SBA can do for the company or, later, if the boss asks that agency for information, advice, and assistance, or applies for an SBA loan.

What Is a Small Business?

There's nothing small about small business! The estimated 20 million small businesses in America today account for 39 percent of the gross national product, provide half of America's workforce, and generate 53.5 percent of all sales.

Since it was established in 1953, the SBA has delivered more than 9 million loans, contracts, counseling sessions, and other forms of assistance—an average of 180,000 in every state—to businesses across the nation. The agency has 110 offices covering every state, the District of Columbia, Guam, Puerto Rico, and the Virgin Islands. With loan authorization of $4 billion, it is the government's most flexible and innovative economic development agency.

All SBA programs and services are extended on a nondiscriminatory basis. These programs and services stimulate capital formation, economic growth, and job creation. They address finance, marketing, production, procurement, and human resources management. Credit programs boost the availability of capital and build the confidence of both lenders and borrowers. Credit programs rely on guarantees of loans made by private lenders, so the cost to taxpayers is minimal.

SBA's General Loan Program

The SBA's prime financial assistance activity is the bank guarantee loan program. The SBA generally does not make loans itself, nor does it have a grant program for starting a small business. Rather, it assists small businesses by guaranteeing commercial loans made by local lenders, generally banks, up to $750,000. There is no theoretical minimum; however, most lenders are reluctant to process commercial loans of less than $25,000.

To obtain an SBA loan, each applicant first obtains a participating lender (bank, savings and loan, or regulated nonbank lender). The SBA loan application is then sent in by this lender. The SBA's guarantee is designed for long-term financial needs (five to twenty-five years, depending on use). Eligible small businesses must be independently owned and operated and engaged in noninvestment, nonspeculative, legal activities. Loans generally can be used for equipment, fixtures, construction, leasehold improvements, inventory, and working capital.

This general loan program represents 90 percent of the agency's total loan effort. It promotes small business formation and growth by guaranteeing up to 90 percent of the amount provided by commercial lenders. Between 1980 and 1990, the SBA provided guarantees for 180,000 loans worth more than $31 billion. A recent study by Price Waterhouse reports that businesses that get these loan guarantees show higher growth than comparable businesses.

Seminars titled "How to Apply for a Business Loan Using the SBA's Loan Guarantee" are presented from time to time in your area. Contact your nearest SBA office for details and dates to pass along to the boss.

How Does the Loan Program Work?

The prospective borrower will be required to provide a capital contribution, normally 30 percent to 50 percent of the total capitalization of the business.

An existing business will be required to provide financial statements showing the business is a profit-making concern, does not have delinquent taxes and, after the loan is made, will have a debt-to-worth ratio not to exceed 3:1 or the industry average.

The SBA charges the lender (usually a bank) a 2 percent guarantee fee on the guaranteed portion of the loan. SBA policy allows the lender (the bank) to pass this guarantee fee on to the borrower (the business owner).

The SBA guaranteed loan program's interest rates are based on the prime rate as advertised in the *Wall Street Journal* according to the following schedule:

- Loans of less than seven years: prime rate plus 2¼ percent.
- Loans of seven years or more: prime rate plus 2¾ percent.

The SBA guaranteed loan maturity (length of loan) is based on the following schedule:

- Working capital loans: five to seven years.
- Fixed asset loans: seven to ten years.
- Real estate and building: up to a maximum of twenty-five years.

The general size standards for SBA-guaranteed business loans are based on the average number of employees for the preceding twelve months or on the sales volume averaged over a three-year period according to the following schedule:

- *Manufacturing*: Varies from 500 to 1,500 employees.
- *Wholesaling*: No more than 100 employees.
- *Services*: From $3.5 million to $14.5 million.
- *Retailing*: From $3.5 million to $13.5 million.
- *Construction*: From $9.5 million to $17 million.
- *Special trade construction*: Not to exceed $7 million.
- *Agriculture*: From $0.5 million to $3.5 million.

Your boss should prepare for an appointment with a lender by having ready answers for the lender's questions. An even better way to prepare is to put all the information into a formal business plan; you can help by gathering and assembling the data. Be sure to include the items listed below:

- ☐ Projected profit-and-loss statement
- ☐ Cash flow projections
- ☐ Market analysis
- ☐ Marketing strategy
- ☐ Description of the business
- ☐ Product or services advantage
- ☐ Management ability (resumés of the key staff)
- ☐ Financial information (both personal and business)
- ☐ Cash requirements

Not all business proposals are eligible for the SBA's guaranteed loan program. The following are ineligible:

- Partial purchase of a business
- Lending institutions
- Real estate held for speculation, investment, or rental
- Opinion molders (magazines, newspapers, trade journals, TV, radio, live entertainment, schools, etc.)
- Religious organizations and their affiliates

The Application Process

After a formal business plan that includes the information suggested above is developed, schedule an appointment for your boss with a local banker to discuss the plan and loan request. (The SBA can furnish a listing of your area's most active SBA lenders). If the boss's plan is acceptable, the bank will provide a loan application package for completion. If professional assistance is needed to complete the application, the lender may be able to refer the boss to several qualified loan packagers.

After the loan application package is complete, return it to the lender. If it's acceptable, the lender will forward the loan application along with the lender's credit analysis to the SBA. After SBA approval, the lender closes the loan and disburses the funds.

Other SBA Loan Programs

Following is a description of other SBA loan programs:

- *504/503 Development Company Loan Program.* Uses public/private partnerships to finance fixed assets. It has produced over $5 billion in investments and more than 300,000 jobs since its beginning in 1980.
- *Small Business Investment Company (SBIC) Program.* Made up of privately owned and operated investment companies licensed by the SBA to provide equity or venture capital and long-term loans to small firms to help them operate, grow, and modernize. Investment companies normally take an actual or potential ownership position in the small business firm to which they provide financing. SBICs have invested nearly $11 billion in more than 70,000 small businesses.
- *Microloan Program.* Helps entrepreneurs in inner-city and rural areas form small, often home-based enterprises.
- *Export finance.* Offers normal and specialized loan guarantees of working capital and longer-term financing to promote exporting.
- *Disaster loans.* Provides low-interest loans to help individuals, homeowners, and businesses rebuild after a disaster.
- *8(a) Program.* Targets socially and economically disadvantaged individuals interested in government contracting. An applicant must be a 51 percent owner and manager of an existing business that has been viable for the past two years. For more information, interested individuals should attend monthly seminars conducted by their nearest SBA office.
- *Procurement assistance.* Ensures maximum competition by encouraging contracts for small businesses. This program saved taxpayers $230 million in 1991.
- *Surety Bond Guarantee Program.* Has provided more than 236,000 surety guarantees (as of 1992) for $19 billion in contracts since 1976, helping businesses win government construction contracts. If the boss needs bid or performance bonds for his or her contracting business, the SBA Surety Bond Guarantee program is administered by your regional Office of the SBA. Contact it by telephone for information.

SBA Business Development Programs

Separate from the loan programs are other programs that provide marketing and training information, serving as a catalyst for small business development and growth. Programs focus on management training, international trade, veterans' affairs, women's initiatives, and resource partnerships. Here are the basic programs.

Business Initiatives, Education and Training Program

This produces a broad range of management and technical assistance publications and audiovisual materials. In 1991, the SBA distributed more than 3 million SBA publications and videotapes.

International Trade

Information, advice, and export financing help prepare businesses to take advantage of the new world market, particularly in Mexico, the Pacific Rim, Canada, and Europe.

Veterans' Affairs

This program provides business management, technical training, and counseling. Every year about 1,200 training conferences are held for prospective and established business owners who were veterans.

Women's Business Ownership Assistance

This pilot program was developed by the SBA for emerging and expanding women businesses through the Women's Business Ownership Act of 1988, to provide long-term training and counseling for women, mentoring programs, and training-counseling centers for women nationwide. Each year more than 100,000 women are counseled and more than 180,000 are trained. For more information, contact the Center for Women's Business Enterprise at the regional SBA office nearest you.

Small Business Innovation Research (SBIR) Program

The SBA is the focal point in helping small businesses gain access to federally funded research and development activities. Any for-profit small business concern may apply directly for competitive research contracts and grants from eleven federal agencies. To obtain a quarterly Pre-Solicitation Announcement containing information on the SBIR solicitations of participating federal agencies, call your nearest SBA office.

Service Corps of Retired Executives (SCORE)

SCORE counselors are experienced former business owners and executives who, free of charge, assist small businesses with problems and prospective owners with counseling and direction. If your boss would like to talk to someone who can and will help his or her business with related questions, you might contact SCORE. There may be SCORE volunteers in your community. Major service activities are located throughout the nation.

SCORE volunteers sponsor and present monthly "Going into Business" seminars at a minimal cost to attendees. From time to time they also present a workshop "How to Start and Manage a Small Business." For a listing of SCORE chapters near you, contact your nearest SBA office.

Small Business Institute (SBI) Program

The SBI program offers small businesses individual help with site location, marketing studies, industry research, industry trends, and many other business challenges through area colleges and universities. Call your nearest SBI office for a list of local participating colleges and universities.

Small Business Development Center (SBDC)

If the boss needs assistance in preparing a business plan, evaluating business prospects, seeking capital, or obtaining specific information on international trade, technical problems, or opportunities in selling to the government, your local SBDC may be the answer. SBDCs are located in many areas, not necessarily only in the city where an SBA regional office is located. The SBDC program provides in-depth training and counseling assistance to small businesses. Call your nearest SBA office for details and locations of a Small Business Development Center near you.

In all, SCORE, SBI, and SBDC handle more than 800,000 counseling and training cases each year.

Selling to the Federal Government

If your employer would like to sell the company's services or products to the federal government, the Small Business Development Center can help through its Center for Government Contracting. A fee may be charged for this help.

You should also contact government contracting agencies such as the Department of Defense in a regional office near you or in Washington, D.C.; the General Services Administration (GSA) in a regional office or in Washington, D.C.; the Regional SBA Procurement Division in a regional office; or the Procurement Automated Source System (PASS) program, which is a computer directory describing the profile of a company interested in competing for federal procurement. Call your SBA office for complete details.

Section Six
Career
Advancement

There are many opportunities for advancement for dedicated secretaries who care about the quality of their work.

Chapter 30
Your Future

Growing as the Company Grows

As you begin or continue your career, you have numerous choices regarding type and size of companies. Which is better to work for: a large or a small one? You'll find as many answers as there are secretaries. A large company often offers the best available salary and benefits, as well as steady advancement within its corporate structure. Yet small companies, too, offer growth potential. They may not always be able to afford as generous a salary or benefit package but often provide a wider range of experience that would otherwise be impossible to get. And when a small company successfully expands, the secretary has the excitement of getting in on the ground floor and growing with the business. In many instances the small business secretary can inherit as much responsibility as he or she wants.

Learn About the Business

It's important that no matter what type of business you work for, what size it is, or where it's located, you should do your best to learn as much about it as possible. In Chapter 1 we discussed learning about the business to make a favorable impression during your job interview. This learning process should never stop. Even if your duties are strictly defined and fairly routine, you should do your best to discover how the business is managed, how customers or clients are obtained, and how the products or services provided are produced. Although you may see no immediate need for this knowledge, it can be invaluable in a later emergency, as you advance, or if you seek work with a different company.

Upgrade Your Skills

No matter what type or size company you work for, focus on acquiring essential business skills, whether or not you need any one of them now. Make sure your skills are top-notch in such office-related areas as keyboarding, maintaining a filing system, handling incoming and outgoing mail, setting appointments, answering telephones, taking dictation, and using office machines. Try to acquire proficiency in correspondence, research, customer service, purchasing, budgeting, bookkeeping, invoicing, training new employees, and supervising an office staff. You should learn how to write and speak effectively and be able to plan and organize your work. And finally, you must be computer literate. Having all these skills will give you the most flexible preparation to meet any challenge you face—either an on-the-job crisis or a career opportunity.

As proof of the level of quality of your skills, you may want to investigate being certified by the National Secretaries Association as a CPS (Certified Professional Secretary). This certification is granted only upon the successful completion of examinations in various aspects of secretarial procedures and skills. Serious secretaries may find it worthwhile to inquire about the activities of this outstanding association. Being certified can be a tremendous boost to your career.

Recognizing a Time for Change

One of the trends in modern business is the changing nature of secretarial work. Today in businesses of all sizes, more managers are doing work on their own desktop computer systems that in the past would have been handled by a secretary. As these trends continue, there will be fewer and fewer secretaries and more office and information specialists. It's up to you to create a place for yourself in this changing world.

Learning new skills and improving your old ones is the best professional insurance you can acquire, and it can put you in the position of being a better secretary than your current position demands. If you cannot expand your current role but are capable of much more than you're doing, your dissatisfaction may lead you to want to change your direction in life and seek out a new job. Your new skills will help you get the best possible situation.

These skills will also prove invaluable if change is forced upon you. Gone are the days when a secretary might work forty-five years for the same *company,* many of those years for the same boss. This is true of both large and small companies. A large company used to provide stability, but no longer. Corporate restructurings, which have affected hundreds of thousands of people over the past years, have been a mixed blessing for secretaries. In the wake of restructuring, some secretaries have to leave their position when their boss leaves, but others are asked to take on greater responsibility, to "take up the slack" as middle managers are phased out. Either situation could be professionally devastating if it was not what the secretary would have chosen himself or herself.

On the other hand, small businesses have their own dangers, particularly in the first eighteen months of operation, though knowing that doesn't make it easier for the secretary who faces possible job loss. Rather than restructure, a small business may just fold completely, perhaps without giving you adequate notice, perhaps even without giving you a final paycheck.

Always be alert to conditions or changes that could affect your job, no matter what size company you work for. In a large company, be wary if your boss is excluded from meetings he or she used to attend, is dropped from routing lists, or is told to cut back on budget and staff. Do people who used to lunch or chat with your boss still do so? These warning signs can also signal that your own position might be in jeopardy.

In a small business where you work directly for the owner, pay attention to details. Has business been slipping lately? Is it just a temporary slump or something more serious? Has the boss paid vendors and other creditors, or are you starting to receive dunning letters and telephone calls? Of critical importance to you is whether the boss has paid payroll taxes and health insurance premiums. If your boss has not and the business folds, the Internal Revenue Service will look to the individual to pay the overdue taxes even though the money was already withheld from earlier paychecks. The individual may have no health care coverage even though deductions for premiums may have been taken. And the individual might not even be able to collect unemployment benefits though taxes for that were deducted too.

What should you do if something like this should happen to you? Your best bet is to consult an attorney; however, be advised that though you might file and win a lawsuit against your former employer, collecting your judgment may prove to be difficult and costly.

The better advice is to be aware of the financial health of your employer so you can take action before it's forced on you. These events are the exception, but it's better to be employed and equipped with this knowledge than to experience it naively when you can least afford it.

Finding a Job

When, for whatever reason, you feel the need to find a new job, explore all possible ways. Don't simply look in the paper or sign up at an employment agency for a position as a secretary, administrative assistant, or office manager. A more aggressive search can find you a more satisfying position.

Start by researching companies you might want to work for or areas where you might like to work. With newspapers and trade journals in hand, you might read about companies that were voted "family friendly," or had instituted company-wide training programs in computers or second languages, or had a strong policy of promoting from within. One company might be known for its laid-back atmosphere and flexible hours. Another might be known for its hard-driving excellence. Which interests you more? Which do you need more? These are the companies to target.

Locally, drive around office or industrial parks or anywhere else businesses are located. Stop in and talk and ask questions. Find out what the business does and if there are any job openings. These cold-call in-person visits are not as difficult as they might sound. If you are friendly and don't take up too much time, you can gain much valuable information.

You can also conduct research by looking through directories available in larger public libraries. The Better Business Bureau and the chamber of commerce of the town or city you're interested in will give you lists of local businesses. Both organizations are also good sources for checking the reputation of a particular business you may be interested in.

Tap your network of relatives, friends, neighbors, and professional associates for information. That insurance agent who calls, that vendor you talk to so frequently, that secretary you met at an office skills conference? These are just some of the people to tell when you're looking for a new position.

Finally, don't overlook temporary placement services. One benefit is that many agencies provide free training on new equipment and software packages, which can make you more desirable to a prospective employer. A second benefit is that temporary work allows you to experience different companies as an insider; once you find a company you like, apply for full-time work. Yet another benefit is that temporary work allows you maximum flexibility in scheduling your personal time.

Presenting Your Credentials

Your Resumé

No matter which path you take to look for a new job, you will need a professional-looking resumé, the document describing your work history and skills to a potential employer. There are two basic formats to follow. One focuses on a history of where you've worked (Figure 30-1) and the other on particular skills you have (Figure 30-2).

All resumés should include:

- ☐ Your name, address, and telephone number.
- ☐ Your educational background (schools attended; degrees, diplomas, or certificates awarded; special training received or courses attended).
- ☐ A listing of all previous employment.
- ☐ Your current job.

One mistake many people make on a resumé is attempting to explain why they left one job and moved on to another. This is not the place to discuss it. You may be asked this question in an interview, so be prepared with an answer, but don't volunteer it in your resumé.

It can be very useful to prepare several versions of a resumé, adapting the basic facts to emphasize the different skills required for different jobs. For example, using the sample here, suppose the secretary were applying for a position in a sales department. She might want to rewrite the skills-format version of her resumé, putting her sales experience as the first item and enlarging upon it wherever possible. Did she work with sales representatives? Did she handle objections or close calls herself? Did she find new prospects for the salespeople? Emphasizing this side of her experience could make her more attractive to the interviewer.

Figure 30-1. Sample resumé in a chronological format.

Jennifer Lee Wauson
12345 Heartside Dr.
Western Branch, GA 31234
(404) 555–1234

Experience

1995–Present	Lyon's Still Photography Acworth, Georgia

Office manager and assistant to business owner
Maintained files and records, accounts receivable, and customer database. Assisted photographer with photo subjects, as well as sales of proofs and prints. Handled scheduling of business activities, all correspondence, and travel arrangements.

1993–1995   Third Coast Video, Inc.
Austin, Texas

Office assistant
Scheduled clients and facilities for video production and postproduction facility. Scheduled freelance crews and equipment rentals. Arranged for shipping of equipment and travel for crews. Also handled invoicing and correspondence.

Education
1990–1993   B.A.—English
University of Texas
Austin, Texas

References furnished upon request.

This in no way means you should make up qualifications. If you do, it could prove disastrous if you are called on to perform a task you claim to be experienced at doing.

The Cover Letter

Along with your resumé you should also include an application or cover letter that states your interest in a particular job, briefly lists your qualifications, and explains why you might like to work for this particular employer (Figure 30-3).

Figure 30-2.   Sample resumé in a skills format.

Jennifer Lee Wauson
12345 Heartside Dr.
Western Branch, GA 31234
(404) 555–1234

Experience

ADMINISTRATION	Maintained files and records, accounts receivable, and customer database. Handled scheduling of business activities, all correspondence, and travel arrangements.
SALES	Worked with customers to set appointments and to sell photography services.
VIDEO PRODUCTION	Coordinated scheduling of crews and facilities. Hired freelance crews and outline equipment rentals.
TECHNICAL SKILLS	Complete understanding of IBM-compatible software including: Windows, Word for Windows, Excel, and WordPerfect. Also, some understanding of Apple Macintosh computers including Microsoft Word and Excel. Good typing skills, 50 wpm. Working knowledge of most office equipment, copiers, fax machines, and typewriters.

Work History

1995–Present	Office Manager and Assistant to Business Owner Lyon's Still Photography Acworth, Georgia
1993–1995	Office Assistant Third Coast Video, Inc. Austin, Texas

Education

1990–1993	B.A.—English University of Texas Austin, Texas

References furnished upon request.

Figure 30-3. Job application cover letter.

12345 Heartside Dr.
Western Branch, GA 31234
December 2, 19X3

Mr. Kevin Wilson
President
Videologies, Inc.
10 North Main St.
Atlanta, GA 30303

Dear Mr. Wilson,

I am very interested in applying for the job of office assistant listed in the *Atlanta Constitution* on December 1.

As you can see from my enclosed resumé, I have worked for both a still photographer and a small video production company. I enjoyed working at both of these companies, and I feel this past experience qualifies me for the position described in your advertisement.

I have a good understanding of the visual medium and the many details you must handle in your work. I believe I can help take responsibility for some of these details with little additional training.

I would appreciate the opportunity for a personal interview. You can reach me at 555–1234.

Thank you for your consideration.

Sincerely yours,

Jennifer Wauson

The Interview

If your resumé and letter are successful, your next step will be an interview with the prospective employer. There are several ways you can prepare and techniques you can use for conducting yourself during it:

☐ Examine your image. How do you look to the outside world? Consider the way you dress, the way you talk, even the way you stand. Can you talk to someone and look that person in the eye, rather than glance around or stare at your feet?

☐   How about your skills? Can you do anything that someone would want to hire you to do?

☐   What about experience? Have you ever practiced these skills in an employment situation?

☐   How much money do you want? What are employers in your area willing to pay for your skills? Find this out before you go to the interview by asking people and checking resources at the library, Chamber of Commerce, or Better Business Bureau.

☐   What do you know about the company where you're going to interview? How does it make money? What does its success depend on?

If you can find out this information, you'll be prepared to show how you can help make the business better. And that's what an employer wants to hear.

The Plus Element

The ending of this book can be brief because the most important instruction of all must come from your own heart and character. You must enlarge on every possibility to keep in rhythm with your employer, work with graceful efficiency, and anticipate the needs of the office. Then with your own pride and pleasure in the work you've done, you'll also see your employer's great satisfaction in having at last found the "right hand" he or she has always needed.

Index

abbots, forms of address, 210, 224
abbreviations
  alphabetizing, 92
  for *number*, 287
  periods in, 266
  postal, 27
  question marks with, 271
  for time, 283–284
accounting, *see* bookkeeping
accounts, 297–298
accounts payable, 295
accrued liabilities, 295
acknowledgment, letters of, 195–196
active cells, 146
address
  cell, 146
  forms of, 188, 210–224
addresses, 23–28, 33, 55–56, 63–66
  commas in, 270
  common problems, 29
  encoding, 28–30
adjectives, in transposed order, 269
affect, effect, 242
age, 285–286
agreements, legal, 227, 231
air express services, 71
air freight, 74
airmail, 67
air-to-ground calls, 21
air travel
  Official Airline Guide, 78
  for, reservations, 79, 81
  telephone calls and, 21
aldermen, forms of address, 210,
    223–224
all right, 242
almost, most, 248
alphabetizing, rules for, 90–93
already, all ready, 242

altogether, all together, 242
ambassadors, forms of address, 210–
    211, 223–224
America Online, 143
among, between, 243
ampersands, in alphabetizing, 93
angry, mad, 248
answering machines, 105
any, either, 243
apostrophes, 275–276
Apple Macintosh operating system,
    130
applications software, *see* software,
    computer
appointments
  letters for, 195–196
  making and tracking, 10, 13–14
apprenticeships, 5–6
archbishops (Roman Catholic), forms
    of address, 211, 224
archdeacons, forms of address, 211
arguments, 136
articles, in alphabetizing, 93
as, like, 247
assembly representatives, forms of ad-
    dress, 219, 223–224
assets, 291, 294–295
at, to, 250
ATMs (automated teller machines),
    315
attention line, 189
attorneys general, forms of address,
    211, 223–224
audit logs, 155
awful, awfully, 243
a while, awhile, 243

backups, 128
badly, 243

balance sheets, 292–296
banking:
  bank tellers, 321
  checking accounts, 312–313, 317–324
  credit cards, 324
  deposits, 319–321
  investment accounts, 314
  other services, 315–317
  petty cash, 313
  savings accounts, 313–314
  trust services, 314–315
  withdrawals, 322
bar-code readers (scanners), 23, 26–27, 122
baud rate, 141
because, 243
be sure and, try and, come and, 250
between, among, 243
bishops, forms of address, 212, 224
bonds payable, 295
bookkeeping:
  accounting statements, 292–296
  accounts, 297–298
  assets, 291, 294–295
  automobile expenses, 299, 302, 304
  cash budgets, 292, 305, 306
  liabilities, 291–292, 295
  payroll, 298–299, 300–301
  reconciling bank statements, 324–325
  records for lenders, 306, 307
  for taxes, 308–311, 327
  travel and entertainment expenses, 299, 303
both, each, 243
both alike, 243
boxes, 32–33
bring, take, 243
brothers (religious order), forms of address, 212
budgets, 292, 305, 306
bulletin board systems (BBS), 143
bus freight, 74
bushel(s), 243–244
business, 244
business licenses, 311

business reply service, 68
busy number redial, 106

cabinet officers (U.S.), forms of address, 213, 223–224
calculators, 102, 103
call-back modems, 155
caller (pickup) service, 55
call forwarding, 106
calling number ID, 106
call waiting, 106
came by, 244
can, may, 248
canons, forms of address, 213, 224
can't seem, 244
capital, 291
capitalization, rules of, 258–260
cardinals (Roman Catholic), forms of address, 213
career advancement, 337–344
  cover letters for, 341, 343
  growth in, 337–338
  interviews and, 4–5, 343–344
  and researching jobs, 339–340
  resumés in, 340–341, 342
car rentals, 79
cashier's checks, 317, 323–324
CD-ROMs, 128
cells, 146, 148
cellular telephones, 107–108
certificates of deposit (CDs), 314
certificates of mailing, 58, 60
certified checks, 323–324
certified mail, 58, 59
chairpersons, U.S., Congress subcommittee, forms of address, 213, 223–224
chancellors, university, forms of address, 222–223
change of address forms, 55–56, 57
chaplains, forms of address, 214, 224
character formatting, 168
character sets, 123
chargés d'affaires ad interim, forms of address, 214, 224
checking accounts, 312–313, 317–324

ciphers, 283, 284
clergy, forms of address, 214, 224
clerks of court, forms of address, 214–215, 224
clock speed, 119
codicils to wills, 227, 230
collect calls, 20
collect-on-delivery (COD) service, 38, 50, 56–58
colons, 272–273, 274
combination, 244
come and, be sure and, try and, 250
commas, 266–270
  in addresses, 270
  in company names, 270
  in compound and complex sentences, 266
  with contrasting phrases, 268
  dashes in place of, 276
  in dialogue, 268
  with infinitive phrases, 268
  with introductory expressions, 267
  with nonrestrictive modifiers, 268
  with numbers, 269, 281
  for omissions, 269
  with other transitional words, 267
  with prepositional phrases, 267
  with questions, 271
  with quotation marks, 268, 274
  with repeated words, 269
  in series, 266
  in titles, 270
  with transposed adjective order, 269
communications protocol, 141
company names
  alphabetizing, 91–92
  commas in, 270
  registering, 326
complimentary close, 191
CompuServe, 143, 145
computer(s), 113–145
  bulletin boards, 143
  communications capabilities of, 139–145
  disaster planning for, 157

electronic mail and, 53–54, 67, 144–145
elements of, 113
glossary of terms about, 172–182
hardware for, 113–119, 144, 156–157
input devices for, 121–123
keyboarding skills, 158–162
location of, 8
for mail services, 23–30
memory, 120–121
modems, 139–141, 155
networking, 139, 141, 143–144
online databases for, 143, 145
output devices for, 123–125, 168–169
security of, 153–157
software, *see* software, computer
storage devices, 125–129
telephones for, 105
types of, 113
and voice mail systems, 105, 106
condolence letters, 198
conference calls, 20–21, 106, 107
conference notes, 206–207
confidentiality, 4, 14
congratulations letters, 197, 200
Congresspersons, forms of address, 220
conjunctions
  in alphabetizing, 93
  omission of, 272
consul, council, counsel, 244
consuls, forms of address, 215, 224
contractions, 275
contractors, independent, 310
contracts, 227, 231
cooperate, 244
copy machines, 100–103
copyright information, 326
cost of goods sold, 296
could of, might of, would of, 248
council, counsel, consul, 244
courier services, 76
credible, credulous, 244
credit cards, 324
credulous, credible, 244
currency, foreign, 316–317

current liabilities, 295
customs inspections, 68–69, 84–85
cutting and pasting, 165–166

daisy-wheel printers, 124
dangling participles, 252–253
dashes, 276
data, 244
data, spreadsheet, 148–149
database management systems,
    132–138
  creating, 132
  defined, 132
  fields, 132–133, 134
  online, 143, 145
  records, 133–134
  reports, 136
  searching, 135–136
  sorting, 134–135
  types of, 136–138
dates, 284
  in letters, 186
  Roman numeral, 288
deal, 244
deans
  of cathedrals, forms of address, 215,
    224
  university or college, forms of ad-
    dress, 223
decimal points, 283
declination, letters of, 199, 204–205
deferred charges to expenses, 294–295
deferred credits to income, 295
demand deposits, 320
depreciation, 296
dictation, 11–13, 225
dictionaries, 9, 12, 253
different from, different than, 244
dimensions, 286
directories
  reference works, 9–10
  telephone, 19–20
disaster planning, for computer sys-
    tem, 157
disk drives, 114, 156
display adapters, 118
doctors, forms of address, 215

documents
  creating, *see* software, computer;
    typewriters; word processing
  filing, *see* filing systems
  legal, *see* legal documents
  letters, *see* letters
  mailing, *see* mail services and
    shipping
  reports, *see* reports
  travel, 55, 82–84
don't, 245
DOS (disk operating system), 130
dot-matrix printers, 124
Dow Jones News Retrieval, 143
drop shipment service, 38, 51

each, both, 243
each, their, 245
effect, affect, 242
either, any, 243
either, neither, 245
electronic mail services, 53–54, 67,
    144–145
ellipses, 276–277
employer
  letters for signature of, 195
  office of, 13–14
  telephone calls of, 16
employment taxes, 309
enclosures, letter, 193
encryption, 155
enthuse, enthusiastic, 245
envelopes
  dimensions of, 24
  facing, 32
  OCR read area of, 24–26
  window, 27
equipment, *see* office equipment
except, unless, 245
exclamation points, 272, 274
expanded memory, 121
expansion boards, 117, 118
expect, 245
Export-Import Bank of the United
    States, 328
exporting, 327–328
Express Mail, 34–45, 66, 67

extended memory, 121
external modems, 139–141

facsimile machines, 109–112
  INTELPOST service, 54, 67
farther, further, 245
Federal Express, 71, 75
federal taxes, 308
feet, foot, 245–246
fewer, less, 247
fields, computer, 132–133, 134
file managers, 136
file servers, 144
filing systems, 88–94
  alphabetical, 89–90
  check list for, 88–89
  computerized, 125–129, 132–138
  decimal, 89
  file cabinets, 93–94
  subject, 90–93
financial records, *see* bookkeeping
financing, sources of, 328–332
first-class mail, 45–50, 51
fiscal period, 296
fix, 245
fixed liabilities, 295
floppy disks, 126–129
follow-up files, 196
fonts, 168
foot, feet, 245–246
foreign currency exchange, 316–317
foreign titles, alphabetizing, 91
formatting
  disks, 129
  documents, 166–168
forms of address, 188, 210–224
formulas, spreadsheet, 148–149
forwarding, mail, 39, 51
401k plans, 315
fourth class mail (parcel post),
  52–53
fractions, 283, 285, 286
franchise taxes, 309
freaking, 154
free forwarding, 39
function keys, 159–161
further, farther, 245

General Services Administration
  (GSA), 334
GEnie, 143
glossaries
  of computer terms, 172–182
  of legal terms, 227, 229–237
got, 246
gotten, 246
government contracting, 334
governors, forms of address, 215–216,
  223–224
grammalogues, 225
graphical user interface (GUI), 123–124
graphics tablets, 122–123
gross profit on sales, 296
ground-to-air calls, 21
guess, 246

hacking, 154
hard drives (fixed disks), 126, 156
hardware, computer, 113–119
  mechanical problems with, 156–157
  network, 144
he, she, 251
her, him, them, 252
high-density diskettes, 129
him, them, her, 252
hospitality letters, 197, 200
hotel accommodations
  Hotel and Motel Red Book listings of,
    78, 79
  reservations for, 78–79, 81, 196
hyphens, in numbers, 284–285

I, 251
immunizations, 84
importing, 68–69, 327–328
inaugurate, 246
income statements, 293, 294, 296
incorporation process, 326
independent contractors, 310
index of files, 90–93
individual retirement accounts (IRAs),
  315
informed, posted, 249
ink jet printers, 124
input devices, 121–123

inside address, 187
inside of, within, 246
insurance, postal, 36, 45, 60, 62, 68
INTELPOST (International Electronic
    Postal Service), 54, 67
internal cache, 119
internal modems, 139–141
international business
    and customs inspections, 68–69,
        84–85
    and Express Mail, 37, 38, 45, 66, 67
    import and export information for,
        327
    mailings, 26, 66–68
    and shipping services, 76
    for small businesses, 332, 333
    trading with other countries as,
        327–328
    travel, 55, 82–87, 316–317
international surface air lift (ISAL),
    67–68
International Trade Administration
    (ITA), 327
interoffice memorandums, 199–200,
    207
interviews, job, 4–5, 343–344
introduction letters, 197, 199, 201
investment accounts, 344
invitations
    acceptance of, 199, 203
    letters of, 199, 202–203
invite, 246
italics, 277–278
itinerary, 81–82, 83
it's, its, 246

Jr., 270
judges, forms of address, 216, 223–
    224
justification, line, 167

Keogh plans, 315
keyboards, 121, 158–162
kind, 246
kind of, sort of, 246
kings, forms of address, 216

labels
    package, 33, 53
    spreadsheet, 148
languages, official, 85–87, 328
laser printers, 125
lawyers, forms of address, 216, 224
lay, lie, 247
learn, teach, 246
leave, let, 247
ledgers, 297
legal documents:
    agreements, 227, 231
    case titles, 226
    codicils to wills, 227, 230
    contracts, 227, 231
    formats of, 225–226
    grammalogues, 225
    notary public forms, 227, 228–229
    proxy, 227, 231
legal terms, 227, 229–237
less, fewer, 247
let, leave, 247
letter-quality printers, 124
letter(s), 185–199
    for acknowledgments, 195–196
    appearance of, 185
    for appointments, 195–196
    attention line in, 189
    beginning of, 186–190
    body of, 190–191
    closing of, 191–193
    complimentary close in, 191
    date line in, 186
    for employer's signature, 195
    enclosures in, 193
    forms of address in, 210–224
    inside address of, 187
    job application, 341, 343
    and mail merging feature, 170–171
    model, 196–205
    paragraphing of, 186
    postscripts to, 193
    reference initials in, 192–193
    salutation of, 190
    signature of, 191–192, 195
    subject line in, 190

titles in, 188–189, 192
written by secretary, 194–195
see also typewriters; word processing
liabilities, 291–292, 295
liable, likely, 247
licenses, business, 311
lie, lay, 247
lieutenant governors, forms of address, 216, 223–224
light pens, 121–122
like, as, 247
likely, liable, 247
line, 247
lists, *see* mailing lists
loan, 247
loans
  bookkeeping for, 306, 307
  small business, 329–332
local area networks (LANs), 139, 141, 143–144
long-distance calls, 20, 21, 106–107
lost, 247
lots, 247

macros
  keyboard, 161
  spreadsheet, 152
  word processor, 171
mad, angry, 248
Mailgram service, 54
mailing lists
  and mail merging feature, 170–171
  maintaining, 200, 205
  postal clean-up service for, 28–30
mail services, 23–76
  addressing for, 23–28, 33, 55–56, 63–66
  alternative, 69–76
  for banking, 316
  and encoding business mailers, 28–30
  labeling for, 33, 53
  metering for, 30–32
  and packaging, 32–33, 38–39, 50, 52
  postal abbreviations for, 27
  sacking for, 53, 68

and U.S. Postal Service, 33–53, 55–69
margins, setting, 166–167
math co-processors, 119
may, can, 248
mayors, forms of address, 216
m-bag, 68
MCI Mail, 143, 145
me, us, 252
measures, weights and, 286
Medicare, 309
meetings, 205–209
  conference notes, 206–207
  minutes of, 205–206, 208
  office, 207, 209
  resolutions, 206
memorandums, 199–200, 207
memory, computer, 120–121
memory chips, 118
merchandise return service, 58
messages, telephone, 16–18
meters, postage, 30–32
might of, would of, could of, 248
military personnel
  forms of address for, 216–217, 224
  mailing to, 37, 39, 45, 66–67
  veterans' business benefits for, 333
ministers, forms of address, 217, 224
minutes of meetings, 205–206, 208
modems, 139–141, 155
money market accounts, 313
money orders, 55, 317, 324
monitors, computer, 121, 123–124
monsignors (Roman Catholic), forms of address, 217, 224
mortgages payable, 295
most, almost, 248
mother boards, 116–117
mouse, 121, 161–162

names of individuals
  alphabetizing, 90–91, 92–93
  and forms of address, 188, 210–224
  in letters, 190, 191
  titles in, *see* titles, courtesy
neither, either, 245

networking, computer, 139, 141,
    143–144
net worth, 291
net worth taxes, 310
never, 248
new address verification card, 63–66
900 telephone numbers, 107
nodes, 144
notary public services, 227, 228–229,
    317
notes payable, 295
NOW accounts, 313
numerals, 279–288
    and age, 285–286
    alphabetizing, 93
    commas with, 269, 281
    and dates, 186, 284, 288
    decimal points in, 283
    and dimensions, 286
    and dollars and cents, 282–283
    hyphens in, 284–285
    large, 280–281
    in page numbering, 287
    and percentages, 286
    plurals of, 287
    in printed text, 279–280
    Roman, 288
    separating digits in, 281
    and spreadsheet, 148
    and time, 281, 283–284, 288
    for weights and measures, 286
    words vs. figures, 279

OCRs (optical character readers), 23–28
off, 248
office equipment:
    answering machines, 105
    calculators, 102, 103
    computer systems, *see* computer(s)
    copy machines, 100–103
    dictation machines, 13
    facsimile machines, 109–112
    printers for OCRs, 28
    typewriters, 8, 97–99, 162
on-demand service, 45
online databases, 143, 145

only, 248
open, 248
operating expenses, 296
operating systems, 129–130
optical character readers (OCRs),
    23–28
optical disks, 128
OS/2 (Operating System Two), 130
output devices, 123–125

packaging, 32–33, 52
    for Express Mail, 38–39
    for priority mail, 50
pagers, telephone, 108–109
paragraphing, 186
parallel ports, 117
parcel airlift mail (PAL), 66–67
parcel post, 52–53, 66
parentheses, 277
    question marks with, 271
participles, dangling, 252–253
party, 248
passports, 55, 82–83, 84
patents, obtaining, 327
payroll
    accounting for, 298–299, 300–301
    taxes on, 309, 310
PBX (private branch exchange), 104
peer-to-peer network, 144
pen interface, 121–122
pen plotters, 125
people, 248–249
percent, 249
percentage, 249
percentages, 286
periods, 265–266
personal letters, 196–197, 200
person-to-person calls, 20
petty cash, 313
photocopiers, 100–103
planning, daily, 10–11
plurals
    of numbers, 287
    rules for, 253–256
popes, forms of address, 217
ports, 117

postage meters, 30–32
postage refund guarantee, 39, 45
postal authorization, 30
posted, informed, 249
post office boxes, 55
postscripts, 193
premiers, forms of address, 217–218
prepositions
    in alphabetizing, 93
    commas with, 267
presidents
    of the United States, forms of ad-
        dress, 218, 223–224
    university or college, forms of ad-
        dress, 223
priests, forms of address, 218, 224
primary field, 134
prime ministers, forms of address, 218
princes, forms of address, 218–219
princesses, forms of address, 219
printers
    computer, 124–125, 168–169
    for OCRs, 28
    postage meter, 31, 32
priority mail, 50–51, 67
processor chips, 118
Procurement Automated Source Sys-
    tem (PASS), 334
Prodigy, 143, 145
professors, forms of address, 219
profit-and-loss statements, 293, 294, 296
pronouns, 251–252
pronunciation, 261–264
proper nouns, 258–260
property taxes, 310
proprietorship, 291
proxy, 227, 231
punctuality, 3–4
punctuation:
    apostrophes, 275–276
    colons, 272–273, 274
    commas, 266–270, 271, 276, 281
    dashes, 276
    ellipses, 276–277
    exclamation points, 272, 274
    italics, 277–278

parentheses, 271, 277
periods, 265–266
question marks, 271, 274
quotation marks, 268, 271, 273–274
semicolons, 272, 274

queens, forms of address, 219
querying the database, 135
question marks, 271
    with quotation marks, 274
quotation marks, 273–274
    colons preceding, 273
    commas with, 268, 274
    double, 273–274
    exclamation points with, 274
    question marks with, 271, 274
    single, 274
    in titles, 274

rabbis, forms of address, 219
raise, rise, 249
RAM (random access memory) chips,
    118–119, 120, 125
real, 249
recorded delivery, 68
records
    computer, 133–134
    see also filing systems
reference initials, 192–193
reference works, 9–10
registered mail, 63, 64, 68
remote computers, 139
removable cartridge drives, 128
reports
    database, 136
    office meeting, 207, 209
representatives
    Congressional, forms of address,
        220, 223–224
    state, forms of address, 219, 223–224
reservations
    hotel and motel, 78–79, 81, 196
    letters for, 196
resolutions, 206
restricted delivery, 59–60
resumés, 340–341, 342

return receipts, 39, 58, 59, 61, 62, 68
return service, merchandise, 58
return to sender, 39
rise, raise, 249
ROM (read-only memory), 121
Roman numerals, 288
round numbers, 280
run, 249

safe deposit boxes, 316
sales tax, 309
salutations, 190
same, 249
savings accounts, 313–314
savings bonds, 314
searching, 135–136, 166
secondary field, 134
second-class mail, 51
secretaries of state, forms of address,
    220, 223–224
security, computer, 153–157
selective call acceptance, 106
selectmen, forms of address, 210,
    223–224
self-employment tax, 309–310
semicolons, 272, 274
senators, forms of address, 220–221,
    223–224
serial commas, 266
serial numbers, 281
serial ports, 117
Service Corps of Retired Executives
    (SCORE), 333–334
set, sit, 250
sets of numbers, 280
shall, will, 249
shape, 249
shareware, 141
she, he, 251
ships
    names of, 277
    ship-to-shore calls, 21
shorthand, 11–13, 225
should, would, 250
signatures
    in letters, 191–192, 195
    waiver of, 39

SIMM (single in-line memory module)
    chips, 118–119, 120
simplified pension plans, 314–315
sisters (religious order), forms of ad-
    dress, 221
sit, set, 250
Small Business Administration (SBA),
    329–334
so, 250
Social Security tax, 309, 310
software, computer
    communications, 141–143
    database management, 132–138
    network, 139, 141, 144
    operating, 129–130
    piracy of, 154–155
    shareware, 141
    spreadsheet, 146–152
    types of, 129–131
    virus protection, 156
    word processing, 163–171
sometime, some time, 250
sort of, kind of, 246
space-available mail (SAM), 66–67
speakers, U.S. House of Representa-
    tives, forms of address, 221,
    223–224
special delivery, 63, 68
special handling, 63
spelling, 12, 253–260
    capitalization and, 258–260
    checkers, 170
    dictionaries for, 9, 12, 253
    irregular, 257
    plurals and, 253–256
    suffixes and, 256–257
spreadsheet software, 146–152
    data, 148–149
    described, 146
    editing, 150–151
    functions, 149–150
    macros for, 152
    multitasking, 151–152
    navigating around, 146–148
    online help for, 152
    templates, 149, 152
Sr., 270

states
  postal abbreviations, 27
  taxes of, 308–309
station-to-station calls, 20
storage devices, 125–129
subject line, 190
suffixes, 256–257
Super NOW accounts, 313
supplies, office, 8–9, 11
Supreme Court justices, forms of address, 221–222, 223–224
surface mail, 68

take, bring, 243
taxes, 308–310, 311, 327
teach, learn, 246
teleconferencing, 107
telegram airport delivery, 21–22
telephone(s), 15–22, 104–108
  and air-to-ground calls, 21
  answering machines for, 105
  bill paying via, 316
  cellular, 107–108
  colleagues', answering, 15–16
  conference calls on, 20–21, 106, 107
  directories, 19–20
  employer's answering, 16
  etiquette for, 15, 18–19
  facsimile machines, 109–112
  and long-distance calls, 20, 21, 106–107
  messages, 16–18
  multiline, 105
  often-used, numbers, 19–20
  other business, 105
  pagers, 108–109
  PBX (private branch exchange), 104
  screening calls on, 18–19
  and ship-to-shore calls, 21
  special services, 106
  and telegrams to airplane passengers, 21–22
  trains, calls to, 21
  transferring, calls, 16
  and voice mail, 105, 106
templates, spreadsheet, 149, 152
thank-you notes, 197, 199, 200

that, who, which, 251
their, each, 245
them, her, him, 252
thesauri, 9
they, 251–252
third-class mail, 51, 52, 53
three-way conferencing, 106
tickler files, 196
time
  abbreviations for, 283–284
  colons and, 273
  deposits, 320
titles
  business, 189
  colons in, 273
  commas in, 270
  italics for, 277
  legal case, 226
  quotation marks for, 274
titles, courtesy, 188–189, 192
  alphabetizing, 91, 93
  forms of address, 188, 210–224
  in letters, 188–189, 192
  of men, 188, 270
  of women, 188, 192
to, at, 250
"to-do" lists, 11
toll-free numbers, 107
track balls, 121
trademarks, obtaining, 327
train travel
  arrangements for, 80, 81
  telephone calls and, 21
travel, 77–87
  agencies, 80–81, 82, 196
  basics, 77–78
  currency exchange for, 316–317
  documents for, 55, 82–84
  itinerary, 81–82, 83
  and languages, 85–87, 328
  reservations, 78–81
  and traveler's checks, 317, 324
trial balance, 297, 298
trucking freight, 74–76
trust services, 314–315
try and, come and, be sure and, 250
type-over mode, 164–165

typewriters, 97–99, 162
  location of, 8
  selecting, 99
  word processing, 98

uninterruptible power supply, 157
United Nations
  delegates, forms of address, 222,
    223–224
  secretaries-general, forms of ad-
    dress, 222
United Parcel Service (UPS), 69–71,
  72–74, 76
U.S. Department of State, 327–328
U.S. Postal Service (USPS), 33–53,
  55–69
  alternatives to, 69–76
  Consumer Advocate, 34
  Express Mail, 34–45, 66, 67
  first-class mail, 45–50, 51
  fourth-class mail (parcel post), 52–53
  list clean-up service of, 28–30
  other services of, 55–66
  priority mail, 50–51, 67
  second-class mail, 51
  third-class mail, 51, 52, 53
university or college officials
  chancellors, forms of address,
    222–223
  deans, forms of address, 223
  presidents, forms of address, 223
UNIX, 130
unless, except, 245
us, me, 252

vaccinations, 84
verbose expressions, 241–242
vice presidents of the United States,
  forms of address, 223
video displays, 121, 123–124
videotext services, 143
virtual memory, 121
viruses, computer, 156
visas, 83–84

vocabulary
  computer terms, 172–182
  developing, 6, 12
  and dictionaries, 9, 12, 253
  legal, 227, 229–237
voice mail, 105, 106
voice recognition, 122

wait on, 250
waiver of signature, 39
warrant officers, forms of address, 223
we, 252
weights and measures, 286
Western Union, 54
where, 250–251
which, 251
which, that, who, 251
will, shall, 249
wills, codicils to, 227, 230
wire transfers, 316
within, inside of, 246
Women's Business Ownership Assistance, 333
word processing, 163–171
  advanced features of, 170–171
  creating documents with, 163–164
  editing documents with, 164–166
  formatting documents with, 166–168
  loading documents on, 169–170
  macros for, 171
  mail merging with, 170–171
  positioning documents with, 164
  printing documents with, 168–169
  saving documents with, 169
  spell checkers for, 170
  and typing documents, 163–164
word wrapping, 159, 164
workers compensation, 310
workstations, 7–8, 93–94
would, should, 250
would of, could of, might of, 248
write-protect notches, 127

zip codes, 28, 33, 46